Crisis

of

Diplomacy:

The Three Wars...
and After....

by Abdul-Hafez M. Elkordy, Ph.D.

Professor of International Politics
Shaw University

The Naylor Company
Book Publishers of the Southwest
San Antonio, Texas

Crisis
of
Diplomacy:
The Three Wars . . .
and After. . . .

TO THE UPROOTED . . . THE REFUGEES
EVERYWHERE . . .

TO NAHED . . . AND OUR CHILDREN

Contents

vii

ix

Introduction

Both as a textbook and an essay, this book is written for all concerned about the game of power and diplomacy in the nuclear age as practiced, directly or indirectly, by the Great Powers, and as "controlled" or "rationalized," effectively or ineffectively, by the new developments in both international politics and international organization.

While the central theme of this work is a crisis of diplomacy, its principal case of study is the Middle Eastern conflict. As such, *Crisis of Diplomacy: The Three Wars . . . and After. . . .* is a contemporary comprehensive study of the Middle Eastern principal impasse in view of the living and the changing political realities not only in that region but also in the world at large. This need has imposed itself at a time when explosions and tensions in the Middle East have overshadowed all other world problems, and have indeed brought the world to the edge of war.

This study addresses itself to the historical, psychological, humanitarian, territorial, legal, political and organizational problems which are at the very roots of the Middle Eastern crisis and, as such, would determine the prospects for peace in that area. A primary focus is placed on the changing diplomacy of the Great Powers, particularly the United States and the Soviet Union, and the United

Nations on the Arab-Israeli impasse. In particular, emphasis is given to the shift from the diplomacy of alienation to the diplomacy of partition; and from the diplomacy of peace-observation to the preventive diplomacy of peace-keeping; and from the diplomacy of conquest to the diplomacy of peacemaking through conciliation.

In the process, the study principally raises certain basic interrelated questions to which it has attempted to respond: (a) Historically, what is the crisis, its roots and dimensions? (b) Functionally, what has been done, by whom and to achieve what? What has not been done? What are the problems of the United Nations' peace-observation and peace-keeping operational diplomacies in the area? What should be done? What could be done, by whom and to secure what? (c) Diplomatically, to what extent, and for how long would the United States and the Soviet Union be willing to "control" their cold war diplomacy in the Middle East? Has any — or all — of the parties directly involved, the Arab States and Israel, changed their strategy and the direction of their diplomacy on the conflict? What would be the implications of Nasser's death? (d) Pragmatically, what is the Palestinian Revolution? What is its place in the Middle Eastern conflict? And, what would be the most feasible solution to the Palestinian national aspirations?

It is hoped that as we understand the problem, we become objectively aware of its dimensions; and that the crisis of diplomacy would eventually develop an imaginative diplomacy humanly committed to the cause of peace and justice.

Abdul-Hafez M. Elkordy
Raleigh, North Carolina
April 17, 1971

Part One
The First War . . .

The greatest prayer of man does not ask
for victory but for peace. . . .

DAG HAMMARSKJOLD

Chapter I

Background to the Crisis: The Diplomacy of Alienation

There is no doubt that the Arab-Israeli case has consti- tuted one of the greatest human and political crises of the postwar world. It is a crisis which the United Nations could not have avoided. As a mandate under the League of Nations, the Palestine problem had long become a matter of great international concern. Chapter XI of the United Nations Charter clearly applied to Palestine as did articles on the international trusteeship system and, as such, Palestine raised the difficulties of international peace and security. The human tragedy in Palestine is also important because of the intense political interests held by the Great Powers, particularly those of the United States and the Soviet Union.

From the beginning, the United Nations tried to pro- tect Arab homes and lands which were situated within the area of the proposed Jewish State by clearly stipulating that the position of the current inhabitants was in no way to be prejudiced by the partition and that they were to retain all their rights and property. But shortly after adoption of Partition Resolution 181 (II) of November 29, 1947, a campaign of terror began in the Holy Land. It aimed at two major objectives: first, to confirm Zionist dominance over the Arabs within the territory assigned by that resolution to the Jewish State; second, to enlarge that territory to include the whole of Palestine.

Before the British Mandate ended on 15 May, 1948, before a single soldier from any Arab State entered Palestine, and two months before the State of Israel could legally be proclaimed according to the Partition Resolution, the Zionists had already illegally occupied much of the territory reserved for the Arab State, as well as the greater part of the Jerusalem International Zone. During the six-month period prior to the creation of Israel, more than 300,000 of the country's 1,380,000 Moslems and Christians were driven out of their homes and now live as refugees on international charity.[1]

Mr. Lilienthal precisely described the situation relative to the majority of the refugees who were huddled together in United Nations camps.

The seven cents a day received from the United Nations for rations and care has kept the refugees alive without lessening one whit their tragic frustration and bitterness. Deserted by all, they are easy prey for anyone who takes the trouble to woo them. As these refugees go, so will go the Middle East.[2]

Consequently, the conflict between Israel and the Arab

---

[1] Sami Hadawi, *Palestine: Loss of a Heritage* (San Antonio, Texas: The Naylor Company, 1963), p. 6.

[2] Alfred M. Lilienthal, *There Goes the Middle East* (New York: The Bookmailer, Inc., 1958), p. 53.

States not only contains the seeds of a bitter war, but it also has brought the Middle East into the arena of the cold war. In fact, this region has emerged in the past few years as the most important area in the military, economic, and political struggle between the Eastern and Western Powers. This reality, coupled with the Arabs' need of both the United States' and Soviet Union's support in case of any Arab-Israeli conflict, explains Mr. Lilienthal's observation that "the Arab world for whose favor the United States and the USSR were competing, was faced with making a choice or risking the hazards of neutralism."[3]

A BIT OF HISTORY

The Sykes-Picot Agreement

To safeguard their interests, the way to India as well as to the oil-rich Arab Gulf countries, and so to defeat the Ottoman Empire which then controlled the Arab World, England and France persuaded the Arab leaders in 1915 to revolt against their Turkish rulers. Toward this common interest they used Sherif Hussein of Mecca as a religious Arab leader. They promised him in return for his support that they would recognize as independent an Arab State covering what they called "Greater Syria," which included Palestine, Jordan, Lebanon, and Iraq.

In the spring of 1916, when the Arab revolt against the Turks began, the British and French on May 9 entered into the secret Sykes-Picot Agreement which split the eastern Arab World (outside Arabia) in two: Iraq and Palestine (which encompassed Transjordan) went to the British, and Syria and Lebanon were placed within the French sphere of influence.

Implementation of the Sykes-Picot agreement would have negated the promises made to Sherif Hussein.

---

3 Ibid., p. x.

5

So also would this implementation have conflicted with promises made by Britain to the Zionists who had been seeking to establish a Jewish homeland in Palestine. Zionist leaders in Europe had been working to secure this since 1897 when the first Zionist Congress took place in Basle, Switzerland. Many British statesmen supported the Zionist goals and during the war pressed the case for establishing a Jewish community in Palestine.[4]

The Balfour Declaration: A Promise

During the First World War, Palestine came into the center of modern world politics when the British conquered it. Yet its significance arose not simply from its own territory but rather from its being detached from Turkey. In this process, the British Government allowed some of the Arab leaders to believe that Britain was freeing them from the Turks so that they might be free from any outside supervision or control. Under the stress of World War I, however, the British Government made promises to Arabs and to Jews in order to get their assistance. On these promises both parties formed certain expectations. While the Arabs were promised independence, the Jews were promised a homeland in a Palestine that was to be redeemed from the Turks. This promise is less subject to doubt since it is found in the Balfour Declaration approved by the British Cabinet in November, 1917.[5]

On November 2, 1917, British Foreign Minister Lord Balfour issued "on behalf of His Majesty's Government, the following declaration of sympathy with Jewish Zionist aspirations which has been submitted to, and approved by, the Cabinet":

---

4 A. G. Mezerik, "Arab-Israel Conflict and the United Nations," *International Review Service*, Vol. VIII, No. 73 (1962), p. 3.

5 For more information see Palestine Royal Commission Report (London: His Majesty's Stationery Office, 1937), pp. 16-21, 278.

His Majesty's Government view with favour the establishment in Palestine of a national home for the Jewish people, and will use their best endeavours to facilitate the achievement of this object. It being clearly understood that nothing shall be done which may prejudice the civil and religious rights of existing non-Jewish communities in Palestine or the rights and political status enjoyed by Jews in any other country.[6]

The Balfour Declaration was endorsed forthwith by the Allies and later confirmed by the Supreme Council of the Allies at San Remo on April 24, 1920. The Balfour Declaration was to become a part of the text of the League of Nations Mandate and other early documents.

The Treaty of Sevres

Section VII, Article 95, of the Treaty of Sevres of August 10, 1920, stated:

> The High Contracting Parties agree to entrust, by application of the provisions of Article 22, the administration of Palestine within such boundaries as may be determined by the Principal Allied Powers. The Mandatory will be responsible for putting into effect the declaration originally made on November 2, 1917, by the British Government and adopted by the other Allied Powers, in favor of the establishment in Palestine of a national home for the Jewish people, it being clearly understood that nothing shall be done, which may prejudice the civil and religious rights of existing non-Jewish communities in Palestine, or the rights and political status enjoyed by Jews in any other country.[7]

After "the Principal Allied Powers had selected His

---

6 A. G. Mezerik, op. cit., p. 85.

7 Maurice Harari, *Government and Politics of the Middle East* (New Jersey: Prentice-Hall, 1962), p. 132.

7

Britannic Majesty as the Mandatory for Palestine,"[8] they indicated in Articles 2 and 6 of the Treaty of Sevres that:

Article 2: The Mandatory shall be responsible for placing the country under such political, administrative, and economic conditions as will secure the establishment of the Jewish national home, as laid down in the Preamble and the development of self-governing institutions, and also for safeguarding the civil and religious rights of all the inhabitants of Palestine, irrespective of race and religion.

Article 6: The Administration of Palestine, while ensuring that the rights and position of other sections of the population are not prejudiced, shall facilitate Jewish immigration under suitable conditions and shall encourage . . . close settlement by Jews on the land including State lands and waste lands not required for public purposes.[9]

While the Turkish Government never ratified the Treaty of Sevres, which was superseded by the Treaty of Lausanne of July 24, 1923, it serves as an illustration of the consistency with which the substance of the Balfour Declaration was infused in international agreements affecting Palestine since November, 1917.

The Mandate for Palestine, which became effective as an official act of the League of Nations on September 29, 1923, was established, however, on the basis of Article 22 of the Covenant of the League of Nations. It, too, incorporated the Balfour Declaration almost verbatim.

---

8 J. C. Hurewitz, *Diplomacy in the Near and Middle East* (Princeton, N.J.: D. Van Nostrand Co., 1956), Vol. II, p. 107.

9 Ibid., pp. 107-108; for more information see General Assembly Official Records (GAOR), Second Session, Supplement No. 11 (Lake Success, N.Y.; 1947), pp. 18-21.

After reading these documents, it is clear that the Palestine dilemma has been the responsibility of all the "Principal Allied Powers," not only the United Kingdom, who helped effectuate the Balfour Declaration. In 1922, for instance, the United States Congress adopted a Joint Resolution supporting the establishment of a Jewish national home in Palestine. Furthermore, the United States, not a member of the League of Nations, gave its approval to the Mandate for Palestine in the Anglo-American Convention of December, 1924. However, one must admit that neither the British declaration, nor the Mandate Covenant, or the United States resolution of support constituted a political "commitment" for the creation of a "Jewish State" in Palestine but rather a "promise" and an "expression of support" for the establishment of a "Jewish Residence" in the Arab State. Indeed, nowhere in these documents one finds a pledge for the creation of a "Jewish State" in the Arab land.

Jewish and Arab Claims to Palestine

The Jews have based their claim to Palestine on the following points:[10]

1. A religious as well as historical background going back four thousand years when God promised Abraham, "Unto thy seed have I given this land, from the river of Egypt unto the great river, the river Euphrates."[11] So, the Jews, most especially the Zionists, have placed special emphasis on the "right" of Jews to "return" to Palestine as "their" ancient and religious homeland.

---

[10] See GAOR, Second Session, Supplement No. 11, op. cit., p. 30.

[11] Sami Hadawi, *Palestine: Questions and Answers* (New York: Arab Information Center, 1961), p. 11.

9

2. A political claim that rests on the Balfour Declaration of 1917 and on the Mandate for Palestine. This second document (a) incorporated the Declaration in its preamble, (b) recognized the historic connection of the Jewish people with Palestine, and (c) upheld the grounds for reconstituting the Jewish National Home there.

3. That the pledges to the Jews in the Balfour Declaration and the Mandate are international "commitments" not to the Jews of Palestine alone, who were at the time only a small community, but to the Jewish people as a whole, who are now often described as the "Jewish Nation."

4. That the Jews have built in Palestine on the basis of faith in the international pledges made to the Jewish people and they cannot be halted in midstream.

5. That the immigrant Jews "displace no Arabs," but rather develop areas which otherwise would remain undeveloped.

6. That the Mandate was to be terminated only when its primary purpose, the establishment of the Jewish National Home, had been fulfilled.

7. That the establishment of the Jewish National Home and "State" will do "no" political injustice to the Arabs, "since the Arabs have never established a government in Palestine."

The Arabs of Palestine have based their case on the following points:[12]

---

12 GAOR, Second Session, Supplement No. 11, op. cit., pp. 33-34; see also Ibid.

1. The natural right of the Arab majority to Palestine should not be disputed because the Arabs are and have been for many centuries in possession of the land. This natural right is based on the historical fact that the Arab connection with Palestine has continued uninterruptedly from early times. The term "Arab" is to be interpreted as connoting not only the invaders from the Arabian Peninsula in the seventh century but also the indigenous population that intermarried with the invaders and their speech, customs and modes of thought in becoming permanently Arabized.

2. That the general promises and pledges officially made to the Arab people in the course of the First World War, in particular the McMahon-Hussein correspondence of 1915-1916, should be fulfilled.

3. That the Mandate for Palestine, which incorporated the Balfour Declaration, is illegal since its terms are inconsistent with the letter and spirit of Article 22 of the Covenant of the League of Nations because (a) the Mandatory Power was given in Article 1 of the Mandate "full powers of legislation and administration" instead of a limited jurisdiction in the form of administrative advice and assistance; and (b) the wishes of the Palestine community had not been "a principal consideration in the selection of the Mandatory" as provided for in Article 22, paragraph 4, of the Covenant.

4. That the principle and the right of national self-determination were violated, for the Partition Resolution of November 29, 1947, was passed without the consent of the majority of the population, the Arabs of Palestine.

11

5. That the Arab States were not members of the League of Nations when the Palestine Mandate was approved, and were not, therefore, bound by it.

6. Since the terms of the Palestine Mandate were illegal and invalid, Jewish immigrants had no legal right to enter the country during the period of the Mandate.

7. From the religious point of view, the promise that was made to "Abraham and his seed," according to Zionist logic, applies equally to Arabs, Moslems and Christians, who are the descendants of Abraham's eldest son Ishmael, and not simply to the Jews who are reputedly the descendants of his second son, Isaac.

Palestine under the Mandate

According to the Sykes-Picot agreement, the Arab areas of the collapsed Ottoman Empire were divided between France and Britain. On April 25, 1920, the Supreme Council of the Allied and Associated Powers assigned the Palestine Mandate to Britain. The terms of the Mandate received the approval of the Council of the League of Nations of July 24, 1922.

Under the Mandate, as under the Treaty of Sevres, the British Government was obliged to place the country "under such political, administrative and economic conditions as will secure the establishment of the Jewish National Home."[13]

In Palestine, Zionist immigration increased rapidly. In the period from 1882 to 1917 more than 75,000 Jews,

---

[13] *Israel and the United Nations*, Report of a Study Group set up by the Hebrew University of Jerusalem, prepared for the Carnegie Endowment for International Peace (New York: Manhattan Publishing Co., 1956), p. 19.

mostly from Central and Eastern Europe, immigrated to that area of the Arab land.[14] In January, 1919, however, an agreement was signed by Emir Feisal of the Arab Kingdom of the Hedjaz and Chaim Weizmann, representing and acting on behalf of the Zionist Organization. The two parties pledged to encourage the immigration of Jews into Palestine and their settlement of the Arab land.[15] But Feisal insisted on adding the following all-important reservation before giving his signature. This reservation was considered a part of the agreement since the signatures of both Feisal and Weizmann were appended to the original agreement as well as to the reservation.[16]

> If the Arabs obtain their independence as demanded in my memorandum of the 4th of January, 1919 to the Foreign Office of the Government of Great Britain, I shall agree to the contents of the above clauses but, if the slightest change or modification is made, I shall not then be tied or bound by any of its provisions and the agreement will then be null and void, not binding and of no account, and I shall not be liable in any manner whatsoever.[17]

In fact, Feisal did not agree to turn Palestine over to the Jews or to establish a Jewish State in Palestine. The Agreement provided instead for "cordial goodwill and understanding" between Arab and Jew. It attempted "to encourage and stimulate immigration of Jews into Palestine." And, an integral part of it was the third provision,

---

14 *Worldmark Encyclopedia of the Nations* (New York: Worldmark Press, Inc., Harper Brothers, 1960), p. 507.

15 Palestine Royal Commission Report (1937), p. 27.

16 Stephen B. L. Penrose, "The Palestine Problem: Retrospect and Prospect," A speech prepared for the World Council of Churches Conference, held in Beirut in May, 1951, p. 6.

17 Ibid.

13

"the Arab peasant and tenant farmers shall be protected in their rights."[18] Thus, it is impossible to argue that the Arabs agreed to fulfill what was proposed in the Feisal-Weizmann Agreement, for the promises of independence that were given to them were never achieved.[19]

When Hitler came to power in Germany, "the Nazi torrent of murder and bestiality, which began in 1933, forced all the Jews in its path to die or to flee.[20] The Jews, escaping the Hitler regime and seeking refuge, immigrated into Palestine in spite of Arab resistance and the opposition of the British, who controlled the military, police and administrative power therein.

As thousands of Jews arrived in Palestine, the Arab majority felt itself threatened. In 1936, the Arabs of Palestine organized politically by forming the Arab Higher Committee, which was to represent six Palestine Arab parties and to act for the Palestine Arabs. Later that year, the Arab Higher Committee appealed to the British Government, as the trustee of Palestine, to end Jewish immigration.

In consonance with the British desire to protect its huge oil interests and its essential access routes in the Middle East, it issued, on May 17, 1939, the "White Paper," thereby indicating a new policy for Palestine. This new policy deferred the Balfour promises and curtailed the existing "rights" of the Jews to immigration and land purchases. It projected an independent Palestine within ten years in which the Jews would be relegated to permanent minority status. Specifically, it envisaged:

1. Participation of both Jews and Arabs in an interim government with a constitution to be drawn up after five years, providing for a Jewish national home.

---

[18] Sami Hadawi, *Palestine: Questions and Answers*, op. cit., p. 17.

[19] For more information see Stephen B. L. Penrose, op. cit., p. 6.

[20] A. G. Mezerik, op. cit., p. 5.

2. The Jewish immigration should be limited to a total of 75,000 during the next five years — which would give the Jews one-third of the total population in 1944 — and that further Jewish immigration would depend on Arab consent; and

3. That further transfer of Arab-owned land to Jewish ownership would be regulated by the proposed interim government.[21]

Both Arabs and Jews rejected this plan. The Arab Higher Committee felt the plan did not solve the problem of the Jews already in Palestine and that it would permit entry of 75,000 more. The Jews felt the British were repudiating the Balfour Declaration which had promised the establishment of a Jewish National Home in Palestine.

As the fighting of World War II continued, the Allies found that their military were more and more dependent on the oil of the Arab World, on the Arab pipelines, and on the Suez Canal. To placate Arab opinion the British instituted harsh measures against Jewish immigration by imposing something of a blockade and by setting up camps on Cyprus to contain those Jews seeking entry into Palestine. Yet, by this time, the Zionist community had organized itself to conduct the fight against the British, to protect the Jews seeking entry, to represent the Palestine Jews before the world, and to take over the reins of government.[22]

To insure a united position on Palestine, the Arab League was created in March, 1945, with the Palestine Arab Committee being admitted as a permanent member with a full vote. "The formation of the Arab League in 1945 confirmed abundantly that Palestine Arabs could count on strong support from outside Palestine."[23]

On May 1, 1946, an Anglo-American Committee of

21 *Israel and the United Nations,* op. cit., p. 20.

22 A. G. Mezerik, op. cit., p. 8.

23 Maurice Harari, op. cit., p. 138.

15

Inquiry recommended that immediate entrance to Palestine should be permitted to 100,000 Jews; that Palestine be kept under mandate until a trusteeship agreement should be negotiated, that is, until it might become a Trust Area under the United Nations; and that Palestine should be neither Arab nor Jewish, but a State cherishing equally the rights of Moslems, Christians, and Jews.[24] This Committee consisted of equal numbers of Americans and British. Because none of its members represented the two groups immediately concerned, the Arabs and the Jews of Palestine, its "recommendations — like all previous compromise plans for Palestine — were denounced by Arabs and Zionists. . . ."[25]

Even as the British blockade against Jewish immigration continued, the Arab resistance against the Balfour Declaration increased under the newly created Arab League. Conversely, Jews in Palestine opposed the British blockade and insisted upon the fulfillment of the Declaration. It was this impasse that led to United Nations participation and direction.

---

[24] Report to the U.S. Government and His Majesty's Government in the U.K. (Washington, D.C., Department of State Publication, 1946), No. 2536, pp. 38-51; for more information see GAOR, Second Session, op. cit., p. 27.

[25] Maurice Harari, op. cit., p. 138.

To develop . . . the principle of equal rights and self-determination of peoples . . . (and to promote and encourage) respect for human rights and for fundamental freedoms for all without distinction as to race, sex, language, or religion. . . .

UNITED NATIONS CHARTER

Chapter II

The United Nations Special Committee on Palestine: The Diplomacy of Partition

By 1936 serious difficulties were apparent. The rapid Jewish immigration caused the Arabs to demand immediate self-government and a cessation of immigration. By the end of April, 1936, a general Arab strike spread throughout Palestine and precipitated violence between Arabs and Jews as well as against the British. In August, 1936, Britain appointed an investigation commission under the leadership of Earl Peel. Partition of Palestine was recommended for the first time by this commission as the only workable alternative. The plan of partition was also regarded by the commission as "the only solution which offered any possibility for ultimate peace."[1] The commission further recommended:

---

[1] GAOR, Second Session, Supplement No. 11, (Lake Success, N.Y.: 1947), p. 39.

1. The termination of the Mandate, as the commission was convinced that under the existing Mandate there was little hope of peace in the Holy Land.
2. Treaties of Alliance should be negotiated by the Mandatory with the Government of Trans-Jordan and representatives of the Arabs of Palestine on the one hand and with the Zionist Organization on the other. These treaties would deal with the partition plan, would guarantee the protection of minorities in each State after partition, and would include military conventions for the maintenance of peace and order of the new States.

Finally, the commission indicated that by partition the Arabs would obtain their independence; the Jews, their National Home in Palestine. Again, Arabs and Jews attacked the Peel Report, thus making its implementation impossible.[2]

In April, 1938, another commission was sent to Palestine under the leadership of Sir John Woodhead. It confirmed the Peel plan of partition, but the situation had long passed the point at which partition was feasible.

By the middle of the 1940's, having repeatedly failed to find a satisfactory solution to the Palestine dilemma, Britain laid the problem before the United Nations. "We have tried for years," the British delegate told a committee of the General Assembly, "to solve the problem of Palestine. Having failed so far, we now bring it to the United Nations, in the hope that it can succeed where we have not."[3]

---

[2] See this and more information in Palestine Royal Commission Report, (1937), pp. 285-297; see also on this point Eugene P. Chase, *The United Nations in Action* (New York: McGraw-Hill, Inc., 1950), pp. 140-147.

[3] L. Larry Leonard, "The United Nations and Palestine," International Conciliation, No. 454 (October, 1949), p. 610.

Financial and administrative strains compelled the British delegation to the United Nations to request, on April 2, 1947, that a special session of the General Assembly be convened to consider the question of "constituting and instructing a special committee to prepare for consideration of the question of Palestine. . . ."[4] The report was to be submitted at the next regular session of the General Assembly.

The majority of the members of the United Nations agreed to this proposal; and the Special Session was held at Flushing Meadow, New York, on April 28, 1947, adjourning on May 15. The General Assembly decided, in its First Special Session, to consider only one item in its agenda, namely, the proposal of the United Kingdom for "constituting and instructing a Special Committee to prepare for the consideration of the question of Palestine at the second regular session" of the General Assembly. It omitted the proposal by Egypt, Iraq, Syria, Lebanon, and Saudi Arabia, which asked for "the termination of the mandate over Palestine and the declaration of its independence."[5]

The convening of the First Special Session of the General Assembly on 28 April 1947 opened the UN's

---

4 "Letter dated 2 April 1947 from the Permanent Representative of the U.K. to the Secretary of the U.N.," U.N. Document A/286, GAOR, First Special Session, p. 183; see also on this point Eugene P. Chase, op. cit., p. 147.

5 U.N. Document A/287-291 and A/298; for more information see GAOR, the First Special Session, pp. 183-186, 194-195; see also U.N. Document A/307 and A/307/Corr. I Ibid., p. 197. U.N. Document A/298 indicates that the General Committee had considered at its twenty-eighth and twenty-ninth meetings the item on the provisional agenda (Document A/293), entitled "constituting and instructing a special committee to prepare for the consideration of the question of Palestine at the second regular session," submitted by the Government of the United Kingdom, and decided not to recommend the inclusion of the item entitled "the termination of the mandate over Palestine and the declaration of its independence," submitted by the Governments of Egypt, Iraq, Syria, Lebanon and Saudi Arabia.

entry into the business of state-making. In the arena of [the] UN at Lake Success, New York, the contending interests met — proposing, refuting, threatening and entreating.[6]

Meanwhile, in Palestine, the fighting began. The Jews fought the British, who were forcibly blockading immigration; the Arabs and the Jews fought each other with each promising that, if there were no satisfactory solution, the fighting would continue and grow.

The committee work was done entirely by the First (Political and Security) Committee and its subcommittees. Hearings were given to two nongovernmental organizations, the Arab Higher Committee and the Jewish Agency for Palestine. Each gave its ideas of the future State it wanted. The Arabs asked for an end to the League of Nations Mandate and the creation of an independent, unpartitioned Palestinian State under the existing Arab majority. The Jewish Agency insisted on a State which gave them their "right" under the Balfour Declaration and the League of Nations Mandate and complained of British restrictions on immigration to Palestine.[7]

One major controversy centered about the right of the Arab Higher Committee to represent the Palestine Arabs and the Jewish Agency for Palestine to represent the Jews. Some representatives believed that "The Arab case is, and should be, represented by the five Arab States which are taking part in our deliberations."[8] The Syrian delegate objected to this view, "We . . . as well as delegations of other Arab States, do not represent the Palestinian Arabs. We of the Syrian delegation represent the Government of

---

6 A. G. Mezerik, "Arab-Israel Conflict and the United Nations," *International Review Service*, Vol. VIII, No. 73 (1962), p. 9.

7 Ibid., p. 50; see also GAOR, Second Session, op. cit., pp. 30-34; and see the claims and views of each side above, pp. 9-12.

8 U.N. Document A/BUR/P, Vol. 32 (May 2, 1947), p. 21.

the Syrian Republic."[9] The Egyptian delegate took a similar position:

> I should like to clarify a point . . . that my Arab colleagues and I represent the Arabs of Palestine. I wish to emphasize at this point that we are representatives of Governments and not of any organizations or bodies. . . . Although our Governments are vitally interested in the question of Palestine, I must affirm nevertheless that the Palestinians have not committed us to take up their case and probably do not approve of our procedure or of our way of defending what we think is right.[10]

The General Assembly, however, made no provision for participation of nongovernmental agencies. The delegation of Ecuador, who supported the right of the Jewish Agency to participate, took this position:

> This . . . is just, because we are dealing with the fate not only of the Arabs but also of the Jews of Palestine, who have an undeniable right to be heard in defence of their vital interests. This procedure is fitting, because the General Assembly ought to obtain as much information as possible and, in particular, ought to become familiar with the outlooks of the two population groups living in Palestine.[11]

The Soviet delegation insisted that the voice of the representatives of the Jewish Organization should be heard. "We have not heard the voice of those organizations which speak for a considerable part of the Jewish population of Palestine." Mr. Gromyko finally told the General Assem-

---

9 GAOR, the First Special Session, Vol. I, Plenary Meetings of the General Assembly (April 28-May 15, 1947), p. 104.

10 U.N. Document A/BUR/P, Vol. 33 (May 2, 1947), p. 114.

11 U.N. Document A/BUR/P, Vol. 30 (April 30, 1947), p. 46.

22

bly that "it would be unjust to deprive the Jewish organizations, or organization of the right to express their views. . . ."[12]

Along with Dr. Fiderkiewicz of Poland, Mr. Pearson of Canada opposed the participation of the nongovernmental groups. He declared that no subject involving the Palestine problem would be discussed. Hence, no opportunity for either the Arabs or the Jews to present their views need be provided. For "it is not the case of Palestine which will be heard before the First Committee but merely the question of setting up a committee to investigate the situation in Palestine."[13]

The official presentation was given when, on May 6, 1947, the President of the General Assembly informed both the Jewish Agency and the Arab Higher Committee of the decision taken concerning their participation:

The General Assembly resolves:
That the First Committee grant a hearing to the Jewish Agency for Palestine on the question before the Committee.[14]

The General Assembly:
Affirms that the decision of the First Committee to grant a hearing to the Arab Higher Committee gives a correct interpretation of the Assembly's intention.[15]

A second difference of opinion was in regard to the constitution of the Special Committee. The main question here concerned the nature of the membership of the Committee. Was it feasible and advisable for the Big Powers (the United States, the Soviet Union, the United Kingdom, and France) to participate in this Committee?

---

12 GAOR, First Special Session, Vol. 1, op. cit., p. 78.
13 U.N. Document A/BUR/P, Vol. 33, op. cit., p. 119.
14 GAOR, First Special Session, op. cit., p. 197; U.N. Document A/305.
15 Ibid.; U.N. Document A/306.

With regard to this issue the Big Powers were divided:[16] The United States held, "We could hardly admit that a body which contains the five Great Powers was entirely independent and removed from bias." France maintained, "The Big Five should be excluded since their presence might introduce the more general difficulties of the world political situation thus adding to the difficulties inherent to the problem of Palestine." The Soviet representative stated:

> I wish to draw the attention of the Committee to the following question: Which alternative will make it easier to come to an agreement on the Palestine problem during the next session of the General Assembly? Will it be if Great Powers participate in the preparation of the decisions or will it be if the Great Powers are compelled to remain aside in the preparation of those decisions? I submit that it would be easier to come to an agreement on the Palestine problem at the next session of the Great Assembly if the five Powers will have participated in the preparation of pertinent recommendations for the General Assembly. I submit that it is difficult to dispute this thesis.

On May 15, 1947, the General Assembly passed a resolution constituting the United Nations Special Committee on Palestine, popularly known as UNSCOP. It was composed of representatives of eleven member states, none of which were permanent members of the Security Council.[17]

The Special Committee was given authority to carry on its investigations "wherever it may deem useful"; "to receive and examine written or oral testimony" from any governments, organizations or individuals "it may deem necessary"; and to make recommendations in a report to

---

16 L. Larry Leonard, op. cit., pp. 623-624.

17 See UNSCOP Report, pp. 5-6. These were Australia, Canada, Czechoslovakia, Guatemala, India, Iran, the Netherlands, Peru, Sweden, Uruguay, and Yugoslavia.

the General Assembly to be submitted in its second regular session by September, 1947.[18]

The resolution for the creation of UNSCOP passed with forty affirmative votes and thirteen abstentions. The latter included the three Soviet Republics, the five Arab League States, Afghanistan, Turkey, Czechoslovakia and Yugoslavia. In response, the Arab States stated that they would boycott UNSCOP.[19] The Iraqi delegate asserted what was later proved a prescient judgment.

> Taking the small land of Palestine, which has its Arab quality and character, and bringing in people there [Jews] and making them a majority, thereby creating a state of people coming from abroad, is certainly a matter of aggression and a matter of war which, in normal times, cannot be solved except by fighting. This is actually an invitation to fighting.[20]

As the situation worsened, the General Assembly passed another resolution calling upon:

> All governments and peoples, and particularly upon the inhabitants of Palestine, to refrain, pending

---

[18] See L. Larry Leonard, op. cit., pp. 627-628. The resolution as adopted covered the following points:

1. An eleven-nation investigating committee was established.
2. This committee was empowered to investigate conditions and to make recommendations.
3. The scope of the committee's investigating authority was broad enough to include the displaced persons, problems in Germany and other issues related to Palestine.
4. Although no specific mention was made of independence, this was generally assumed by the delegates to be the objective.

[19] See U.N. Document A/RES/196 (S-1) in "Resolutions Adopted by the General Assembly during Its First Special Session from 28 April to 15 May 1947" (Lake Success, New York: 1947), p. 6; see also A. G. Mezerik, op. cit., p. 50.

[20] GAOR, The First Special Session, Vol. III, Main Committees (April 28-May 13, 1947), p. 261.

action by the General Assembly on the report of the Special Committee on Palestine, from the threat or use of force or any other action which might create an atmosphere prejudicial to an early settlement of the question of Palestine.[21]

On May 26, 1947, the United Nations Special Committee on Palestine held its first meeting at Lake Success. It chose as chairman, Emil Sandstrom of Sweden, and as vice-chairman, Dr. Alberto Ulloa of Peru. After preliminary meetings in New York, the Committee traveled to Palestine, accompanied by members of the United Nations Secretariat.

The Arab Higher Committee detailed its position in a cable of June 13, 1947, addressed to the Secretary General.

> After thoroughly studying the deliberations and circumstances under which the Palestine fact-finding committee was formed and the discussions leading to terms of reference they resolved that Palestine Arabs should abstain from collaboration and desist from appearing before said committee for following main reasons — firstly United Nations refusal adopt natural course of inserting termination mandate and declaration independence in agenda special UN session and in terms of reference; secondly failure detach Jewish world refugees from Palestine problems; thirdly replacing interests Palestine inhabitants by insertion world religious interests although these are not subject of contention — furthermore Palestine Arabs natural rights are self-evident and cannot continue to be subject to investigation but deserve to be recognized on the basis of principles of United Nations Charter ends.[22]

---

21 Resolution adopted by the General Assembly (April 28-May 15, 1947), p. 7.

22 UNSCOP Report, A/364/Add. I, p. 14.

On August 31, 1947, the members of the Committee signed their report and transmitted it to the Secretary-General for presentation to the second session of the General Assembly. It was a long report describing in great detail the activities of the Committee. Included was a review of the factual evidence along with observations and conclusions.[23]

In Chapter V of its Report the Committee unanimously recommended some general principles:[24]

1. The Mandate for Palestine shall be terminated at the earliest practicable date.

2. Independence shall be granted in Palestine at the earliest practicable date.

3. There shall be a transitional period preceding the grant of independence in Palestine which shall be as short as possible, consistent with the achievement of the preparations and conditions essential to independence.

4. During the transitional period the authority entrusted with the task of administering Palestine and preparing it for independence shall be responsible to the United Nations.

5. In whatever solution may be adopted for Palestine, the sacred character of the Holy Places shall be preserved and access to the Holy Places for purposes of worship and pilgrimage shall be ensured in accordance with

---

[23] Vol. I, Report to the General Assembly, U.N. Document A/364; Annexes 1 to 21 and Appendix, U.N. Document A/364/Add. I; Annex A: Oral Evidence Presented at Public Meetings, U.N. Document A/364/Add. 2; Annex B: Oral Evidence Presented at Private Meeting, U.N. Document A/364/Add. 3; see also Index to the Report and Annexes, U.N. Document A/364/Add. 4 (October 9, 1947).

[24] GAOR, the Second Session, Supplement No. 11, op. cit., pp. 42-46.

existing rights, in recognition of the proper interest of millions of Christians, Jews and Moslems abroad as well as the residents of Palestine in the care of sites and buildings associated with the origin and history of their faiths.

6. The General Assembly shall undertake immediately the initiation and execution of an international arrangement whereby the problem of the distressed European Jews, of whom approximately 250,000 are in assembly centers, shall be dealt with as a matter of extreme urgency for the alleviation of their plight and of the Palestine problem.

7. In view of the fact that independence is to be granted in Palestine on the recommendation and under the auspices of the United Nations, it is a proper and an important concern of the United Nations that the constitution or other fundamental law as well as the political structure of the new State or States shall be basically democratic.

8. It shall be required, as a prior condition to independence, to incorporate in the future constitutional provisions applying to Palestine those basic principles of the Charter of the United Nations.

9. The economic unity of Palestine as a whole is indispensable to the life and development of the country and its peoples.

10. States whose nationals have in the past enjoyed in Palestine the privileges and immunities of foreigners, including the benefits of consular jurisdiction and protection as formerly pro-

vided by capitulations or usage in the Ottoman Empire, shall be invited by the United Nations to renounce any right pertaining to them or to the reestablishment of such privileges and immunities in an independent Palestine.

11. The General Assembly shall call on the peoples of Palestine to extend their fullest cooperation to the United Nations in its effort to devise and put into effect an equitable and workable means of settling the difficult situation prevailing there, and in the interest of peace, good order, and lawfulness, to exert every effort to bring to an early end the acts of violence which have for too long beset that country.

With regard to the future government of Palestine, the Committee was divided on two plans. The majority, consisting of the representatives of Canada, Czechoslovakia, Guatemala, the Netherlands, Peru, Sweden, and Uruguay, proposed that Palestine be partitioned into an Arab State, a Jewish State, and the City of Jerusalem — all linked in economic union. This plan included the following principal features:[25]

1. Palestine to be partitioned into an Arab State, a Jewish State, and an independent City of Jerusalem.

2. The Arab and Jewish States to become independent after a transitional period of two years from September 1, 1947. During this interval, the United Kingdom to continue to govern Palestine but under the general auspices of the United Nations.

---

[25] UNSCOP Report, A/364, op. cit., pp. 122-140.

3. A stated number of Jewish immigrants to be admitted during the transitional period.

4. The population in each of the States to elect an interim assembly to draw up a constitution. This to provide for democratic institutions and guarantees for the Holy Places and minority rights.

5. The Constituent Assembly in each State to establish a provisional government empowered to make a declaration protecting the Holy Places, and to sign a treaty of economic union between the Arab and Jewish States.

6. The objectives of economic union to be administered by a joint economic board consisting of members from each of the States and members appointed by the Economic and Social Council of the United Nations.

7. The boundaries of each of the States were specified.

8. Each of the States was to be recognized as independent only after the declaration concerning the protection of the Holy Places had been made and the treaty of economic union had been signed.

9. Jerusalem after the transitional period was to become a Trust Area under the International Trusteeship System with the United Nations as the administering authority.

The minority, consisting of the representatives of India, Iran, and Yugoslavia, while opposed to the majority's recommendations concerning the future government of Palestine, outlined a plan for the establishment of a federal state which included the following provisions:[26]

---

26 Ibid., pp. 147-164.

1. An independent federal state consisting of an Arab State and a Jewish State with Jerusalem as the capital to be established after a transitional period not to exceed three years.

2. During this interval, responsibility for governing Palestine and preparing for its independence to rest with an authority designated by the General Assembly.

3. In the transitional period, the people of Palestine to elect a constituent assembly to draw up a constitution providing for a federal government. Powers to be specified for federal government, and local autonomy provided for the Arab and Jewish States. In addition to the basic democratic institutions of government, the constitution to provide for free access to the Holy Places and the protection of religious interests.

4. For a period of three years Jewish immigration to be permitted only to the extent to which the country could absorb the immigrants without hardship on the population. The absorptive capacity of Palestine to be determined by an international commission consisting of three Arab, three Jewish, and three United Nations representatives.

5. The boundaries for the Arab and Jewish areas of the federal state were specified.

The Australian member of UNSCOP abstained from voting since he believed the terms of reference of the Committee confined its activities to recording, reporting, and fact-finding; that it was for the General Assembly to decide what was feasible in the light of all factors, including the political factors.

The minority plan was basically satisfactory to the Arabs who opposed the majority plan which was accepted by the Jews, excepting the extremists who remained unsatisfied, for the plan did not include the whole land of Palestine in a Jewish State.[27]

---

27 A. G. Mezerik, op. cit., pp. 12, 51.

Chapter III

The Partition Resolution

In September, 1947, the General Assembly met for its second regular session. The Assembly set up an ad hoc Committee to consider the report of the United Nations Special Committee on Palestine. The ad hoc Palestine Committee met for the first time on September 25, elected Dr. Herbert V. Evatt of Australia as Chairman, and invited the Arab Higher Committee and the Jewish Agency for Palestine to be present at its deliberations.

The ad hoc Committee was divided into two subcommittees, one favoring the majority report of UNSCOP (the Subcommittee on Partition)[1] and the other supporting the minority plan of UNSCOP (the Subcommittee on the

---

1 The Subcommittee on Partition was composed of Canada, Czechoslovakia, Guatemala, Poland, South Africa, the United States, the Union of Soviet Socialist Republics and Venezuela.

Federal State).[2] Also established was a Conciliation Group which tried to find an acceptable middle position. This was a select body composed of the chairman, vice-chairman, and rapporteur of the ad hoc Committee.

On September 29, 1947, in the third meeting of the ad hoc Committee, the Arab Higher Committee offered these recommendations as alternatives to the UNSCOP report:

1. An Arab State should be established in the whole of Palestine.
2. This State would respect the rights and the fundamental freedom of all persons before the law.
3. The Arab State would protect the legitimate rights and the interests of all minorities.
4. The Arab State would recognize freedom of worship and access to the Holy Places, including Jerusalem.[3]

On October 2, 1947, in the fourth meeting of the ad hoc Committee, the Jewish Agency pledged to accept the UNSCOP recommendation for partition of Palestine "although this falls short of Balfour Declaration's promises which referred to the whole of Palestine." The Agency stated that Jerusalem was heavily populated by Jews and so should be the capital of the Jewish State, and in no case, was Jerusalem to be under international administration.[4]

---

[2] The Subcommittee on the Federal State was composed of Afghanistan, Colombia, Egypt, Iraq, Lebanon, Pakistan, Saudi Arabia, Syria and Yemen. Colombia resigned from the Subcommittee when the Chairman of the ad hoc Committee refused Colombia's request that neutral states be included in its membership.

[3] U.N. Document GAOR, Second Session, ad hoc Committee, Third Meeting.

[4] U.N. Document GAOR, Second Session, ad hoc Committee, Fourth Meeting.

34

On October 13, the Soviet Union informed the ad hoc Committee that it would support the UNSCOP recommendation for the partition of Palestine, but with economic union. It charged that bloodshed between Arabs and Jews was the result of the British failure to properly execute the Mandate.[5]

On October 14, 1947, Iraq submitted a draft resolution to the ad hoc Palestine Committee requesting that the following legal question be referred to the International Court of Justice:

> Did not the pledges given by Great Britain to the Sherif Hussein of Mecca and its subsequent declarations, promises and assurances to the Arabs that, in the event of Allied victory, the Arab countries would obtain their independence, include Palestine and its inhabitants?[6]

This proposed resolution failed to secure passage.

On October 16, Great Britain told the Committee that it would cooperate with any plan for Palestine only if the plan was acceptable to Jews and to Arabs.[7] On the same day Syria submitted the following draft resolution to the Committee asking that the considerations contained therein be referred to the International Court of Justice:

> Having considered the contentions of several delegations against the competence of the General Assembly to adopt and execute by force the plan of Partition on Palestine dividing Palestine into three sovereign states, namely, Arab, Jewish, and City of Jerusalem, against the wishes of the Arab majority, arguing that the provisions of the Charter and the Mandate itself

5 U.N. Document GAOR, Second Session, ad hoc Committee, Twelfth Meeting.

6 U.N. Document A/AC.14/21.

7 U.N. Document GAOR, Second Session, ad hoc Committee, Fifteenth Meeting.

do not enable the General Assembly to adopt any plan
of Partition and enforce it upon the Arabs, who form
the majority of the population, without their consent. . . . [the Committee] requests the International
Court of Justice to give an advisory opinion . . . on
the following question. . . . Does the plan of Partition . . . in its adoption and forcible execution fall
within the Jurisdiction of the General Assembly?[8]

Like the Iraqi attempt, the Syrian-proposed resolution was
abortive.

On October 23, 1947, the Subcommittee on Partition
began its deliberations.

Invitations were accepted by the United Kingdom
and the Jewish Agency to attend the sessions. The
Arab Higher Committee refused to attend on the
grounds that it was prepared only to give information
on the question of the termination of the mandate
and on the creation of a unitary state of Palestine.[9]

Dr. Evatt, as head of the Conciliation Group, reported
on November 19, the failure of his group to bring the
parties together. "It was subsequently alleged by some
delegates that this Conciliation Group had never actually
functioned."[10]

Almost simultaneously, each of the two subcommittees
reported its conclusions to the ad hoc Committee. While
the Subcommittee on Partition submitted a plan based
upon the proposals of the UNSCOP majority plan, the
Subcommittee on the Federal State suggested a plan for the
recognition of Palestine as an independent unitary State.

The full Committee, after a long debate, adopted the
work of the first subcommittee and presented a partition
plan to the General Assembly. On November 29, 1947, the

---

8 U.N. Document A/AC. 14/25.

9 L. Larry Leonard, "The United Nations and Palestine," International Conciliation, No. 454 (October, 1949), p. 641.

10 Ibid., p. 642.

General Assembly, by two-thirds vote, adopted a resolution on the "Plan of Partition with Economic Union of Palestine."[11] The vote was thirty-three in the affirmative, thirteen in the negative, and ten abstentions.[12] The plan provided:

1. The British Mandate over Palestine was terminated.
2. British armed forces were to leave the country by August 1, 1948.
3. The Arab State, the Jewish State, and the International regime for Jerusalem were to come into being two months after departure of the British armed forces.
4. The boundaries of the three territories were defined as follows:[13]

---

[11] GAOR, Resolutions, 181-II, pp. 132-137. For full text, see Appendix B; see also Map I— Partition and Conquest.

[12] The vote was as follows: in favor: Australia, Belgium, Bolivia, Brazil, Byelorussia, Canada, Costa Rica, Czechoslovakia, Denmark, Dominican Republic, Ecuador, the Netherlands, New Zealand, Nicaragua, Norway, Panama, Paraguay, Peru, Philippines, Poland, Sweden, Ukraine, Union of South Africa, the Soviet Union, United States, Uruguay, and Venezuela; against: Afghanistan, Cuba, Egypt, Greece, India, Iran, Iraq, Lebanon, Pakistan, Saudi Arabia, Syria, Turkey, and Yemen; abstained: Argentina, Chile, China, Colombia, El Salvador, Ethiopia, Honduras, Mexico, United Kingdom, and Yugoslavia.

[13] For more information, see J. C. Hurewitz, *Diplomacy in the Near and Middle East* (Princeton, New Jersey: D. Van Nostrand Co., Inc., 1950), Vol. II, pp. 289-292. It is to be noted, however, that the Jewish State would include most of the coastal strip, populated with Jews and economically well-developed. It would include another fertile and populous area, eastern Galilee. And it would include most of the Negev, the sandy southern area of the country which is large and empty but intended by the Jews for future settlement. The important Arab areas were the southern part of the coastal strip and a slice of the Negev, running from the coast south along the Egyptian border, and most of the interior of Palestine going as far east as the border of Transjordan. Jerusalem was to be internationalized. Tel Aviv was Jewish and to remain so. Haifa, with a majority of Jews, was in the Jewish coastal strip Jaffa, with a majority of Arabs, was to be an Arab enclave in the Jewish State. Gaza was Arab and would remain so.

Map I — Partition and Conquest

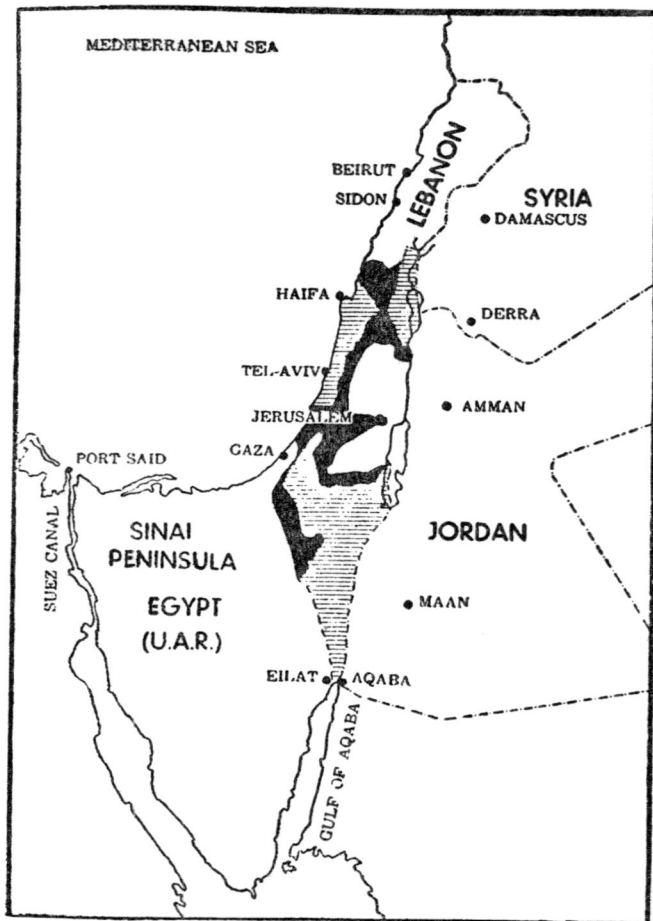

(horizontal lines)	The Jewish State under the Partition Resolution of November 29, 1947
(black)	Further annexation by Israel after the first Arab-Israeli War of 1948-49
- - -	International Boundaries and Armistice Lines

The Arab State would include three separate areas: western Galilee, the central part of Palestine from the valley of Esdraelon down to Beersheba, and a strip of land along the Mediterranean coast (including Gaza) and along the Egyptian border about halfway from the Mediterranean to the Red Sea. It would also include Jaffa, which would be geographically an enclave in the Jewish State. Apart from Jaffa, the Arab State would consist of three areas, each touching other Arab areas at points where separate areas of the Jewish State would also meet.

The Jewish State would also be composed of three separate areas, meeting at corners: eastern Galilee and the valley of Esdraelon, a coastal strip from Haifa to below Jaffa, and for the third area, that part of the Negev not assigned to the Arabs.

Jerusalem, including Bethlehem and other suburbs, would be a separate unit outside both States.

5. The Trusteeship Council was instructed to prepare a Statute for the City of Jerusalem.

6. Economic union was to be achieved through a Joint Economic Board composed of three representatives appointed by each of the two States, in addition to three members appointed by the Economic and Social Council of the United Nations.

7. A United Nations Palestine Commission of five States was established to implement the General Assembly resolution.

8. The Security Council was called upon to assist in the implementation of the plan, determine

whether the situation in Palestine constituted a threat to the peace, and take measures to preserve peace. It was specifically requested by the General Assembly to interpret as a threat to peace any attempt to alter the partition plan by force.

9. Arab human, civil, political, economic, religious, and property rights, including fundamental freedoms in religion, language, speech, publications, education, assembly and association in the territory reserved for the Jewish State were to be guaranteed.

10. No discrimination of any kind was to be made between the inhabitants on the grounds of race, religion, language, or sex.

11. "So expropriation of land owned by an Arab in the Jewish State shall be allowed except for public purposes. In all cases of expropriation, full compensation as fixed by the Supreme Court be paid previous to dispossession."[14]

It should be noted, however, that the United Nations Resolution on Partition of Palestine, which was adopted and which became the basic document guiding the United Nations program and policy in Palestine, was not the same as recommended by UNSCOP.

The Partition plan as it stood after adoption by the General Assembly, made the following principal changes in the UNSCOP proposal. A Palestine Commission was established with responsibilities for implementation. The United Kingdom, as the Mandatory Power, was relieved of all administrative and enforce-

---

14 GAOR, Resolutions (September 16-November 29, 1947), 181-II. pp. 132-137.

ment responsibilities during the transition period except those which flowed from its membership in the United Nations. The Security Council was called upon to aid in the enforcement of Partition.[15]

However, to determine whether the General Assembly had the requisite authority in approving the partition resolution, it is necessary to look at the problem from the different angles: legal, political and moral.

Legally, it is generally understood that the General Assembly is not a legislative or a judicial body. As provided in the Charter,[16] the General Assembly is the main body of deliberation, discussion, and recommendation. It has the power to discuss any questions within the scope of the Charter and to make recommendations on any such questions. It may recommend measures for the peaceful adjustment of any situation. Therefore, the resolution on the partition of Palestine, being a recommendation and a measure for peaceful adjustment in Palestine, lay within its scope and was legally valid. The General Assembly did not exceed its authority when it recommended,

> to the United Kingdom as the Mandatory Power for Palestine, and to all other Members of the United Nations the adoption and implementation, with regard to the future government of Palestine, of the plan of Partition with Economic Union. . . .[17]

Furthermore, as the Mandatory Power, the United Kingdom had relinquished responsibility on April 2, 1947, to the General Assembly. Hence, the Assembly carried this responsibility on behalf of the people of Palestine, not of the Mandatory Power. This responsibility was assumed

---

15 L. Larry Leonard, op. cit., p. 646.
16 See U.N. Charter, Chapter IV (Articles 10, 11/2, 14).
17 U.N. Resolution on Partition of Palestine, op. cit., p. 131.

41

within the limitation that had been given to Britain under the Mandate for Palestine which had been approved by both the Council of the League of Nations and the Principal Allied Powers. Article 2 of the text of the Mandate for Palestine is the most relevant document pertinent to the point now discussed. This Article reads as follows:

> The Mandatory shall be responsible for placing the country under such political, administrative and economic conditions as will secure the establishment of the Jewish national home, as laid down in the preamble, and the development of self-governing institutions, and also for safeguarding the civil and religious rights of all the inhabitants of Palestine, irrespective of race and religion.[18]

Politically, the belief that there was no other peaceful alternative came to be the decisive consideration. It is also interesting to note two other things: (a) As there was no indication that the two conflicting groups would live together in peace, the partition of Palestine was considered the most practical solution; and (b) As the General Assembly represents the world opinion, and reflects the world conscience, the majority vote behind the resolution showed that it was politically convenient for the maintenance of peace and stability in that area.

Morally, however, the consent of the Arab inhabitants of Palestine, being the majority, relative to the future of their country was a necessary action consistent with principles and the spirit of the Charter and should have been implemented.

The Status of the Population and Land Ownership before and after the Partition Resolution

In 1918, when British forces occupied the Holy Land, there were 56,000 Jews in the country, representing about

---

18 For the complete text of the Mandate of Palestine, see J. C. Hurewitz, op. cit., pp. 106-111.

42

8 percent of the total population of 700,000. They owned only 2 percent, or 162,500 acres of a total land area of 6,580,755 acres. In 1948, when Great Britain left Palestine, the Jews numbered 700,000 or 33 percent of the total population which was estimated to have reached 2,155,000 (Moslem and Christian Arabs were 1,380,000 with others numbering 35,000). When the partition resolution was adopted, Jewish ownership of land in Palestine had risen from 2 percent to 5.67 percent.[19]

The Partition Plan envisaged an Arab State with an area of 4,476 square miles or 42.88 percent of the total area of Palestine, inhabited by 725,000 Arabs and 10,000 Jews. The Jewish State was to comprise 56.47 percent or 5,893 square miles of the total area, inhabited by 498,000 Jews and 407,000 Arabs. Jewish landholdings in the proposed area of the Jewish State were to be 9.38 percent, or 345,964 acres of a total land area of 3,815,412 acres, while the Arab landholdings in this area were to be 24.24 percent or 894,456 acres. In the Arab State, Jewish landholdings would have been 0.84 percent or 23,885 acres of a total land area of 2,897,467 acres while the Arab landholdings in their area were to be 77.69 percent or 2,212,075 acres.

Finally, the International Zone of Jerusalem was to comprise 0.65 percent or 68 square miles of the total area of Palestine, and to be inhabited by 100,000 Jews and 105,000 Arabs. Whereas the Arab landholdings in Jerusalem were to be 84.70 percent or 37,165 acres of a total land area of 43,876 acres, the Jewish landholdings in that area would have been 7.01 percent or 3,074 acres.[20]

---

19 Sami Hadawi, *Palestine: Loss of Heritage* (San Antonio, Texas: The Naylor Company, 1963), pp. 12-25; and Eugene P. Chase, *The United Nations in Action* (New York: McGraw-Hill, Inc., 1950,) pp. 152-153.

20 The figures given for the distribution of the settled population in the two proposed States were estimated on the basis of official figures up to the end of 1946. See on this point the GAOR, Supplement No. 11, Vol. 1 (1947), p. 54; see also for more information Sami Hadawi, op. cit., pp. 25, 135.

43

The Arab Reaction to the Partition Resolution

The Palestine Arabs, supported by the Arab States, rejected the partition from the very beginning. "The Palestine Arabs were not unaware that the partition plan was not the end but the beginning of bloodshed and strife in the Holy Land."[21] The Arabs of Palestine, as well as the neighboring Arab States, saw that:

> Part of an Arab country was to become, without the consent of the majority of its population and against their expressed will, subject to an alien authority. The United Nations had violated the principle of national self-determination in making such a recommendation. The General Assembly in particular had exceeded the scope of its competence as defined in the Charter. To the Arabs, the establishment of a Zionist State in part of the Arab country was a gross act of injustice.[22]

Moreover, the Arabs of Palestine, as well as all Arab States, saw that it was not fair or just that "the area awarded to the Jewish State comprised 56.47 percent of the total area of Palestine. Only half of its inhabitants were Jews and they owned only 9.38 percent of its land area."[23]

The sum of these considerations caused the Arab countries to declare that they would not recognize the United Nations resolution and served notice that if it were implemented, they would war on the new Jewish State.[24] Earlier, on September 1, 1947, the Arab Higher Committee had said that any attempt to carry out the UNSCOP

---

21 Sami Hadawi, op. cit., p. 29.

22 Fayez A. Sayegh, *The Arab-Israeli Conflict* (New York: The Arab Information Center, November, 1956), p. 15.

23 Ibid.

24 U.N. Document A/PV. 128.

44

plan "will set Palestine and the Arab world on fire. . . ."
An Iraqi representative said, immediately after the resolution had passed, "My country will never recognize such
a decision. It will never agree to be responsible for it. Let
the consequences be on the heads of others, not on ours."[25]
In similar fashion, Jordan rejected the United Nations
actions:

> In San Francisco, we had high hopes for the world.
> Today, these hopes are shattered. . . . In the name of
> my Government, I wish to state that it feels that
> this decision is anti-democratic, illegal, impractical
> and contrary to the Charter. . . . I wish to put on the
> record that Iraq does not recognize the validity of
> this decision, will reserve freedom of action towards
> its implementation.[26]

The Jewish Reaction to the Partition Resolution

The Jews accepted the resolution on Partition of
Palestine, but extremists remained unsatisfied. The Jewish
Agency favored the plan, saying that it accepted, in principle, the partition, although this fell far short of the
original area promised to the Jews in the Balfour Declaration.[27] Chaim Weizmann, then President of the World
Zionist Organization and first President of the State of
Israel, expressed the Jewish dissatisfaction and intention to
expand and occupy more areas in Palestine when he defended the noninclusion of southern Palestine within the
proposed Jewish frontiers, remarking, "It will not run
away."[28] David Ben-Gurion, then Chairman of the Jewish

---

[25] GAOR, Second Session (1947), Vol. 2e, p. 1427.

[26] Ibid.

[27] GAOR, Second Session, ad hoc Committee on the Palestine Question (1947), pp. 12-19.

[28] George Kirk, *A Short History of the Middle East* (New York:
F. A. Praeger, 1959), pp. 186-187.

Agency and the first Prime Minister of the State of Israel, also admitted that the expansion over the whole of Palestine was the intention and the ultimate goal when he wrote that the State "has been resurrected in the western part of the land of Israel,"[29] and that "independence" has been reached "in a part of our small country."[30] Mr. Ben-Gurion wrote:

> Every State consists of a land and a people. Israel is no exception, but it is a State identical neither with its land nor with its people. It has already been said that when the State was established it held only six percent of the Jewish people remaining alive after the Nazi cataclysm. It must now be said that it has been established in only a Portion of the Land of Israel.[31]

The Attitudes of the Big Powers

First, it should be noted that the decision — that Palestine should be partitioned into two States and an international Jerusalem, linked in economic union for the entire country — was a decision of the majority of the United Nations Committee in which none of the Big Five had a seat. But it was hardly a secret that ". . . the combined support of the United States and the Soviet Union won many doubtful States to vote for the plan. Particularly, however, the United States Government used its influence to gain votes."[32] A most conspicuous example of influence, here of a congressional nature, is given by Mr. Lilienthal: "Twenty-six pro-Zionist Senators joined in a telegram drafted by New York's Robert F. Wagner. That telegram, sent to the Philippines and to twelve other U.N. delega-

---

29 Government of Israel, Israeli Yearbook (1952) p. 63.

30 Ibid., (1951-1952), p. 64.

31 Ibid., (1952), p. 65.

32 Eugene P. Chase, op. cit., p. 151.

tions, changed five votes to yes, and seven voted from no to abstention."[33]

The United Kingdom: The United Kingdom, the Mandatory Power, did not participate in the vote but expressed dissatisfaction with the partition plan:

> After years of strenuous but unavailing effort, His Majesty's Government has reached the conclusion that it is not able to bring about a settlement in Palestine based upon the consent of both Arabs and Jews and that the mandate is no longer workable. . . . it is with deep regret that my Government recognizes that an acceptable settlement has still not been found.[34]

The British Government subsequently declared that it would do nothing to carry out the General Assembly decision since it was not satisfactory to both Jews and Arabs.[35] The British representative in the General Assembly remarked that his Government did not believe that:

> . . . the Mandate required it to establish either a Jewish State or an Arab State in Palestine by force, or to coerce either people in the interests of the other; nor is it prepared now to accept any responsibility which would involve the use of British troops as the means of enforcing a decision against either people.[36]

The United Kingdom advocated any peaceful solution which was based upon the consent of all parties concerned. At the same time, its representative said it would not

---

33 U.S. Congressional Record (December 18, 1947), p. 1176; and Walter Millis, *The Forrestall Diaries* (New York: Viking Press, 1951), p. 363.

34 GAOR, Second Session, op. cit., p. 1323.

35 L. Larry Leonard, op. cit., p. 646.

36 GAOR, Second Session, op. cit., pp. 1323-1324.

"obstruct the carrying out of any decision which the General Assembly may take."[37]

France: The French representative justified support of the partition by saying if the Assembly failed to vote "in favor of partition, there will be no decision at all. We have been led to think that we must choose between the plan of partition, with its obvious difficulties, and the absence of any plan, which may mean chaos."[38] The French representative felt the partition of Palestine might lead to an agreement on a final settlement in the area.[39]

The United States: While the United States supported the resolution, its representative to the United Nations told the member states that his Government would participate in any United Nations plan toward the establishment of a workable settlement in Palestine. The American ambassador further maintained that the plan of partition offered the best practical opportunity and possibility of obtaining a peaceful settlement in Palestine.

> It is the sincere belief of the United States delegation that the partition plan . . . with all its imperfections admitted, provides for the people of Palestine in that land the best practicable means by which high objectives may be attained.[40]

The United States representative then turned to a constitutional point when he discussed the jurisdiction of the General Assembly in partitioning Palestine. The United States delegate held that the action fell "properly within the scope of the Charter and within the power and responsibilities of the organs of the United Nations."[41] Additionally, Mr. Johnson stated:

---

37 Ibid., p. 1324.
38 Ibid., p. 1403.
39 Ibid., p. 1401.
40 Ibid., p. 1328.
41 Ibid., p. 1326.

48

Palestine, as a territory under mandate, is not a State. It is not an international community. In the circumstances now prevailing, the General Assembly of the United Nations is the effective voice of the international community in determining the new forms and structures of government which should prevail in Palestine when the Mandate is terminated.[42]

The United States Government suggested that, in order to meet the problem of international law and order during the transitional period, the establishment of a special United Nations peace force serving in Palestine might be required. The United States also promised to offer, through the United Nations, assistance to meet economic and financial problems.[43]

The Soviet Union: The Soviet Union supported the resolution and expressed its sympathies for the creation of the Jewish State — a feeling which it did not retain after 1952. The Soviet representative told the General Assembly that in the view of his country the partition of Palestine was "the only workable solution."[44] Mr. Gromyko then reminded the delegations that "the Jews, as a people, have suffered more than any other people."[45] Therefore, the Soviet representative said, the establishment of a Jewish State in Palestine was "in keeping with the basic national interests not only of the Jews but also of the Arabs."[46]

Regarding the constitutional question as to the jurisdiction of the General Assembly in partitioning Palestine, the Soviet delegate told the Assembly that "the decision to

42 Ibid., p. 1327.

43 GAOR, Second Session, ad hoc Committee on the Palestinian Question, op. cit., p. 64.

44 GAOR, Second Session, op. cit., p. 1359.

45 Ibid., p. 1360.

46 Ibid.

partition Palestine is in keeping with the high principles and aims of the United Nations. It is in keeping with the principle of the national self-determination of peoples."[47] He added:

> It was just because the system of governing Palestine by mandate had failed, had proved inadequate, that the United Kingdom Government turned to the United Nations for help. The United Kingdom asked the Assembly to take the appropriate decision and thus to undertake itself the settlement of the problem of the future of Palestine.[48]

It seemed that the main political reasons for Soviet support were: (a) its desire to oust the United Kingdom from its strong position in the Middle East; and (b) its unwillingness to leave the United States alone as the dominant power in the area. The Soviet Union, therefore, rightfully placed the blame for the difficulties, including the bloodshed between Arabs and Jews, on the failure of the British in Palestine. To the United States, however, the Soviet objectives in supporting the partition of Palestine were:

> to strengthen the Soviet Union among Zionists everywhere; to gain a military foothold in the Middle East, on the assumptions that partition must be imposed by force and that force used for this purpose by (the) UN must involve Russian participation; and most important, to ensure chaos and confusion in the Middle East by creating against Arab opposition, a Jewish State surrounded by Arabs.[49]

---

47 Ibid., pp. 1360-1361.

48 Ibid., p. 1361.

49 Kermit Roosevelt, *Partition of Palestine: A Lesson in Pressure Politics* (Broadway, New York: The Institute of Arab-American Affairs, February, 1948), p. 7.

50

THE UNITED NATIONS PALESTINE COMMISSION

Having passed its Palestine resolution, the General Assembly placed primary responsibility for assuring its implementation on the United Nations Palestine Commission. However, since the Security Council was called upon to assist in enforcement should this be required, the actual implementation would depend primarily upon the policies of the permanent members of the Council.

The General Assembly elected Bolivia, Czechoslovakia, Denmark, Panama, and the Philippines as members of the Palestine Commission. When the Commission met for the first time on January 9, 1948, at Lake Success, it decided that its major task in implementing the partition resolution included:[50]

1. Arrangement for the progressive transfer of administrative authority from the Mandatory Power to the Commission and the establishment of Provisional Councils of Government (in the Arab and Jewish states).

2. Supervision of the function of the Provisional Councils of Government, including the maintenance of public order in the transitional period following the termination of the Mandate.

3. Delimitation of frontiers of the Arab and Jewish states and the City of Jerusalem.

4. Exercise of political and military control over the armed militia in each of the projected states, including selection of their high commands.

---

[50] United Nations Palestine Commission, First Monthly Progress Report to the Security Council, U.N. Document A/AC. 21/7 (January 29, 1948), p. 4.

5. The preparatory work in connection with the establishment of the Economic Union, including the creation of the preparatory Economic Commission and the maintenance of the economic services with which it would be concerned in the transitional period.

6. Negotiations on the allocation and distribution of assets.

7. Maintenance of administration and essential public services, following the termination of the Mandate.

8. Preparation for the application of the United Nations Statute to the City of Jerusalem.

9. Protection of Holy Places.

Because the United Nations Palestine Commission would have legislative as well as executive powers, it possessed a character essentially different from that of UNSCOP, which was only a deliberative and an investigative body. Also, instead of establishing subcommittees as had UNSCOP, individual members were given official assignments, but with the specific understanding that they would be responsible to the Commission at all times.

The Commission invited the Arab Higher Committee, along with the United Kingdom, the Mandatory Power, and the Jewish Agency, to send representatives to "be available to the Commission for such authoritative information and other assistance as the Commission may require in the discharge of its functions."[51] While both the Mandatory Power and the Jewish Agency accepted the invitation and appointed representatives, the Arab Higher Committee refused and issued, on February 6, 1948, the following statement:[52]

---

51 U.N. Document A/AC.21/SR.1, p. 4.

52 United Nations Palestine Commission, First Special Report to the Security Council: The Problem of Security in Palestine, U.N. Document A/AC. 21/9 (February 19, 1948), pp. 5-6.

A. The Arabs of Palestine will never recognize the validity of the extorted partition recommendations or the authority of the United Nations to make them.

B. The Arabs of Palestine consider that any attempt by the Jews or any Power or group of Powers to establish a Jewish State in Arab territory is an act of aggression which will be resisted in self-defense by force.

C. It is very unwise and fruitless to ask any commission to proceed to Palestine because not a single Arab will cooperate with the said commission.

D. The United Nations or its commission should not be misled to believe that its efforts in the partition plan will meet with any success. It will be far better for the eclipsed prestige of this organization not to start on this adventure.

E. The United Nations prestige will be better served by abandoning, not enforcing such an injustice.

F. The determination of every Arab in Palestine is to oppose in every way the Partition of that country.

G. The Arabs of Palestine made a solemn declaration before the United Nations, before God and history, that they will never submit or yield to any power going to Palestine to enforce partition.

H. The only way to establish partition is first to wipe them [the Arabs] out — man — woman — and child.

In Palestine the situation grew worse. The extent of hostilities from the passage of the General Assembly resolution to February 1, 1948, was revealed in the casualties, which totalled 2,778 and of whom 869 were killed. The Arabs suffered 1,462 casualties; the Jews, 1,106; the British, 181.[53] By April 10, 1948, the Palestine Commission reported to the General Assembly that:

> As a result of Arab armed opposition to the resolution of the General Assembly, counter or preventive measures taken by the organized Jewish community, and the continued activity of Jewish extremist elements, Palestine is now a battlefield.[54]

By April 3, casualties had risen to 6,187, of whom 4,210 were wounded and 1,977 were killed.[55]

As the Palestine Commission attempted to cope with these hostilities, it met further difficulties in securing British acceptance of the Assembly's timetable which provided that:[56]

1. The Mandatory Power should "use its best endeavors" to have an area in the Jewish State evacuated by February 1, 1948, the Area to include a seaport and hinterland to provide facilities for substantial immigration.

2. The Commission shall have selected and established by April 1, 1948, in the Arab and Jewish States, Provisional Councils of Government.

---

53 Ibid., p. 5.

54 United Nations Palestine Commission, Report to the General Assembly, U.N. Document A/432 (April 10, 1948), p. 10.

55 Ibid., p. 13.

56 L. Larry Leonard, op. cit., p. 652.

54

3. The latest date for the approval by the Trusteeship Council of the statute for the City of
Jerusalem was set as April 28, 1948.

4. August 1, 1948, was the final date for the termination of the Mandate and for the complete
withdrawal of British armed forces from Palestine.

5. Finally, October 1, 1948, was assigned as the
date for the establishment of independent
Arab and Jewish States and the special international regime for the City of Jerusalem.

The British Government then informed the Palestine
Commission that it unilaterally set May 15, 1948, instead
of August 1, 1948, as the date for the termination of the
Mandate. It also refused to open a Jewish seaport, holding
that unlimited immigration and the possible unregulated
importation of arms would produce a deterioration of the
situation in Palestine. The Commission informed the
General Assembly that:

> The Commission could not change this position of
> the United Kingdom. It has had to accommodate itself
> to it and to negotiate with a view to adopting its
> plans for carrying on in Palestine after 15 May to
> the plans of the United Kingdom Government to aban-
> don its responsibilities as a whole, while affording the
> successor authority no assistance which, in their view,
> would constitute implementation of the Assembly
> resolution.
> The Palestine Administration has accordingly been
> unable to take any steps or to pursue any measures
> which would be designed to prepare the ground for
> the plan. This has been particularly serious in view
> of the inability of the Commission itself to be in
> Palestine. The refusal of the Mandatory Power to
> cooperate in implementing the plan, its rejection of
> any progressive transfer of authority, and the inability

55

of the Commission to be in Palestine, constitute a serious jeopardy to the discharge of the Commission's responsibilities.[57]

In step with the war preparations, the fighting in Palestine increased. Soon it became clear that "the UN plans for any kind of union of the two prospective states look completely unrealistic and the problem became more one of seeking to restore peace rather than to implement the elaborate partition plan."[58]

In its first special report to the Security Council, the Palestine Commission expressed (1) the problems in obtaining the cooperation of the Mandatory Power, (2) the inability to fulfill its responsibilities "unless military forces in adequate strength are made available to the Commission when the responsibility for the administration of Palestine is transferred to it,"[59] and (3) the inability to implement the 1947 resolution because "powerful Arab interests, both inside and outside Palestine, are defying the resolution of the General Assembly and are engaged in a deliberate effort to alter by force the settlement envisaged therein."[60] The Commission criticized "certain elements of the Jewish Community" for "irresponsible acts of violence which worsen the security situation."[61] It concluded:

It is the considered view of the Commission that the security forces of the Mandatory Power, which at the present time prevent the situation from deteriorating completely into open warfare on an organized

---

[57] U.N. Document A/532 (April 10, 1948), p. 9.

[58] A. G. Mezerik, "Arab-Israel Conflict and the United Nations," *International Review Service* (1962), p. 14.

[59] U.N. Document A/AC. 21/9 (February 16, 1948), p. 2.

[60] Ibid., p. 3.

[61] Ibid.

basis, must be replaced by an adequate non-Palestinian force which will assist law-abiding elements in both the Arab and Jewish communities, organized under the general direction of the Commission, in maintaining order and security in Palestine, and thereby enabling the Commission to carry out the recommendations of the General Assembly. Otherwise, the period immediately following the termination of the Mandate will be a period of uncontrolled, widespread strife and bloodshed in Palestine, including the City of Jerusalem. This would be a catastrophic conclusion to an era of international concern for that territory.[62]

The Security Council and the Partition Resolution

For the purpose of implementing the Partition Resolution, the General Assembly requested the Security Council to assume a dual responsibility: (1) to provide the Palestine Commission with guidance and instructions, and (2) to provide such force as might be required to implement the partition plan. The Partition Resolution specifically provided that:[63]

A. The Security Council take the necessary measures as provided for in the plan for its implementation.

B. The Security Council consider, if circumstances during the transitional period warrant such consideration, whether the situation in Palestine constitutes a threat to peace. If it decides that such a threat exists, and in order to maintain international peace and security, the Security Council should supplement the authorization of the General Assembly by

---

[62] Ibid., pp. 18-19.

[63] GAOR, Resolutions (September 16-November 29, 1947), 181 (II), pp. 131-132.

taking measures under Articles 39 and 41 of the Charter, to empower the United Nations Commission, as provided in this resolution, to exercise in Palestine the functions which are assigned to it by this resolution.

C. In accordance with Article 39 of the Charter, the Security Council consider as a threat to the peace any attempt to alter by force the settlement envisaged by this resolution. . . .

The relationship of the Palestine Commission to the Security Council envisioned by these provisions was discussed at several meetings of the Commission. The Palestine Commission called upon the legal advisor of its Secretariat to prepare a memorandum clarifying its role vis-à-vis the Security Council. His working paper, "Relations Between the United Nations Commission and the Security Council," dealt not only with the delimitation of powers between the two bodies but also scrutinized the question "whether the Security Council has the power to accept the responsibilities assigned to it by the General Assembly." Among the conclusions were:

> The Resolution leaves a very wide margin of discretion both to the Commission and the Security Council as to the extent of their mutual relationship. The Security Council may, or may not, consider necessary to issue instructions to the Commission on its own initiative. The Commission may ask for the guidance, but it does not need authorization from the Security Council in order to take action.[64]
>
> It is submitted that if the Security Council deemed that it was within its competence to accept responsibilities for the carrying out of certain provisions of a treaty negotiated and concluded outside the United

---

64 U.N. Document A/AC. 21/13 (February 9, 1948), p. 2.

58

Nations, it is still more appropriate that it should accept responsibilities for the implementation of a plan adopted by the General Assembly.[65]

Despite the urgency of the situation, the Council failed to consider its responsibilities for more than two months after the General Assembly resolution had been passed. It was not until February 24, 1948, that the Security Council examined the question of Palestine.

The United Nations Commission reported to the Security Council on military developments in Palestine. These reports provided the basis for the Council's deliberations during February and March, 1948. When the United States introduced a resolution calling upon the parties "to cease acts of violence immediately," it was unanimously adopted on April 1, 1948.[66] The resolution also requested the President of the Council to negotiate a truce. On April 17, the Security Council agreed to a truce resolution calling for a cease-fire and requesting the Mandatory Power to aid in its implementation.[67] But, even though the first truce resolution was passed on April 1, 1948, the Security Council did not create the machinery for implementing its resolution until April 23, 1948, when the Council appointed the three-member Truce Commission "to assist the Security Council in supervising the implementation by the parties of the . . . [cease-fire and truce resolutions]."[68]

The continuous fighting made obvious the impossibility of any peaceful implementation of the Partition Plan and led the United States representative to the United Nations to suggest an alternative scheme, a temporary trusteeship

---

65 Ibid., p. 7.

66 SCOR, Third Year, Supplement for April, 1948, S/714 (April 1, 1948), p. 4.

67 Ibid., S/723 (April 16, 1948), p. 7.

68 SCOR, Third Year, No. 62, p. 33.

59

for Palestine. To this end he proposed that a special session of the General Assembly should be called by the Security Council (under Article 20), and that the Council instruct the Palestine Commission to suspend its efforts to implement partition. "The Arabs favored this plan because it implied a single, not a partitioned, state; the Jews opposed it."[69] Also in opposition was public opinion in the United States. In consequence, "this formula quickly withered under political pressures exerted on the President, his cabinet, and Congress."[70]

On April 1, 1948, the Security Council passed two resolutions. In the first of these the Council referred to "the increasing violence and disorder in Palestine." The Council stated, "It is of the utmost urgency that an immediate truce be effected in Palestine." Therefore, it called upon "Arab and Jewish armed groups in Palestine to cease acts of violence immediately," and, with this objective in mind, requested both the Arab Higher Committee and the Jewish Agency to make representatives available to the Council to discuss arrangements for truce.[71] In the second resolution, the Security Council agreed to the United States proposal for a Special Assembly.[72]

Meanwhile, the United Nations Palestine Commission continued its efforts to implement the partition resolution, unaided by the Council. On April 10, 1948, the Commission submitted its report to the General Assembly, stating that:

> The Commission . . . has the duty to report to the General Assembly that the armed hostility of both Palestinian and non-Palestinian Arab elements,

69 A. G. Mezerik, op. cit., p. 15.

70 Alfred M. Lilienthal, *There Goes the Middle East* (New York: The Bookmailer, Inc., 1958), p. 11.

71 SCOR, Third Year, op. cit., S/714 (April 1, 1948), p. 4.

72 SCOR, Third Year, (April 1, 1948), No. 52, S/PV. 277, pp. 34-35.

the lack of cooperation from the Mandatory Power, the disintegrating security situation in Palestine, and the fact that the Security Council did not furnish the Commission with necessary armed assistance, are the factors which have made it impossible for the Commission to implement the Assembly's resolution.[73]

The Commission concluded:

> The steadily deteriorating situation in Palestine leads to the inescapable conclusion that, in the absence of force adequate to restore and maintain law and order in Palestine following the termination of the Mandate, there will be administrative chaos, starvation, widespread strike, violence and bloodshed in Palestine, including Jerusalem. . . . These calamitous results for the people of Palestine will be intensified unless specific arrangements are made regarding the urgent matters outlined above well in advance of 15 May, 1948.[74]

Second Special Session of the General Assembly

In accordance with the decision of the Security Council at its meeting on April 1, 1948, the Secretary-General, acting under the provisions of rules seven and nine of the rules of procedure of the General Assembly, convoked the second special session of the General Assembly to meet on April 16, 1948, "to consider further the question of the future Government of Palestine."

On April 16, the Second Special Session of the General Assembly convened. The Political Committee of the General Assembly entered on a long discussion which touched upon three aspects:[75]

---

73 United Nations Palestine Commission, Report to the General Assembly (April 10, 1948), p. 39.

74 Ibid., pp. 41-42.

75 L. Larry Leonard, op. cit., p. 662.

1. The termination of hostilities in the Holy Land;
2. An interim arrangement for governing Palestine when the United Kingdom withdrew on 15 May; and
3. The means of achieving a permanent settlement and the status of the partition resolution.

The United States proposed a temporary trusteeship with the United Nations as the administering authority and the Trusteeship Council as supervisor of the administration, and, therefore, that the Palestine Commission suspend its efforts until the General Assembly had an opportunity to reexamine the problem. The United States representative stated, however, that:

> The temporary trusteeship should not be considered as a substitute for the plan of partition with economic union or for any other solution which might be agreed upon by the Jews and Arabs of that country. It was an emergency measure to ensure public order and the maintenance of public services.[76]

The United States proposal was an attempt to find an acceptable solution following the failure of the Partition Resolution. It was hoped that a temporary trusteeship would provide a much needed cooling-off period. Moreover, the United States considered that a temporary trusteeship would furnish a Government, essential public service, and protection for the Holy Places. Mr. Austin, the United States representative to the United Nations, told the member states that:

> In favoring the plan for partition with economic union, the United States Government was aware that

[76] GAOR, The Second Special Session, Vol. II (April 16-May 14, 1948), p. 9.

the Arabs of Palestine were unwilling to agree to it in advance. . . . At present, however, the United Nations was faced with a demand for emergency action. The trusteeship proposal was intended to insure order and government, and thereby to make possible the working out of peaceful settlement and constructive development in Palestine. . . . The United States was willing to undertake its share of responsibility for the provision of police forces which would be required during a truce and a temporary trusteeship. . . .[77]

The reaction of the Great Powers ranged from support by China and France to rejection by the Soviet Union. While Chinese support was based upon an unwillingness to see force applied to achieve partition, France saw in the United States proposal a way of gaining time for achieving a settlement during a "cooling-off" period. The Soviet Union took the position that "the only legitimate activity of the United Nations would be to carry out the duly adopted partition resolution of the previous November."[78] The two parties most directly concerned, the Jewish Agency and the Arab Higher Committee, reaffirmed their previous positions with rejection by the former and approval by the latter.

Some states pointed to the probability that as much force would be required to implement the trusteeship arrangement as partition.[79] The Arab States found in the United States proposal the "fair" solution for Palestine, which might provide the time and atmosphere required for peaceful negotiations. The Arab States continued to

---

77 Ibid., pp. 5, 10.

78 Eugene P. Chase, op. cit., p. 158. This partition resolution provides, as mentioned before, for the partition of Palestine into three separate areas linked in economic union of the entire country: the Arab State, the Jewish State, and the International City of Jerusalem.

79 For more information, see GAOR, Second Special Session, op. cit., pp. 10-31; the States were Australia, Czechoslovakia, New Zealand and Poland.

urge the Jews to abandon the idea of a Jewish State and to accept a unitary State built upon joint Arab-Jewish cooperation.[80]

THE CREATION OF THE STATE OF ISRAEL

On May 14, 1948, just before the vote on the draft resolution — based upon the recommendations of the Political Committee — was taken, the representative of the Jewish Agency informed the delegates that a Jewish State had been proclaimed. In fact the Mandate was to expire on the same day at 6:00 P.M. In the so-called "Proclamation of Independence," on the same day Israel announced that it was willing "to cooperate with the organs and representatives of the United Nations in the implementation of the Resolution of the Assembly of November 29, 1947."[81]

This action no doubt precluded compromise and complicated the process of reconciliation. The circumvention was made more serious when the United States, after proposing and leading debate for the temporary trusteeship, granted de facto recognition to the State of Israel. The United States representative read the following statement from the President of the United States:

> This government has been informed that a Jewish State has been proclaimed in Palestine, and recognition has been requested by the Provisional Government thereof. The United States recognizes the Provisional Government as the de facto authority of the new State of Israel.[82]

Both the proclamation and the recognition were unexpected. "The Soviet Union nevertheless seized the oppor-

---

80 Ibid., pp. 68-69.

81 For full text of proclamation, see State of Israel Government Yearbook 5711 (Jerusalem: The Government Printer, 1950), pp. 43-45.

82 GAOR, Second Special Session, Vol. I, Plenary Meetings of the General Assembly (April 16-May 14, 1948), p. 42.

tunity to accuse the United States of opposing partition within the United Nations but supporting it on the outside."[83] While the Arab delegation criticized that action, the representative of Egypt considered that the United Nations was being "shamelessly betrayed."

The Validity of the Proclamation of the State of Israel

To ascertain the validity of the unilateral establishment of the State of Israel two facts are to be weighed: First, the Mandate for Palestine was declared terminated on May 14, 1948, and the status of Palestine was, therefore, subject to determination by the majority of its population, not the minority. From the democratic as well as the moral point of view, it is generally recognized that the voice of the majority, if not prevailing, should be considered, especially in vital matters.

Second, as the Partition Resolution provided, the establishment of the Jewish State was to take effect two months after the withdrawal of the British forces, that is to say, not before July 15, 1948. In that period (between May 15, and July 15) the Mediator was responsible for assuming the administration of Palestine from the Mandatory Power. So, with this understanding, the said proclamation was juridically and morally invalid.

Unable to take any other action to enforce its resolution on November 29, 1947, the General Assembly adopted on May 14, 1948, by thirty-one votes in favor, to seven against, with sixteen abstentions the following resolution:

The General Assembly,
Taking account of the present situation in regard to Palestine. . . .

1. Empowers a United Nations Mediator in Palestine . . . to exercise the following functions: . . .
   (III) Promote a peaceful adjustment of the future situation of Palestine; . . .

---

83 L. Larry Leonard, op. cit. p. 667.

65

3. Directs the United Nations Mediator to conform in his activities with the provisions of this resolution, and with such instructions as the General Assembly or the Security Council may issue; . . . Relieves the Palestine Commission from the further exercise of responsibilities under resolution 181 (II) of 29 November, 1947.[84]

THE WAR

On May 15, 1948, just after the withdrawal of the Mandatory forces and the proclamation of the State of Israel, the forces of the Arab States entered Palestine. As Mr. Sami Hadawi put it:

Unprepared for such an emergency, the Arab states were faced with political, economic and social problems in their territories beyond their means and ability to cope with. It was at this state and in answer to the pleadings of the remaining Palestine Arabs that the Arab armies decided to march into Palestine.[85]

The Arab States had cabled the Secretary General of the United Nations informing him that they

were compelled to intervene in Palestine because the disturbances there constituted a serious and direct threat to peace and security, within the territories of the Arab states, and in order to restore peace and establish law in Palestine.[86]

Egypt told the Security Council that her forces had entered Palestine "to establish security and order in place of the

---

[84] GAOR, Third Session: Supplement No. 1, U.N. Document A/565 (1948), pp. 5-6.

[85] Sami Hadawi, op. cit., pp. 39-40.

[86] GAOR, Third Session, Supplement No. 1 (1948), U.N. Document A/565, p. 9.

66

chaos and disorder which prevailed and which rendered the country at the mercy of the Zionist terrorist gangs who persisted in attacking peaceful Arab inhabitants."[87] Jordan said her forces had been "compelled to enter Palestine to protect unarmed Arabs against massacres."[88]

From both the legal and the moral angles, was the entry of the Arab armies legally and morally justified? As the generally recognized rules of International Law as well as the United Nations Charter provide, war has been considered not only illegal but also a crime against humanity except in case of self-defense against "immediate" aggression. The question then becomes, was the entry of the Arab armies into Palestine for the purpose of self-defense against "immediate" aggression? Certainly, there was an "immediate" aggression against "the Arabs of Palestine" by neglecting their consent and depriving them of their natural rights to live in their homes and to determine their future. Furthermore, under the law of nations as well as the United Nations Charter, there was legal justification for the Arab entry, since there was real reason for self-defense in the presence of an "immediate" aggression against all of them.

The Arab States informed the Secretary General in the aforesaid cable that they "were compelled to intervene in Palestine because the disturbances there constituted a serious and direct threat to peace and security, within the territories of the Arab States, and in order to restore peace and establish law in Palestine." From this cable two things are apparent: First is the fact that the Arab States decided to enter the war because of the "direct threat to peace and security" within their territories. Here, the "direct threat to peace," as the "act of aggression," provides for the right

<hr />

[87] Text of Cable from Egypt to the U.N. Security Council, SCOR (May 15, 1948), U.N. Document S/743, p. 26.

[88] Text of Cable from Transjordan to the U.N. Security Council, SCOR (May 16, 1948), U.N. Document S/748, p. 90.

of self-defense and justifies preparatory measures as well. Second, the Arab States decided to march into Palestine "in order to restore peace and establish law in Palestine." This in the first place was, and still is, not only the responsibility of the World Organization under its Charter; but the League of the Arab States, being a regional arrangement, has had under the United Nations Charter a definite responsibility and right in undertaking a collective self-defense action for the maintenance of peace and justice in Palestine.

Therefore, the entry of the Arab armies into Palestine had an undisputed legal ground. Moreover, from the moral point of view, the military action of the Arab States was justified as a demonstration of an emergent Arab Nationalism vis-à-vis Zionism as a new and aggressive phase of imperialism and racism.

It should be noted here, furthermore, that when the Arab armies entered Palestine the Jewish forces were already in occupation of key positions well within the territory assigned to the Arab States. This situation was confirmed by Sir John Glubb, a British officer commanding the Jordanian Legion in 1948, who wrote that "the Jews were already in the Arab areas when the Arab Legion arrived."[89] Mr. David Ben-Gurion, former Prime Minister of the State of Israel, confirmed that the Zionists started war on the Palestine Arabs even before the creation of the Jewish State. He wrote:

> Until the British left, no Jewish settlement, however remote, was entered or seized by the Arabs, while the Haganah . . . captured many Arab positions and liberated Tiberias and Haifa, Jaffa and Safad. So, on the day of destiny (May 15, 1948) that part of Palestine where the Haganah could operate was almost clear of the Arabs.[90]

---

[89] Sir John Bagot Glubb, *A Soldier with the Arabs* (New York: Harper Brothers, 1947), p. 302.

[90] David Ben-Gurion, *Rebirth and Destiny of Israel* (New York: The Philosophical Library, 1954), pp. 530-531.

Chapter IV

The United Nations Truce Supervision Organization: The Diplomacy of Peace-Observation

As the fighting started in Palestine, the role of the United Nations came to be that of truce seeker, mediator, conciliator and truce observer. Five basic actions were taken in this direction:

1. The establishment of the United Nations Truce Commission for Palestine.
2. The appointment of a Mediator.
3. The signing of the Armistice Agreements.
4. The establishment of the United Nations Conciliation Commission for Palestine (UNCCP).
5. The establishment of the United Nations Truce Supervision Organization (UNTSO).

The United Nations Truce Commission For Palestine

When the United States introduced a resolution calling upon the parties "to cease acts of violence immediately," it was unanimously adopted on April 1, 1948.[1] This resolution also called upon the President of the Council to negotiate a truce. But the Security Council did not create the machinery for implementing its resolution until April 23, 1948, when Columbia proposed that three members be appointed from the Secretariat to observe the truce. A United States proposal, however, was adopted in that resolution which established:

> A Truce Commission for Palestine composed of representatives of those Members of the Security Council which have career consular officers in Jerusalem, noting however, that the representative of Syria has indicated that his Government is not prepared to serve on the Commission. The function of the Commission shall be to assist the Security Council in supervising the implementation by the parties of the . . . [cease-fire and truce resolutions].[2]

Accordingly, the Truce Commission for Palestine was established with Belgium, France and the United States as its members. In fact, the consuls were appointed because they were in the area and were acquainted with the situation.

The members of the Truce Commission, though they did all that the circumstances and the means at their disposal allowed, never succeeded in reaching the principal objective of their mission — the conclusion of a long-term and an effective truce. This does not necessarily mean,

---

1 U.N. Document S/714 (April 1, 1948), SCOR, Third Year, pp. 4-5.

2 SCOR, Third Year, No. 62, p. 33. It may also be called "The Consular Truce Commission"; see Azcarate, *Mission in Palestine 1948-1952* (Washington, D.C.: The Middle East Institute, 1966), pp. 80-91.

however, that the Commission had no contribution at all to the efforts of maintaining quiet in Palestine; it demonstrated, through its short experience, that, in order to pacify the area and, thus have a truce, a greater international authority was needed — that authority must be better equipped in order to be able to command on the spot and to prevent violations of the truce.

The Mediator

As the General Assembly had placed responsibility for the appointment of the Mediator on the permanent members of the Security Council, Count Folke Bernadotte of Sweden, Vice-President of the International Red Cross, was chosen United Nations Mediator on May 20, 1948.

The Mediator acted primarily on the basis of a cease-fire resolution of the Security Council of May 29, 1948, and secondarily on the basis of the General Assembly's resolution of May 14, 1948. Mr. Bernadotte, nonetheless, interpreted his authority in the following terms:

1. His role was one which did not involve
   . . . the handing down of decisions on the future of Palestine, but . . . was one of offering suggestions to the parties on the basis of which further discussions might take place and possible counter-suggestions be put forth looking toward a peaceful settlement of this difficult problem.[3]

2. He did not consider himself bound by the provisions of the November 29 resolution which recommended the partition of Palestine since, if this was done, there would be no meaning to his mediation.[4]

---

3 U.N. Document S/863 (June 27, 1948), p. 2.

4 Progress Report of the U.N. Mediator on Palestine to the Security Council (September 16, 1948), U.N. Document A/648, p. 9.

71

3. He did not have authority to recommend to the Members of the United Nations a proposed course of action on the Palestine Question. He should, on the other hand, accumulate information and draw conclusions from his experience which "might well be of assistance to Members of the United Nations in charting the future course of United Nations action on Palestine." It was his

> . . . duty to acquaint the Members of the United Nations . . . with certain of the conclusions on means of peaceful adjustment which have evolved from frequent consultations with Arab and Jewish authorities.[5]

On June 27, 1948, Count Bernadotte submitted proposals to Arabs and Jews for "a possible approach to the peaceful adjustment of the future situation in Palestine."[6] This was the first effort made to reexamine the partition plan. Consultations with the Arab and Jewish experts aided in the formulation of the suggestions which provided:

1. Palestine, including Transjordan, should become a "Union" including two "members," one Arab and the other Jewish;

2. The members should agree upon the boundaries;

3. Each member should have complete sovereignty over its area and people, although the union would seek to promote close economic relations and operate common services;

---

5 Ibid., p. 17. See also Azcarate, op. cit., p. 92.

6 Ibid., p. 7.

4. Each member should control immigration into its area; and

5. A series of modifications should be made in the territory allotted to Arabs and Jews under the Partition Plan. The Mediator justified the proposed modifications in the following terms:

> The indispensable condition for the attainment of . . . [a peaceful adjustment of the future situation of Palestine] would be to find some common framework of reference within which the parties would be willing to accept further mediation. In accepted international usage the employment of "good offices" involves offering friendly suggestions to facilitate adjustment of a controversy between conflicting parties. Mediation is a consequence of the tender of good offices, and the primary task of the Mediator is to initiate proposals calculated to harmonize conflicting interests and claims. In the very nature of the case, therefore, the Mediator must strive to encourage compromise rather than strict adherence to legal principles. . . .

> The suggestions which I offered on 27 June as a possible focus of discussion, had been formulated on the basis of the equities involved in the Palestine dispute; the aspirations, fears, and motivations of the conflicting parties; and the realities of the existing situation in Palestine. . . .

> As Mediator, I had to seek possible solutions which would be voluntarily accepted by both parties. I sought, therefore, arrangements which might reveal some

common denominator in the relations between Arabs and Jews in Palestine.[7]

Under the modifications proposed by the Mediator, all of Galilee should be Jewish, but the Negev, or most of it, should be Arab. Still these proposals were rejected by the Arabs and the Jews. The Soviet delegate commented in the Security Council on July 7, 1948, that the suggested territorial modifications of the Partition Plan violated the General Assembly action and thereby weakened the authority of the United Nations. The Syrian representative commented that the Mediator had not been sent to Palestine to enforce partition in any way.

In his report to the Security Council on September 16, 1948, the Mediator said:

> A Jewish State called Israel exists in Palestine and there are no sound reasons for assuming it will not continue to do so. . . . The boundaries of this new state must finally be fixed either by formal agreement between the parties concerned or failing that, by the United Nations. . . . Adherence to the principle of geographic homogeneity and integration which should be the major objective of the boundary agreements, should apply equally to Arab and Jewish territories, whose frontiers should not, therefore, be rigidly controlled by the territorial arrangements envisaged in the resolution of 29 November. . . . The right of innocent people, uprooted from their homes by the present terror and ravages of war, to return to their homes, should be affirmed and made effective, with assurance of adequate compensation for the property of those who may choose not to return. . . . International responsibility should be expressed where desirable and necessary in the form of international

---

7 U.N. Document S/888 (July 12, 1948), pp. 10-12.

guarantees, as a means of allaying existing fears, and particularly with regard to boundaries and human rights.[8]

This report was dated September 16, 1948. The next day, while driving through a section of Jerusalem under Jewish military control, the Mediator was shot by men in Israeli uniform.

> Count Bernadotte played a significant and tragic role in the Arab-Israel drama, being assassinated on September 17, 1948, by Jewish terrorists who felt that the Count was partial to the Arabs.[9]

The Security Council immediately appointed Dr. Ralph J. Bunche, an American and the personal representative of the Secretary-General to the Mediator, as the Acting Mediator.

On October 28, 1948, in his report to the Security Council, Dr. Bunche said:

> In my view, the critical stage has now been reached where bolder and broader action is required. Such action as an indispensable condition to an eventual peaceful settlement of the political issues might well take the form of a clear and forceful declaration by the Security Council that the parties be required to negotiate either directly or through the Truce Supervision Organization a settlement of all outstanding problems of the truce in all sectors of Palestine, with a view to achieving a permanent condition of peace in place of the existing truce.[10]

---

8 U.N. Document A/648, GAOR, Third Session (1948), p. 153.

9 James MacDonald, *My Mission in Israel 1948-1951* (New York: Simon and Schuster, 1951), p. 81.

10 Dr. Bunche, Verbatim Record of the Three Hundred Seventy-Fourth Meeting of the Security Council (October 28, 1948), U.N. Document S/PV. 374.

It was apparent that neither the four-week truce of June 11, 1948, (the truce which had been negotiated through the efforts of Bernadotte and which organized the United Nations Truce Supervision Organization, "UNTSO," whose duty was to observe the truce and to investigate violations), nor the truce which was imposed by the Security Council on July 18, 1948, was able to bring peace into the unhappy land. It was clear, too, that although Israeli forces achieved military victory in the war of 1948 (see Map I — Partition and Conquest), they had failed to maintain peace and justice in Palestine.

The Armistice Agreements

In his Progress Report to the General Assembly on September 16, 1948, Mediator Bernadotte concluded:

> The truce is not an end in itself, its purpose is to prepare the way for a peaceful settlement. There is a period during which the potentiality for constructive action, which flows from the fact that a truce has been achieved by international intervention, is at a maximum. If, however, there appears no prospect of relieving the existing tension by some arrangement which holds concrete promise of peace, the machinery of truce supervision will in time lose its effectiveness and become an object of cynicism. If this period of maximum tendency to forego military action as a means of achieving a desired settlement is not seized, the advantage gained by international intervention may well be lost.[11]

On November 4, 1948, acting on the advice of Dr. Bunche, the Security Council adopted a resolution asking Egyptian and Israeli forces to withdraw from Negev and

---

[11] Progress Report of the United Nations Mediator (September 16, 1948), U.N. Document A/648, p. 44.

to negotiate permanent truce lines and demilitarized zones. Failing agreement of these parties, these lines and zones were to be demarcated by the Mediator.[12]

Five days later Dr. Bunche urged the Security Council to take action for a more permanent arrangement than the truce. He stated:

> The demand for an armistice would differ from the truce in that it would specifically and firmly provide for a separation of the forces engaged in the conflict in Palestine and for their withdrawal and reduction to peace-time status.[13]

On November 16 the Security Council adopted a resolution whose major concern was a call for armistice negotiations by the disputants. It reads in part:

> The Security Council. . . .
> Taking note that the General Assembly is continuing its consideration of the future government of Palestine in response to the request of the Security Council of 1 April 1948 (S/714) . . .
> Decides that, in order to eliminate the threat to the peace in Palestine and to facilitate the transition from the present truce to permanent peace in Palestine, an armistice shall be established in all sectors of Palestine:
> Calls upon the parties directly involved in the conflict in Palestine, as a further provisional measure under Article 40 of the Charter, to seek agreement forthwith, by negotiations conducted either directly or through the Acting Mediator on Palestine, with a view to the immediate establishment of the armistice, including:

---

12 U.N. Document S/1070, SCOR, Third Year (November, 1948), p. 7.

13 Report of Security Council to the General Assembly (1948-1949), U.N. Doc. A/945, p. 48.

a. The delineation of permanent armistice demarcation lines beyond which the armed forces of the respective parties shall not move;

b. Such withdrawal and reduction of their armed forces as will ensure the maintenance of the armistice during the transition to permanent peace in Palestine.[14]

The provisional Government of Israel indicated on November 23, 1948, that it would prefer direct negotiations through United Nations intermediaries. The Arab States rejected the idea. But, on January 6, 1949, when Egypt accepted a cease-fire order in the southern Negev region, it also agreed to armistice negotiations. Other Arab States acted similarly. The negotiations proceeded as follows:

1. Preliminary discussions were held separately by the Acting Mediator with each delegation;

2. Informal meetings were held between the heads of delegations and the Acting Mediator; and

3. Joint formal meetings of the delegations were convened under the chairmanship of the Acting Mediator. The Egyptian delegation made it clear that negotiating an armistice did not imply any sort of recognition of the State of Israel.

As Mr. Azcarate puts it:

The minister [the Egyptian Minister of Defense] apparently successfully argued that Egyptian delegates were already negotiating with official representatives of the State of Israel around the table of the Security Council and other United Nations organizations, with-

---

14 U.N. Doc. S/1080 (November 17, 1948), pp. 21-25.

out this implying recognition, either direct or indirect, of that State.[15]

On February 24, 1949, the first Armistice Agreement was signed between Egypt and Israel. This was followed by agreements with Lebanon on March 23, with Jordan on April 3, and with Syria on July 20, 1949.

Agreements with other Arab States followed the pattern of the Egyptian agreement which provided for:

1. The establishment of a Mixed Armistice Commission comprising three representatives from each of the parties, to be headed by the Chief-of-Staff of the United Nations Truce Supervision Organization or his representative. The Mixed Armistice Commission may employ observers "who may be from among the military organizations of the parties, or from the military personnel of the United Nations Truce Supervision Organization." United Nations observers are to remain under command of the Chief-of-Staff of UNTSO.

2. Supervision by the Commission of the execution of the provisions of the agreement.

3. A mutual nonaggression clause and the establishment of Demarcation Lines and a Demilitarized Zone in the Gaza Strip.

Evaluation of the Armistice Agreements: The Legal Status

All four Armistice Agreements were, as stated in their preambles, "to facilitate the transition from the present

---

15 Azcarate, op. cit., p. 113.

truce to permanent peace."[16] As such, they were not final steps in ending hostilities, nor did they comprise a final boundary settlement. Indeed, the armistice agreements were envisaged as a step to permanent peace. Dr. Ralph Bunche's leadership was the object of high praise, and his success reflected favorably on the whole United Nations concept.[17]

It was recognized, since the agreements were concluded in accordance with the Security Council Resolution of November 16, 1948, that the bases on which permanent peace would be made, including primarily the question of the future Government of Palestine, were still the subject of consideration by the General Assembly in response to the request of the Security Council of April 1, 1948. Such bases were not to be defined by the Armistice Agreements themselves. Thus, the Armistice Agreements were designed merely to (a) delineate "armistice demarcation lines" and b) agree on "withdrawal and reduction" of armed forces to "ensure the maintenance of the armistice."

Furthermore, the Armistice Agreements reaffirmed the limited character of their function and purpose in accordance with the resolution on which they were based. The Egyptian-Israeli Armistice Agreement pointed out in Article IV, paragraph 3, that:

> . . . The provisions of this Agreement are dictated exclusively by military considerations and are valid only for the period of the Armistice.

---

[16] For Armistice Agreements, see U.N. Doc. S/1264, Corr. I, S/1264 Add. I (Egypt); S/1296, S/1296, Corr. I, S/1296 Add. I (Lebanon); S/1302, S/1302 Corr. I, S/1302 Add. I (Transjordan); see also U.N. Treaty Series No. 42, Treaties No. 653, 655-657; and see GAOR, Fourth Session, Special Supplements Nos. 1-4.

[17] It is worth noting that the efforts of Dr. Bunche in concluding the Armistice Agreement between the Arab States and Israel gained for him the Nobel Peace Prize in 1950.

80

Article XI stated:

> No provision of this Agreement shall in any way prejudice the rights, claims and positions of either party hereto in the ultimate peaceful settlement of the Palestine Question.[18]

Similarly, Article II, paragraph 2, of each of the Armistice Agreements with Lebanon, Jordan and Syria stated:

> It is also recognized that no provision of this Agreement shall in any way prejudice the rights, claims and positions, of either party hereto in the ultimate peaceful settlement of the Palestine question, the provisions of this Agreement being dictated exclusively by military, and not by political considerations.[19]

As such, the Armistice Agreements could be interpreted as temporary pacts of nonaggression; for, different from the traditional practice in the conclusion of armistices, the four agreements were signed on behalf of the respective governments, and not on behalf of the commanders-in-chief of the fighting armies. This character of nonaggression pacts is what makes these documents original; for traditionally, the conclusion of a nonaggression agreement would have been inconceivable between states which had not recognized, in any form, one another and which, if they did, would be in a state of war, as a result of the refusal by one of them (Israel) to implement the United Nations resolutions.

It follows then that the Arab-Israeli General Armistice Agreements were neither "armistice agreements" in the classical definition of the term, nor "nonaggression pacts" in the political or the legal sense. They were purely mili-

---

[18] See the text of this Armistice Agreement in SCOR, Fourth Year, Supplement No. 3, pp. 1-14.

[19] See the text of these Agreements in SCOR, Fourth Year, Supplements No. 1 and 4, pp. 1-10 and 1-7.

tary arrangements made with a view to extending the cease-fire and establishing demarcation lines separating the fighting forces of the parties until final political settlement could be achieved. In other words, the Armistice System must be considered transitional, provisional, tentative, and without prejudice to the claims or rights of either party in the final settlement of the Palestine crisis.

Does an Armistice Agreement Terminate the State of War?

The main question which arises is in which way the Armistice Agreement is to be interpreted. In the opinion of Israel, the Armistice Agreement did terminate the war and consequently the Arab States had no right to exercise belligerent rights in their relations with Israel. The Arab States, on the other hand, took the view that an Armistice Agreement does not imply the end of the state of war. "An armistice, an agreement between belligerents, has never been considered to put an end to a state of war or to create a state of peace."[20]

Traditionally, a general armistice agreement has been considered only as a temporary suspension of hostilities which may be resumed at a later date. This view was reflected in the Annex to the Hague Convention of 1899 on the regulations concerning the laws and customs of war on land.

Article 36 states as follows:

An armistice suspends military operations by mutual consent between the belligerent parties. If its duration is not fixed, the belligerent parties can resume operations at any time, provided always that the enemy is

---

20 B. Selak, Jr., "A Consideration of the Legal Status of the Gulf of Aqaba," A.J.I.L. (1958), p. 668.

82

warned within the time agreed upon, in accordance with the terms of the armistice.[21]

Sharing the same view, Colonel Levie states:

> As long ago as the days when Greece and Rome were at the Zenith of their power, it became accepted law, that, although the indutiae (armistice or truce) resulted in a cessation of hostilities, it did not, as did the foedus (treaty of peace), result in a termination of the war. The early writers on international law concurred in this conclusion. The great majority of contemporary writers likewise do so.[22]

The same view is taken by Lauterpacht:

> Armistices are in no wise to be compared with peace, and ought not to be called temporary peace, because the condition of war remains between the belligerents themselves and between the belligerents and the neutrals, on all points beyond the mere cessation of hostilities. In spite of such cessation the right of visit and search over neutral merchantmen therefore remains intact, as does likewise the right to capture neutral vessels attempting to break a blockade, and the right to seize contraband of war.[23]

Professor Castren, although rejecting the identification of "armistice" with "temporary peace," maintains that a blockade can be exercised during it.[24]

To conclude, one may say that according to the gen-

---

21 David Brook, *Preface to Peace: The United Nations and the Arab-Israel Armistice System* (Washington, D.C.: Public Affairs Press, 1964), p. 2.

22 H. S. Levie, "The Nature and Scope of the Armistice Agreement." A.J.I.L. (1956), p. 885.

23 L. Oppenheim, H. Lauterpacht, *International Law* (London, 1958), Vol. II, pp. 546-7.

24 E. Castren, *The Present Law of War and Neutrality* (Helsinki, 1954), pp. 128-130.

erally recognized rules of international law, an armistice does not put an end to a state of war. It may also be said that the de facto hostilities between the Arab States and Israel resulted in a de facto state of war. However, what would be the effect of the Charter on the traditional doctrine of war and belligerent rights, particularly when some or all of the belligerents are members of the United Nations, is a moot question. L. M. Bloomfield rejects the existence of a state of war between members of the United Nations and eo ipso considers the Egyptian blockade a violation of the Charter of the United Nations.[25]

However, one might argue that if the normal relationship of peace is disrupted by illegal acts of hostility, with the cessation of these acts the situation reverts to the original state of peace. Here, states' practice has not always been uniform, and in some cases, the cessation of hostilities has ended the state of war itself. It is, therefore, far more important to examine the intended effect and scope of particular armistice agreements ending particular hostilities, than the general question of the effect of an armistice on the existence of a state of war. It may well be that an armistice agreement, even without ending the state of war in the legal sense, puts an end to certain hostile acts. In this respect, it is of a special significance to differentiate between a general armistice involving a cessation of all hostilities and a partial armistice which affects only a limited theater of operations. The former has a more permanent character, pending a final peace settlement, than the latter.

In briefly discussing and evaluating the Egyptian blockade of the Gulf of Aqaba after the Armistice Agreement of 1949, it is of interest to relate to the resolution of the United Nations Security Council of September 1, 1951, in which the blockade was rejected:

---

25 L. M. Bloomfield, *Egypt, Israel and the Gulf of Aqaba in International Law* (Toronto, 1957), p. 164.

. . . Considering that since the Armistice regime which has been in existence for nearly two and a half years is of a permanent character, neither party can reasonably assert that it is actively a belligerent or requires to exercise the right of visit, search and seizure for any legitimate purpose of self-defence; . . . Finds further that such practice is an abuse of the exercise of the right of visit, search and seizure. . . . Finds further that practice cannot in the prevailing circumstances be justified on the grounds that it is necessary for self-defence. . . .[26]

Now, although the United Nations Security Council ruled the Egyptian blockade as unlawful, it is most important to recall the nature of the armistice agreement recognized by the Council. "This action of the Security Council has been construed as indicating that a general armistice is a kind of de facto termination of war."[27] However, one may argue that the resolution of the Security Council was based upon a desire to pacify the situation for facilitating new conditions for peace rather than to change a long established rule of international law. For it is obvious that the Arab-Israeli General Armistice Agreements have not yet brought about a de facto termination of the state of war between the parties involved.

It may be argued, however, in examining the Security Council resolution of September 1, 1951, that although the four General Armistice Agreements between Israel and the Arab States contain a general clause prohibiting all military actions by one of the conflicting parties against the other — a clause that gives the agreements the character of nonaggression pacts — it is only in the Armistice Agreements with Lebanon, Jordan, and Syria that this prohibition extends to all acts of hostility without specifying that the acts referred to are military acts carried out by land, sea or air forces. This paragraph does not appear in the Armistice Agreement with Egypt, where all the clauses

---

26 SCOR, 6th year, 558th meeting, p. 2.
27 Levie, op. cit., p. 886.

prohibiting acts of hostility refer explicitly to military acts carried out by land, sea or air forces. This means that Egypt did not commit itself in the Armistice Agreement with Israel to abstain from taking certain measures against the latter, save purely military actions. It may be legally argued, therefore, that Egypt did not violate the Armistice Agreement when it imposed restrictions on the passage through the Suez Canal and the Gulf of Aqaba of Israeli ships and ships with cargoes for Israel.

In summation, two schools of thought regarding the nature of a general armistice agreement may be distinguished. One takes the position that during an armistice a belligerent may legally do in the actual theater of war only such things as the enemy could not have prevented him from doing at the moment when actual hostilities ceased.[28] The other school maintains that during a general armistice, the belligerent must refrain from only those acts which are explicitly forbidden by it.[29]

Indeed, this latter school has behind it the weight of both reasoning and practice; it is generally recognized that during a general armistice agreement the state of war remains, with all its juridical consequences, between the belligerents themselves, and between the belligerents and neutrals, on all points beyond the mere cessation of hostilities. This is in conformity with the classical theory of international law regarding the juridical nature of an armistice: a provisional suspension by treaty of military operations and other hostilities leaving the condition of war in existence.

The United Nations Conciliation Commission for Palestine (UNCCP)

The General Assembly, on December 11, 1948, adopted a comprehensive resolution establishing the Conciliation Commission for Palestine (CCP) to "take steps to assist

[28] Lawrence, *The Principles of International Law*, 7th ed., (New York, 1927), p. 558.

[29] E. Castren, op. cit., p. 130.

the Governments and authorities concerned to achieve a final settlement of all questions outstanding between them."[30] France, Turkey and the United States were chosen (by a committee composed of the permanent members of the Security Council) as CCP members.[31] The Commission was eventually to assume the functions given by the General Assembly to the Mediator, and, at the request of the Security Council, any or all functions of the Mediator or of the Truce Commission. Indeed the Commission may be considered as the successor to the conciliatory role of the Mediator. On January 24, 1949, the Commission met and organized in Geneva, subsequently establishing its headquarters in Jerusalem. However, since 1952, the main activities of the CCP have taken place in New York.

With the conclusion of the Armistice Agreements, the Acting Mediator, on July 21, 1949, requested the Security Council to terminate his office and transfer the remaining functions to the Conciliation Commission. In his last report to the Security Council, Dr. Bunche said:

> With the Armistice Agreements concluded, there is no longer any useful function to be performed by the Mediator. Any further activity by me would inevitably impinge upon the work of the Palestine Conciliation Commission. This could create only confusion and duplication of effort and would serve no useful purpose whatsoever. Under the terms of the several Armistice Agreements, I have no responsibility for their implementation or supervision, since this responsibility, by mutual agreement, is assumed by the parties themselves. With the truce obsolete, the Armistice Agreements concluded, and the Palestine Conciliation Commission conducting peace negotiations, the mission of the Mediator has been fulfilled.[32]

[30] GAOR, Third Session, Part I (21 Sept.-12 Dec., 1948), U.N. Doc. A/RES/194-III, p. 21. For full text of the resolution, see Appendix D. See also Azcarate, op. cit., pp. 139, 140.

[31] U.N. Doc. A/PV. 186.

[32] U.N. Doc. S/1357 (July 26, 1949), p. 7.

Accordingly, on August 11, 1949, the Security Council relieved him of his responsibilities in Palestine under the Council resolutions, and the Conciliation Commission carried on.[33]

In fact, after the Armistice Agreements had been signed, "the year 1949 saw the coming of peace to Palestine, though it was not in every way peace with justice. The fighting seemed unlikely to be resumed."[34] In keeping with the General Assembly Resolution of December 11, 1948, the Conciliation Commission for Palestine began its efforts "to achieve a final settlement of all questions" outstanding between the parties. After brief exchanges of views with the Governments concerned in the early months of 1949, in Lausanne, the Commission submitted to the conflicting parties a protocol, "which would constitute the basis of work," and asked them to sign it. The protocol was signed on May 12, 1949, by all parties concerned, the Arab States, Israel and the Conciliation Commission. To this document was annexed a map on which was indicated the boundaries defined in the General Assembly resolution of November 29, 1947, which had been taken as the basis of discussion with the Commission.[35]

---

[33] Eugene P. Chase, *The United Nations in Action* (New York: McGraw-Hill, Inc., 1950), p. 163.

[34] Ibid., p. 164.

[35] See GAOR, Fourth Session, ad hoc Political Committee, Annex, Vol. II (A/819, A/838, A/927, A/992), pp. 1-85. The text of the protocol read: "The United Nations Conciliation Commission for Palestine, anxious to achieve as quickly as possible the objectives of the General Assembly resolution of 11 December 1948, regarding refugees, the respect for their rights and the preservation of their property, as well as territorial and other questions, has proposed to the delegations of the Arab States and to the delegation of Israel that the working document attached (a map) hereto be taken as a basis for discussions with the Commission." "The interested delegations have accepted this proposal with the understanding that the exchanges of views which will be carried on by the Commission with the two parties will bear upon the territorial adjustments necessary to the above-indicated objectives."

88

Unfortunately, the CCP failed to fulfill its responsibility mainly because:

a. Instead of assisting the parties concerned to achieve "a final settlement of all questions outstanding between them" in 1951 the Commission decided to limit its jurisdiction to the problem of Arab refugees. Even in dealing with only this major problem, the Commission was unable to find a solution. Perhaps the most recent effort of the CCP was the appointment in August 1961 of Joseph W. Johnson as its special representative to visit the Arab States and Israel. His purpose was "to explore with the host governments and with Israel practical means of seeking progress in the Palestine Arab Refugee Problem."[36] This effort was unsuccessful. However, Mr. Johnson's mission was a constructive step toward the right direction: the peacemaking effort. Its failure meant that the political situation was still not ready for a solution of the Palestine problem mainly because of the continuing refusal of Israel to comply with the United Nations resolutions. In its 1965 Session, the United Nations General Assembly, after it had prolonged the mandate of UNRWA until June 1969, noted

> with regret that repatriation or compensation of the refugees has not been effected, that no substantial progress has been made in the program for the reintegration of refugees either by repatriation or resettlement.

---

[36] GAOR, Seventeenth Session, Supplement No. 1, A/5201.

The General Assembly once more "called upon the United Nations Conciliation Commission to intensify its efforts for the implementation of paragraph 11 of the Resolution 194 (III) . . ."[37]

b. Since the Conciliation Commission's headquarters was moved to New York in 1952, it became rather difficult for the Commission to play, on the spot, an effective peacemaking role. It seems more appropriate, however, to initiate and conduct the conciliation efforts on the spot where the conciliators are more acquainted with all aspects of the situation and more familiar with all living and changing circumstances that may affect the process of mediation as well as the ability to do it.

c. And perhaps this was the most important limitation affecting the CCP's role, the composition of the Commission. It was an important factor in introducing the cold war into the Arab-Israeli conflict. The U.S.S.R. had opposed the Commission as a Western-oriented group, composed only of France, Turkey and the United States, and had suggested a broader membership to include Poland.[38] Indeed, the United States, by agreeing to membership in the Commission, had accepted the responsibility for the conciliation effort in the Arab-Israeli conflict.[39] The Commission, on the other hand, did not include the conflicting parties among its

---

37 Resolution 2053 (XX), adopted by the General Assembly in its 20th Session (December 15, 1965).

38 Third Session, First Committee, pp. 772 and 829.

39 See Hurewitz, "United Nations Conciliation Commission for Palestine," International Organization, VII (November 1953).

members. This would have enabled the Commission to play an effective peacemaking role.

d. The lack of cooperation between the Conciliation Commission and UNTSO. As Mr. Azcarate precisely puts it:

> Although the Security Council had expressly directed that the Chief-of-Staff of the United Nations in Palestine, the official head of the TSO, should keep the Commission regularly informed of anything in his sphere of action that might be of interest to it, this was never done. . . .[40]

Furthermore, the Security Council supported General W. Riley, UNTSO Chief-of-Staff, in excluding the Commission from the negotiations with the conflicting parties.

> During the discussion in the Security Council about the incidents at Lake Hule [which occurred in March 1951 between Syria and Israel when the later began works in the demilitarized zone of Lake Hule in the upper valley of the Jordan], not the slightest allusion was made to the Commission.[41]

Finally, with all these limitations in mind, the Conciliation Commission reported to the Sixth Session of the General Assembly:

> The Commission is of the opinion, however, that the present unwillingness of the parties fully to implement the General Assembly resolutions under which

---

40 Azcarate, op. cit., p. 170.
41 Ibid., p. 171.

the Commission is operating, as well as the changes which have occurred in Palestine during the past three years, have made it impossible for the Commission to carry out its mandate, and this factor should be taken into consideration in any further approach to the Palestine problem. . . . It is desirable that consideration be given to the need for coordinating all United Nations efforts aimed at the promotion of stability, security and peace in Palestine.[42]

The United Nations Truce Supervision Organization

The Security Council having called for a truce on Aprli 1, 1948, established on April 23, 1948, a Truce Commission composed of representatives of members of the Security Council having career consular officers in Jerusalem. But it quickly became apparent that the observer personnel were totally inadequate to the size of the task confronting them. Hence the Commission itself requested the United Nations to send out the officers necessary for control and supervision of the truce.[43] By May 29, 1948, the Council had instructed the Mediator and the Truce Commission to act in concert in supervising the truce. It was decided that they should be provided with a sufficient number of military observers. This was the origin of the United Nations Truce Supervision Organization.

When the first truce expired on July 9, 1948, the situation had clearly deteriorated. It was not until July 15, 1948, that the Security Council passed its resolution invoking Articles 39 and 40 of the United Nations Charter, which relate to threats to the peace and security, ordering the parties concerned to cease fire and to observe the truce until a peaceful solution could be reached.

With the second truce the duties of the new Organiza-

---

[42] GAOR, the Sixth Session, Supplement No. 18, U.N. Doc. A/1985.
[43] SCOR, 3rd year, 291st Meeting, p. 21.

tion increased. The fighting in Palestine did not cease and it became necessary to increase the Group's strength to about three hundred officer observers; the other ranks and civil staff attached to it were also augmented. The first and second truce agreements were enforced on the ground by some 700 United Nations military observers working under the United Nations Mediator and the Chief-of-Staff. Originally most of the officers came from the United States, France and Belgium, but since 1953, officers were recruited from other states such as Denmark, Sweden, Canada, New Zealand and others.

However, only with the conclusion of the Armistice Agreements between the Arab States and Israel in the period from February 24 to July 20, 1949, in response to Security Council resolutions of November 4 and 16, 1948, the functions of the Mediator were regarded as having been discharged. The United Nations Truce Supervision Organization achieved formal and separate recognition by the Security Council in its resolution of August 11, 1949. This resolution reaffirmed the previous cease-fire order, relieved the Acting Mediator of further responsibilities, laid the basis for establishing the MACs, and requested the Secretary-General to arrange for UNTSO personnel and to assist the conflicting parties in supervising the application and observance of the terms of the Armistice Agreements. Finally the resolution requested the Chief-of-Staff to report to the Council on the observance of the cease-fire and to keep the Palestine Conciliation Commission (PCC) informed of matters affecting its work.[44]

In fact, this action achieved a separation between the function of conciliation, which was surrendered by the Acting Mediator to the Conciliaiton Commission (a General Assembly body established by the Assembly on December 11, 1948) and that of observation and supervision of the Armistice Agreements. The coincidence of these two

---

44 S/1376-I.

functions had, according to the Acting Mediator, seriously impeded the task of political conciliation.[45] Accordingly, UNTSO, while organized and developed by the Mediator, acting in consultation with the Secretary-General, became a separate organ of the Security Council based essentially on Article 40 of the United Nations Charter. "The UNTSO was no longer subordinated to the Mediator, but became a subsidiary organ of the United Nations with its own well-defined functions."[46]

The Nature of UNTSO

The very nature of the observers' functions demands that the observers have an authority which will ensure respect; for they have no armed forces, in a sense of a police force, on which to rely for authority. The nature of UNTSO, therefore, derived from its functions and was shaped by its role. The Organization was expected to be of a temporary function, and hence of a transitional nature. It was established not to "supervise the truce" for there was no longer a truce. The latter had been superseded by the four armistice agreements of 1949 with which a transitional armistice system was established.

This marked the end of one aspect of Arab-Israel relations and the beginning of a new era. The armistice was intended to provide a cooling-off period in which tempers would cool, thus creating an atmosphere conducive to further discussions. An armistice machinery was then established to reduce tension along the hot frontiers. This new machinery was composed of two organs: (a) The Mixed Armistice Commissions (MACs) and (b) the United Nations

---

45 SCOR, 4th Year, No. 36, p. 7. Here Dr. Bunche describes how the Armistice Agreement had supplemented the Truce and General Assembly Resolution 194 (III) of December 11, 1948 had provided for the transfer of the Mediator's conciliation functions to the Conciliation Commission.

46 E. L. Burns, *Between Arab and Israeli* (New York: Ivan Obolensky, Inc., 1962), p. 26.

Truce Supervision Organization (UNTSO). Those two organizations were inseparably linked and the maintenance of quiet in the area depended too much upon their cooperation.

The role of UNTSO was envisaged to be a temporary observation and supervision of the armistice until a final peace would be achieved. It was not intended to be of a permanent character or to take an enforcement action in the sense of a police force under Chapter VII of the United Nations Charter.

However, as a long series of events extended the life of the armistice agreements far beyond the period intended by its framers, the armistice regime adapted itself to conditions never envisaged at the agreements. Accordingly, the Organization — the armistice machinery — acquired a "permanent" character pending final settlement. This practical change did not, however, have any effect on the nature of the functions of the machinery itself. Its role remained limited to regulating the work of the observers in supervising the armistice, to assisting the parties in preventing any hostilities, to investigating and to reporting to the United Nations Secretary-General. It was there to determine, with the Mixed Armistice Commissions, whether a violation of the armistice had occurred, to interpret the armistice agreements, and to facilitate cooperation among the conflicting parties for the purpose of reducing tension.

The Functions of UNTSO

The Arab-Israeli General Armistice Agreements provide that "no aggressive action by the armed forces — land, sea, or air — of either party shall be undertaken, planned or threatened against the people or the armed forces of the other" and that "the right of each Party to its security and freedom from fear of attack by the armed forces of the other shall be fully respected."[47] Assisting the parties in

---

[47] SCOR, 4th Year (1949), Special Supp. No. 3.

ensuring that these provisions would be carried out and in preventing any renewal of general hostilities in the period of transition from armistice to peace, was the function of the United Nations Truce Supervision Organization.

The functions of the observers are generally limited by their terms of reference which may stem directly either from the resolutions of the United Nations or from the instructions of the Mediator or Chief-of-Staff controlling the observers and defining their mandate. In Palestine the Security Council repeatedly directed the Mediator, and through him the observers, to assume specific tasks. The terms of reference may also stem from agreements between the parties. Hence, the Truce of Armistice Agreements constituted a consent by them to certain functions being assumed by the UNTSO observers.

The Mediator's instructions to United Nations Observers supervising the truce summarized their functions in the following terms:

> The primary function of the observer is to supervise observance of terms of truce in the area to which he is assigned. To discharge this function properly, observer must be completely objective in his attitudes and judgement and must maintain a thorough neutrality as regards political issues in the Palestine situation. Fundamental objective of terms of truce is to ensure to fullest extent possible that no military advantage will accrue to either side as result of application of truce. Observer is entitled to demand that acts contrary to terms of truce be not committed or be rectified but has no power to enforce such demands and must rely largely upon his ability to settle disputes locally by direct approaches to local commanders and authorities. . . . It is the responsibility of the observer to call promptly to attention of appropriate local commanders and authorities every act which in his opinion is contrary to letter and spirit of truce.[48]

---

48 U.N. Doc. S/928 (July 28, 1948), p. 1.

Indeed, if the United Nations Conciliation Commission could be regarded, as was mentioned, as the successor of the conciliatory role of the Mediator, UNTSO should be considered as the successor of his peace-observation role. Accordingly, it seems correct to say that:

> . . . the peace-observation functions granted to the MACs, UNTSO, and the Chief-of-Staff were far less than those held by the Mediator and the Truce Commission. To some extent, this was inevitable. The existence of armistice lines meant that the chief activity of peace observation would be directed to detecting violations of those lines. [49]

In Palestine, however, the situation was confused and no single truce line was ever definitely established, so that the problem became one of agreeing on lines to which each side would withdraw, leaving a "no-man's-land" between them. The Armistice Agreement fixed a Demarcation Line beyond which the respective forces could not proceed. The extremely comprehensive formula used was:

> No element of the land, sea or air military or para-military forces of either party, including non-regular forces, shall commit any warlike or hostile act against the military or para-military forces of the other party, or against civilians in territory under the control of that party; or shall advance beyond or pass over for any purpose whatsoever the Armistice Demarcation Line. . . .[50]

They also provided for certain Demilitarized Zones and even Defensive Areas in which only limited defensive

---

[49] David W. Wainhouse, *International Peace Observation: A History and Forecast* (Baltimore: The Johns Hopkins Press, 1966), p. 258.

[50] See Egyptian-Israeli Armistice Agreement of 24 February, 1949 (SCOR, 4th Year Special Supp. No. 3); Israel-Lebanon Armistice Agreement of 23 March, 1949, Ibid., Supp. No. 4.

forces, as defined in an Annex to the Agreements, could be maintained. The execution of the Armistice Agreements was entrusted to the Mixed Armistice Commissions (MACs) under Article X and these commissions were empowered to employ observers either from the military organizations of the parties or from UNTSO, the latter observers remaining under the command of the Chief-of-Staff of UNTSO.

Whatever the manner by which and in which the demarcation lines were agreed upon, such lines constituted an essential element in the supervision system; for violations of the armistice would in many cases, although not entirely, consist of transgressions of these lines. To take, by way of illustration, the Progress Report of the Mediator in Palestine of 16 September 1948, the complaints of breaches of the cease-fire included: troop movements, traffic in war materials, military training, attacks on positions, abductions, seizure of positions, firing on United Nations personnel, harvesting incidents, work of fortifications, mine-laying and illegal aircraft fights.[51]

The general functions of the observers are really twofold: (a) the checking of breaches; and (b) the prevention of violations. However, UNTSO was given, in addition to making routine observations and the investigation of alleged breaches of the truce, the responsibilities of dealing with complaints and incidents as they occurred in the theater of its operation. But the organization did not have the authority to enforce decisions they might make or to prevent violations of the truce.[52]

In supervising the Arab-Israeli Armistice Agreements the test adopted was that instituted in Article IV of the Agreements: "The principle that no military or political advantage should be gained under the truce ordered by the

---

51 GAOR, 3rd Session, Supp. No. 11, p. 39.

52 Ibid., p. 33.

Security Council is recognized."[53] However, in the main, the difficulty was simply one of ascertaining the facts through observations and investigations. Therefore, the freedom of movement of observers was absolutely essential and as such, the denial of this freedom by Israel was one of the main obstacles to observation in Palestine.

Furthermore, prevention of violations clearly involves more positive action than mere checking of violations. The Israelis in Palestine denied that the observers had a preventive function, and attempted to restrict the observers to investigating an incident once it had occurred and had been reported to them for investigation by the MAC.[54] Being unarmed, the observers had to rely for their "preventive" power on the fact of their recognized and active presence and on the fear of the parties that, should they violate the armistice, action would be taken by the Security Council. In other words, especially in a tense military and political situation, the preventive effect of the observers, although essential to peace-observation, would be minimal once the parties believed that no sanctions would ensue upon a violation of the truce. The Security Council had, of course, by its resolution of 15 July 1948, determined that the situation constituted a threat to the peace within the meaning of Article 39 and declared specifically that:

> . . . failure by any of the Governments or authorities concerned to comply with the [cease-fire order] would demonstrate the existence of a breach of the peace within the meaning of Article 39 of the Charter requiring immediate consideration by the Security Coun-

---

53 A very difficult problem arose from the Israeli plans for the division of the River Jordan in the Israel-Syrian Demilitarized Zone. General Bennike, as Chief-of-Staff of UNTSO, ordered the work to stop, and his decision was endorsed by the Security Council. However, the only effective sanction which had any effect on the Israelis seems to have been the United States' threat to cease economic aid: See Burns, op. cit., p. 111.

54 Ibid., p. 54.

cil with a view to such further action under Chapter VII of the Charter as may be decided upon by the Council.[55]

However, this threat of ultimate sanctions had little effect on irregular forces, and its effects on regular forces diminished, as with the passage of time, it became clear that the Council would not initiate any coercive action to restore peace in Palestine. The result was, necessarily, a weakening of the authority of the observers to prevent armistice violations. Indeed, the absence of effective United Nations sanctions for a breach of the armistice led to many violations as was demonstrated in the Qibya raid of 14-15 October 1953, the Gaza raid of 28 February 1955, which had been regarded as having destroyed any possibility of achieving a peace settlement, and the attack at Lake Tiberias in December 1955, and again in March 1962, the October 1956 invasion of Egypt, and the June 1967 war against the United Arab Republic, Syria and Jordan.

The Problem of the Egyptian-Israeli General Armistice Agreement

Although a useful institution for observation and a practical mechanism for the airing of complaints,[56] the

---

[55] U.N. Doc. S/801 (May 29, 1948); and U.N. Doc. S/902 (July 15, 1948).

[56] Each General Armistice Agreement provides for a Mixed Armistice Commission to be composed of an equal number of Israeli and Arab delegates presided over by the Chief-of-Staff of UNTSO or his designee. These Commissions are invested with duties of investigation and observation. Usually when the chairman of the pertinent MAC is notified by the complainant party, meetings are held and decisions, whenever possible, are made with unanimous approval. Failing unanimity, the MAC comes to agreement "by a majority of the members present and voting, which for all practical purposes means that the chairman votes for one or the other side." See Hurewitz, "The Israeli-Syrian Crisis in the Light of the Arab-Israel Armistice System," International Organization, V (1951), pp. 459-462.

Egyptian-Israeli armistice machinery-comprising UNTSO and the MAC,[57] was unable to prevent violation of the armistice and fighting across the demarcation lines. Therefore, in February 1957, the prevention of these incidents was designated as UNEF's task.

While members of the UNTSO and the MAC, unarmed and small in number, were mainly authorized to engage in activities of observation and investigation,[58] UNEF troops were, in addition, competent to establish observation posts, patrol the demarcation lines and actively prevent movement across the frontiers. To prevent duplication in their task, however, arrangements were made for the Egypt-Israel Mixed Armistice Commission to be placed under the operational control of UNEF's commander.[59] The legal status of both organs remained unchanged. In March 1958, at the time of the appointment of a new Chief-of-Staff for UNTSO, these arrangements were confirmed by the Secretary-General. The Commander of the Force, said Hammarskjöld,

> . . . would continue to exercise his functions as the Chief-of-Staff in respect of the Egypt-Israel General Armistice Agreement, i.e. as Chairman ex officio of the MAC, in accordance with Article X of that Agreement.[60]

These measures were instituted despite the fact that the Government of Israel had denied the validity of the Armistice Agreement between Israel and Egypt:

---

[57] The Egypt-Israel Commission is composed of seven members. Each of the parties chooses three of these members, while UNTSO's Chief-of-Staff — or a senior aide designated by him — chooses the seventh.

[58] Hurewitz, op. cit., p. 464.

[59] U.N. Doc. A/3500 and Add. I. p. 43.

[60] U.N. Doc. A/3943, p. 43.

Israel's view is . . . that the General Armistice Agreement has been consistently violated by Egypt both in letter and in spirit ever since it was signed on 24 February 1949. Its central purpose of non-belligerency and its character as a transition to a peaceful settlement have been constantly repudiated by Egypt. Egypt has even held, most incongruously, that the Agreement could co-exist with a "state of war" against Israel. This policy of Egypt and the actions flowing therefrom have brought the Agreement to naught, with the result that a new system of relationships must now be constructed.[61]

The absence of an Armistice Agreement, declared the Prime Minister of Israel, did not signify the existence of a state of war with Egypt. To confirm this position, he said, "the Israeli government is at all times prepared to sign an agreement of non-belligerency and mutual non-aggression." But, "the Armistice Agreement, violated and broken, is beyond repair."[62]

Israel's position on this matter was not accepted by the United Nations or by Egypt. "United Nations action," declared the Secretary-General, "must respect fully the rights of Member States recognized in the Charter, and international agreements not contrary to the aims of the Charter, which are concluded in exercise of these rights."[63] International agreement may not be broken unilaterally.[64]

The Armistice Agreement was signed by both parties and, according to Article XII, remains in force until a peace settlement between them is achieved. It was

---

61 "Letter dated 25 January 1957 from the Permanent Representative of Israel, addressed to the Secretary-General," U.N. Doc. A/3527, Annex V, (Feb. 11, 1957), GAOR, 11th Session, Annexes Vols. II-III, p. 62.

62 Quoted by Mr. Abba Eban from a speech by Prime Minister Ben-Gurion in the Knesset on January 23, 1957. Ibid.

63 U.N. Doc. A/3512, p. 47.

64 U.N. Doc. A/3943, p. 17.

approved by the Security Council. Whatever arrangements the United Nations may now wish to make in order to further progress toward peaceful conditions, the Agreement must be fully respected by it.[65]

The Egyptian Government, however, expressed its desire to implement the provisions of the Armistice Agreement with Israel, as indicated in its acceptance of resolution 977 (ES-I) of November 2, 1956, provided that implementation would be reciprocal.[66]

The Government of Israel, on the other hand, chose to maintain the position of refuting the Armistice Agreement with Egypt and, accordingly, preferred to submit any complaints against Egypt to UNEF, rather than to the Egyptian-Israeli Mixed Armistice Commission, although UNEF consistently maintained that official investigations of incidents should be carried out only through the MAC.[67] This situation is precisely explained by Mr. David Wainhouse as follows:

> While Israel refuses to recognize UNTSO on this border (the Egyptian-Israeli frontier), five to seven UNTSO observers remain, supplementing UNEF. Since the United Arab Republic correctly refused to recognize UNEF as supplementing UNTSO, the channel of communications on border incidents and exchange of prisoners is Israel — UNEF — UNTSO — UAR.[68]

As a result, however, UNEF was stationed on the Egyptian-Israeli armistice demarcation line, along that part of the line which separated the Egyptian troops from the Israeli troops, and along the International frontier south of the Gaza Strip.

---

65 U.N. Doc. A/3512, p. 48.
66 U.N. Doc. A/3527, p. 59.
67 U.N. Doc. A/3943, p. 17.
68 David W. Wainhouse, op. cit., p. 284.

Indeed, the obligation upon a State to admit international observers into its territory is one which could only stem from an agreement between the States concerned, as in the Yemeni case, from a decision of the Security Council under Chapter VII of the Charter, or from an action by the General Assembly under the "Uniting for Peace" resolution. It is clear that an observer group formed under Article 34 of Chapter VI, for example, has no right of entry into a State's territory without the consent of that State. But the Security Council could always order a State to admit such a group under Chapter VII, as part of the mandatory provisional measures under Article 40 of the Charter. That order could, if necessary, be enforced by enforcement action. However, for the cause of peace, the States have generally been prepared to admit in good faith international observation, and to concede "freedom of movement" to observers. This is obviously essential to the proper functioning of the observer group, and, by and large, the most frequent cause for complaint by the observer groups has been that they were not in fact accorded the freedom of movement which had been promised.

In Palestine complaints of restrictions upon freedom of movement made by the Israeli authorities were numerous, hence on 19 October 1948 the Security Council reminded all parties of their duty:[69]

> (a) to allow duly accredited United Nations Observers and other Truce Supervision personnel bearing proper credentials, on official notification, ready access to all places where their duties require them to go including airfields, ports, truce lines and strategic points and areas;

---

[69] U.N. Doc. S/1045. This Resolution reiterated the Resolutions of 15 July and 19 August 1948 (S/902, S/983). Further admonitions on freedom of movement were made by the Council on 29 December 1948 (S/1169), 18 May 1951 (S/2157).

(b) to facilitate the freedom of movement of Truce Supervision personnel and transport by simplifying procedures on United Nations aircraft now in effect, and by assurance of safe-conduct for all United Nations aircraft and other means of transport;

(c) to co-operate fully with the Truce Supervision personnel in their conduct of investigations into incidents involving breaches of the truce, including the making available of witness, testimony and other evidence on request;

(d) to implement fully by appropriate and prompt instructions to the Commanders in the field all agreements entered into through the good offices of the Mediator or his representatives;

(e) to take all reasonable measures to ensure the safety and safe-conduct of the Truce Supervision personnel and the representatives of the Mediator, their aircraft and vehicles, while in territory under their control;

(f) to make every effort to apprehend and promptly punish any and all persons within their jurisdictions guilty of any assault upon or other aggressive act against the Truce Supervision personnel or the representatives of the Mediator.

The Armistice Agreements eventually embodied a formal agreement to freedom of movement; Article X (10) of the Israeli-Egyptian Agreement provided:

Members of the Commission and its Observers shall be accorded such freedom of movement and access in the areas covered by this Agreement as the Commission may determine to be necessary, provided that when such decisions are reached by a majority vote United Nations Observers only shall be employed.[70]

---

70 See U.N. Doc. S/1264, Corr. I, S/1264, Add. I.

Problems of freedom of movement continued to occur long after the Armistice Agreements; as late as 4 June 1956 the Security Council was still passing resolutions declaring that full freedom of movement of United Nations observers should be respected in all areas along the Demarcation Lines, in the Demilitarized Zones and in the Defensive Areas.[71] Despite this United Nations observers were expelled from El Auja by the Israeli army on the eve of the attack against Sinai.[72] On 20 April 1957 the Chief-of-Staff was still reporting Israel's refusal to allow observers to enter the Demilitarized Area.[73]

Israel had issued identity cards which would alone permit freedom of movement; in principle the United Nations identity card should be a sufficient guarantee of the status of the individual.

The attempt by Israel in November 1956, after it had closed UNTSO's radio, to force UNTSO's withdrawal from the Gaza area by informing the Chief-of-Staff that the Armistice Agreements were no longer valid was promptly met by the General Assembly's Resolution of 2 November 1956[74] reaffirming the validity of the Armistice Agreements and, accordingly, UNTSO must stay and perform its duties.

Evaluation

As has been indicated, the four Arab-Israeli Armistice Agreements of 1949 were enforced by some 700 United Nations military observers working under the United Nations Truce Supervision Organization. Such operations have given service, and the building up of this experience is in itself an important fact. Indeed, UNTSO provided a nucleus for the United Nations Emergency Force (UNEF)

---

71 U.N. Yearbook (1956), pp. 9-11.

72 Burns, op. cit., p. 179.

73 U.N. Yearbook (1957), pp. 33-34.

74 GAOR, Resolution 997 ES-I (November 2, 1956).

later established as a result of the Suez crisis in 1956, the Congo Operation in 1960 (ONUC) and the Yemen Mission of 1963 (UNYOM). It also furnished the pattern for logistic arrangements used in other areas.

The observer groups so far established by the United Nations have not been considered fighting forces. Basically they have operated with conciliation efforts by the Organization and often, as in Palestine until the termination of the Mediator's role on August 11, 1948, they have been commanded by the person who conducted the conciliation effort.

Indeed, the function of the observer group becomes easier to fulfill as the situation, in both political and military terms, becomes less tense. This has never been the case in Palestine. Moreover, the task of supervising a truce becomes more and more difficult as time passes if it is only a temporary suspension of hostilities. On the other hand, the authority and efficacy of supervision by observers is likely to be greater when there is a prospect of a peace settlement reasonably soon. This again, has never been the case in Palestine. The situation was further complicated by the fact that UNTSO was not a fighting force, and, therefore, was understaffed and underequipped. Thus, one may conclude, the Organization really suffered from all the drawbacks and the weaknesses of any force of a similar nature operating in this kind of environment.

In Palestine the United Nations had achieved a limited and temporary success only with the conclusion of the four Armistice Agreements in 1949 and the establishment, as a result, of a general, but limited, armistice between the Arab States and Israel. However, the armistice regime itself failed to achieve its primary goal: the maintenance of "quiet" in the area and the creation of conditions that would be conducive to peaceful settlement.

Undoubtedly, there have been several factors and limitations that affected the functions of UNTSO and made

107

it difficult for the Organization to play an effective role in the Arab-Israeli conflict; these are:

    a. Internal factors and constitutional limitations:

        (1) The Organization "had no power to impose any sanctions for breaches of the General Armistice Agreements; and the conciliatory spirit which was supposed to inspire them, if it ever existed, by 1954 was not in evidence."[75] As ad hoc peace-observation groups, UNTSO and MACs were authorized neither for enforcement action nor peacemaking function.

        (2) The Organization was understaffed and underequipped.

Certainly, however, it is of great importance to separate the conciliatory function from the responsibility of observation. For the former having the nature of peacemaking cannot be combined with the latter which has the nature of peace-keeping. It may be difficult for a mediator who condemns a party for violating an armistice to try at the same time to make peace with that party. As Dr. Ralph Bunche once stated:

> . . . the separation of the functions of mediation or conciliation from the functions of supervision and enforcement, whether of cease-fire, or truce or armistice, is a very sound and practical principle. . . . Our experience in Palestine with the mediation and truce supervision was that the duties of truce supervision and enforcement often conflicted with the functions of mediation. . .[76]

---

75 Burns, op. cit., pp. 27-28.

76 See the testimony of Dr. Bunche before the Security Council, SCOR, 4th Year, No. 36, pp. 27-28; see also David Wainhouse, op. cit., p. 273.

b. External factors and psychological limitations:

(1) The time element: In this state of affairs the passing of time is an element against peace, not for it. It is unfortunate that when an armistice fails to become a peace after a long period of time, the prestige of the organization conducting the truce supervision lessens. This is evidence by the experience in Palestine. Disregarding the armistice, incidents of violence, and occasional breakdowns of the truce agreements lead to the ultimate collapse of the armistice system. Perhaps equally unfortunate is the diminished respect for international authority in this case.[77]

(2) The credibility gaps: The wars of 1948, 1956, and again, but on a wider scale and scope, in 1967, have widened the long existing credibility gaps to the point of irreparability.

(3) Israel's refusal to implement the United Nations resolutions pertaining to the three major problems previously mentioned: the boundaries; the status of Jerusalem; and the problem of the Arab refugees which has been "the most important cause of the failure of efforts to transform the armistice to a peace settlement."[78] The refugees continue to maintain what they rightfully consider to be their lawful right to return to their former homes, and to emphasize that the United Nations has given assurances regarding repatriation or compensation which remain unfulfilled. In-

---

77 David Wainhouse, op. cit., p. 272.
78 Ibid., p. 273.

deed, the implications for peace and stability in the Middle East remain as grave as ever with the continued existence of the Arab refugee problem.

(4) The Great Powers' political investment in the Arab-Israeli dilemma: It is this impasse which has dragged the cold war's two principal opponents into the Middle Eastern affairs. Indeed, one of the most significant manifestations of the American-Soviet Middle Eastern cold war diplomacy has been their Israeli-Arab armaments policy. This particular phase of the arms race has seriously encouraged aggressions, hindered both the peace-keeping and the peacemaking efforts of the international community, and subsequently prolonged the conflict.

However, as on-the-spot fact-finding and peace-observation organizations, UNTSO and MACs under the Chief-of-Staff succeeded, at least, in arranging cease-fires "after" violations had already occurred. As Mr. David Wainhouse states:

> . . . once shooting had started, neither side would ask for a cease-fire for fear of appearing to be weaker. Without the presence of UNTSO to make the initiative to call for cease-fires, there would have been no one to perform this vital role. They presented unbiased reports to the United Nations Security Council as a basis for its resolutions. They acted as a trip wire, so to speak, to limit the activities of both parties.[79]

Indeed all these factors, limitations, and forces led to the problems of peacemaking through mediatory measures,

---

79 Ibid., pp. 272-273.

and of both peace-observation and peace-keeping through and by UNTSO and, of course, UNEF. Unfortunately, none of these three inseparable tasks has been effectively and satisfactorily accomplished.

Each of the General Armistice Agreements starts with these words:

> With a view to promoting the return to permanent peace in Palestine . . . the establishment of an armistice between the armed forces of the two parties is accepted as an indispensable step towards . . . the restoration of peace in Palestine.

These agreements were concluded as temporary procedures envisaging that a final settlement of the whole case of Palestine would shortly be achieved. But, regrettably, this goal remains unrealized mainly because of:

(a) The termination of the Mediator's office: the presence of the United Nations in the area lacked the effective and persuasive personality of such a man as Dr. Ralph Bunche or Dag Hammarskjöld.

(b) Confining the role of UNTSO to only observing and supervising the armistice and the demarcation lines and "to investigation of incidents brought to the attention of the MAC's 'after' they had occurred";[80] and

(c) The internal and external factors that have been associated with the crisis.

Because of all these factors, what was expected has not been achieved and with the increasing hostilities, what was probable became rather impossible. It became even

---

80 Ibid., p. 272.

more clear that with the growing violations of the armistice, UNTSO not only lost its efficiency but also its effectiveness and prestige. In fact, the following statement shows to what extent the armistice regime has always been disregarded and completely ignored:

> In the end, Israel had no alternative but to hit back. It will always be debated whether the means she chose were the best. They did not help her in the eyes of world opinion, which disliked "reprisals," especially when they appeared indiscriminate. But what was the alternative? Protest to the MACs? This was done times without number, to no effect. All the Commissions could do was to establish guilt and censure the guilty. They could not take preventive or even deterrent action. The night after a Commission's meeting, the raids would start again, setting off anew the futile round of accusation, investigation, discussion and censure. Might Israel not have complained to the Security Council? This was not possible over the heads of the MACs and would . . . have been fruitless.[81]

The fact of the matter is that UNTSO, with a history of twenty-one years, has failed to bring peace and Justice to Palestine. It failed even to stop hostilities and violations of the temporary armistice and, accordingly, to maintain quiet in the area. Some of the violations were very serious and led to a real war. Israeli occupation of the Gaza Strip in November 1956 and its unilateral denunciation of the armistice and the war of June 1967 are two cases in point.

In his report to the Security Council on October 13, 1956, General Burns, then UNTSO Chief-of-Staff, stated that:

> At present the situation is that one of the parties to the General Armistice Agreement makes its own in-

---

[81] Ibid., pp. 266-267. See also Fred J. Khouri, "The Policy of Retaliation in Arab-Israeli Relations," *The Middle East Journal*, Vol. 20, No. 4 (Autumn 1966), pp. 436-441.

vestigations, draws its own conclusions from them and undertakes actions by its military forces on that basis. This is of course, a negation of vital elements of the Armistice Agreement.[82]

Indeed, the situation in Palestine, because of its special nature which involves the creation of a new state and matters of boundaries and refugees, required from the very beginning more than a group of observers. It needed a force together with a special peacemaking team highly supported by a unified and impartial Great Powers' commitment to the principle of "Just Peace" in the Middle East. In fact, in February 1948, the Palestine Commission warned against the dangerous "vacuum" likely to ensue from the withdrawal of the Mandatory's force and asked the Security Council to establish "an adequate non-Palestinian force."[83] It is regrettable that the Council did not see fit to comply with this request. It is equally regrettable, furthermore, that Secretary-General Trygve Lie's proposals for a United Nations Guard Force in 1948 received such scant regard. Mr. Trygve Lie stated that he was ". . . acutely conscious of how different things in Palestine could have been had the United Nations had an international force at its disposal."[84]

---

82 U.N. Doc. S/3670 (October 13, 1956), p. 7.

83 SCOR, 3rd. Year, Supplement No. 2, U.N. Doc. A/Ac. 21/7 and 9.

84 Trygve Lie, *In the Cause of Peace* (New York: Macmillan, 1954), p. 102.

Part Two
The Second War...

Our quarrel is not with Egypt, it is
with Colonel Nasser. . . .
ANTHONY EDEN

Chapter V

The United Nations Emergency Force: The Diplomacy of Peace-Keeping

In an Emergency Special Session on November 5 and 7, 1956, the General Assembly brought into being the United Nations Emergency Force (UNEF) to help pacify a severe crisis in the Middle East and stem the invasion of Egypt by the troops of the United Kingdom, France and Israel. As such, UNEF was charged by the General Assembly with a dual role: initially to secure and supervise the cease-fire and withdrawal of armed forces from Egyptian territory, and later to maintain peaceful conditions and quiet in the area along the Egyptian-Israeli armistice demarcation lines in the Gaza Strip and Sharm el-Sheikh areas. This dual role determined the size, organization, equipment and deployment of the Force as well as its very nature.

In its years of service, however, the Force was concerned with a great number of duties and responsibilities, and has

117

been recognized as an important contribution to the international organization's technique of peace-observation and peace-keeping. In fact UNEF, although "a new and in many ways unique experiment by the United Nations in a type of operation which previously it had not been called upon to conduct,"[1] represented the prototype of a small police force which the international organization might well find useful at other times of crisis. It was the experience gained from the Emergency Force which encouraged and facilitated the establishment on July 14, 1960, of the United Nations Force for the Republic of the Congo (ONUC). The late Secretary-General Hammarskjöld stated that:

> . . . the organization of the United Nations force in the Congo was considerably facilitated by the fact that it was possible for the Secretary-General to draw on the experience of the United Nations Emergency Force in Gaza and on the conclusions regarding various questions of principle and law which had been reached on the basis of that experience.[2]

With the help of UNEF, a local war in the Middle East was pacified, quiet and reasonable stability became possible in the Suez Canal area and on the Egyptian-Israeli frontier. The risk of active interference in the area by the Soviet Union and the United States was eliminated. Creation of the Force, however, was a positive step in the United Nations' "preventive diplomacy." This diplomacy aims at keeping newly arising conflicts outside the sphere of Great Powers' differences, or in the case of conflicts already within this sphere, at localizing the area of hostilities. It proposes to fill a power vacuum between the major powers, if such

---

[1] "Report of the Secretary-General," U.N. Doc. A/3943 (October 9, 1958).

[2] "Introduction to the Annual Report of the Secretary-General on the Work of the Organization, 16 June 1959 — 15 June 1960," GAOR, 15th Session (1960-1961), Supplement No. 1A, p. 4.

should exist. It seeks to prevent military initiative by either of the "super-powers." This kind of new diplomacy — an invention of the late Secretary-General Hammarskjöld — was clearly demonstrated in the Suez crisis of 1956.

The experience of UNEF, on the other hand, was essential for the international organization in developing a new system of peace-keeping relevant to the living realities in the United Nations. Without building this kind of experience, therefore, the World Organization would have to

> go back again to the situation in which we found ourselves last November (1956), when everything had to be improvised, when there was no precedent for making units available, no administrative and financial procedure, and no organization to which the Secretary-General could turn in the task given him by the Assembly of putting a United Nations Force into a dangerous and delicate situation.[3]

The experience of the United Nations Emergency Force, however, may provide insights to an important question for the World Organization: Would the maintenance of international peace and security be substantially furthered by the creation of a standing United Nations military force? In this connection, however, it may correctly be stated that had the United Nations possessed a peace force before the time of the Anglo-French invasion of Egypt, that invasion might never have taken place. For in 1956, the pretext used by the United Kingdom and France was that the United Nations was incapable of effective action in halting the fighting between Israel and Egypt and protecting the Suez Canal. Would these pretexts have been persuasive if a United Nations police force had been standing by, ready to perform those tasks for the maintenance of international peace and security?

---

[3] Lester B. Pearson, "Force for U.N.," *Foreign Affairs*, XXXV (April, 1957), p. 402.

This chapter is a comprehensive appraisal of the United Nations Emergency Force from the historical, political, and constitutional points of view. The study will also include the organization of the Force, its functions, legal status, and an evaluation of its operations. Particular attention will be given to the problem of the Gaza Strip and to the status of the Gulf of Aqaba since the Force was stationing and operating in both areas.

I. THE HISTORICAL AND POLITICAL BACKGROUND

In the years following the establishment of the temporary Arab-Israeli armistice system, the deferred humanitarian, territorial, political and legal issues represented fearful sources of Arab-Israeli animosity. The Armistice Agreements which are transitional and temporary in nature and purely military have not yet opened a door for political settlement of fundamental questions of nonmilitary nature.

The problem of the Arab refugees has not yet been solved, and the General Assembly resolutions regarding the partition of Palestine, and giving the Arab refugees a choice either to return home or to be compensated, have not been implemented. The Israeli inhabitants, on the other hand, remained nervously poised for encounter with what they believed would be the "second-round" — the Arab insistence on restoring Palestine to its rightful owners.[4] Accordingly, no peace has been achieved, and violations of the armistice agreements have always been commonplace.

---

4 Israel interpreted the military agreement between Egypt, Jordan and Syria, signed October 25, 1956, which provided for unified military command in case of war with Israel, as evidence, "in the words of Al-Gamhouria on October 27, that the Arab peoples were endeavoring to tighten the noose around their enemy and to strangle him." See statement by Israel's Ambassador to London, *The Times* (London, November 3, 1956).

The economic boycott of Israel by the Arab League States is also another factor which has gained intensity with the years. After the creation of the State of Israel, the Arab boycott soon covered many aspects of economic and commercial life of the new state. Regional boycott offices have been established and strict rules have been applied. Egyptian blockade and restrictions in the Gulf of Aqaba and the Suez Canal, however, were those most seriously felt by Israel and were the cause of much concern for many years. By closing the two waterways to Israeli trade, it became rather difficult and costly for Israel to maintain contact and to promote commercial ties with Africa and Asia. The Egyptian Government rightfully justified these restrictions by maintaining that the state of war between Egypt and Israel has continued to exist ever since May 15, 1948, and the Armistice Agreement of February 24, 1949, because of its very nature, has not changed this fact. Egypt rightfully argued that from this state of war certain rights of belligerency were derived, such as the right to visit, search, and seizure. Furthermore, in agreement with Saudi Arabia, Egypt erected a number of military installations in the Gulf of Aqaba region to prevent commerce to and from the Israeli port of Elath.[5] These restrictions led to a series of grave incidents in the Gulf of Aqaba.[6]

The mutual hatred and distrust between the Arab States and Israel gave rise to increasingly belligerent "border" violations. Since 1948, hundreds of incidents had occurred in which exchanges of fire took place between the two sides. On the forty-mile frontier the State of Israel and the Egyptian-administered Gaza Strip, fighting was commonplace. On March 20, 1956, the United States called a meeting of the Security Council to consider the

---

5 SCOR, 9th Year, 659th meeting (February 15, 1954), p. 19.

6 For more information about these incidents, see Bloomfield, *Egypt, Israel and the Gulf of Aqaba in International Law*, (Toronto: Carswell Co., 1957), pp. 11-15.

status of compliance with the Armistice Agreement between Egypt and Israel. The Security Council asked Secretary-General Hammarskjöld to survey the situation and submit a report. On May 9, 1956, Mr. Hammarskjöld reported that a "chain of actions and reactions" had occurred in the area which, if not broken, would lead to war.[7] He took the position, at that time, that the cease-fire was an obligation independent from other terms of the Agreement and, therefore, violation of these terms would not justify a violation of the cease-fire. It was in the middle of trying to pacify the situation and reduce tension when the event occurred which, according to Sir Anthony Eden, then British Prime Minister, transformed everything in the Middle East[8] — the nationalization of the Suez Canal Company on July 26, 1956.

Nationalization of the Suez Canal Company

Before the Suez crisis of 1956, three very important events had taken place in Egypt; those events had brought about radical changes in different ways:

a. The Egyptian Revolution of July 23, 1952, had ousted the King, changed the constitutional status of the State as well as the type of the Government and formulated a new Egyptian foreign policy. It has become a turning point in the history of the Arab World.

b. The Anglo-Egyptian Evacuation Agreement of July 27, 1954, had provided for the total evacuation of the Canal Zone within twenty months, and so had brought the 72 years of British oc-

---

7 U.N. Doc. S/3596 (May 9, 1956).

8 Joseph P. Lash, *Dag Hammarskjöld* (New York: Doubleday, 1961), p. 76.

cupation to its end. In his book, *The Road to Suez*, Erskine B. Childers indicated that this Agreement had reduced the British influence in the area and "its halting called for the most profound reckoning since the withdrawal from India."[9] The author, therefore, emphasized the necessity of "a re-thinking about Arab Nationalism."[10]

c. The Aswan High Dam: The idea of building a High Dam near Aswan had been in hydrologists' minds for decades. The idea matured in Egyptian experts' minds, not only as the answer to any one need, but as a complex of best answers to many needs. Egypt, her population exploding by 500,000 every year, was living on six million acres of cultivated land. The problem, therefore, was the need of water at the time when every year, an average of 30 million cubic meters of Nile water were flowing uselessly into the Mediterranean, and there was no hope of pushing this water back into the desert without a high dam.

It was a highly wise decision when both the United States and the United Kingdom announced in December, 1955, their readiness to help finance the Dam, and offered together 70 million dollars. "The International Bank had announced its readiness to lend Egypt up to 200 million dollars, which with the grants made up one-quarter of the total sum sought by Egypt."[11] The Soviet Union had an-

9 Erskine B. Childers, *The Road to Suez* (London: Macgibbon & Kee, 1962), pp. 111-112.

10 Ibid., p. 112.

11 Alfred Lilienthal, *There Goes the Middle East* (New York: The Bookmailer, Inc., 1958), p. 176; see also Herman Finer, *Dulles Over Suez: The Theory and Practice of His Diplomacy* (Chicago Quadrangle Books, 1964), pp. 20-60; and see "Suez Canal Problem July 26 - September 22, 1956," *A Documentary Publication* (Washington, D.C., The Department of State, October 1956).

nounced in October, 1955, that it was willing to finance the Dam.

Unfortunately, on July 19, 1956, both the United States and the United Kingdom together with the World Bank, announced the withdrawal of their offer and readiness. What happened as a result?

1. The Soviet Support: The Soviet Union got the best chance to gain friends by showing its interest in the welfare of the Arabs. This gave Arab Nationalism a new trend.

2. The reaction throughout the Arab World: The nationalist movement throughout the Arab World began to change its trend and to reconsider its foreign policy. As Mr. Alfred Lilienthal explains:

> The reaction of the Arab world, held up momentarily by a religious holiday was violently explosive. From North Africa to Iraq, a stream of abuse was directed against the United States and the alleged reasons of the withdrawal of Western support.[12]

It was the kind of blow that had invariably brought down a government either by resignation, or at some early stage by further and finally overwhelming the Great Powers' pressure. President Nasser and his colleagues, who were the focus of attention in those few days after July 19, felt that his Government and Egypt had been locally as well as globally insulted; and the Dam was badly needed to

_____
12 Ibid., p. 178.

solve — at least to some extent — the problems arising from population explosion. Furthermore, it was necessary for Nasser to convince all the Arabs that Egypt was still strong enough to reply and play, under his leadership, the leading role in the Arab Nationalist Movement.

3. Nationalization of the Suez Canal Company: Having no alternative, Nasser's response was prompt and dramatic. In a highly emotional speech at Alexandria on July 26, 1956, the President announced:

> Today, citizens, the Suez Canal Company has been nationalized. This order has been published in the Official Journal. It has become a matter of fact. . . .[13]

The nationalization of the Suez Canal Company afforded precisely the kind of opportunity that was needed to destroy Nasser and to eliminate his policy and the philosophy he represented.

To the United Kingdom: Nasser had already cut — to a great extent — its influence in the Arab States; he supported the British colonies in Africa and South Arabia in their struggle for independence. The nationalization of the Canal meant only two things:

1. The reduction — if not the elimination — of British influence in Africa and the Middle East;

---

13 See the text of the Nationalization Speech in Carol A. Fisher and Fred Krinsky, *Middle East in Crisis: A Historical and Documentary Review* (Syracuse University Press, 1959), pp. 136-140; see also Mohamed Khalil, *The Arab States and the Arab League: A Documentary Record Vol. II* (Beirut: Khayats, 1962), pp. 151-152.

2. More prestige to Nasser and, therefore, the domination of Arab Nationalism as a revolutionary concept.

To France: It was believed in France that Nasser was the biggest factor behind the Algerian revolution. Thus, she was anxiously waiting for a moment when she could give him a blow that would end his influence. The nationalization of the Canal, however, would give Nasser a greater chance to develop his policy against France, while the latter would lose economically and politically.

To Israel:

1. The Arab people justifiably looked to Nasser as the leader who could redeem their homeland in Palestine. He developed and strongly supported the idea of Arab unity and the concept of Arab Nationalism; and he carried this responsibility to the danger of Israel, as a new state that was created in the heart of the Arab World.

2. The problem of Israeli shipping through the Canal since 1948.

3. The nationalization of the Canal and the withdrawal of the Canal Zone force would be withdrawal of a vital potential buffer against major war or threat of war between Israel and the largest Arab State.[14]

These were the main causes of the Suez Crisis and of the war of 1956. The fact then was that the nationalization of the Suez Canal was not the main or the single cause, but only a golden opportunity to destroy Nasser. As Sir Anthony Eden, in August 1956, precisely declared: "Our

---

14 Erskine B. Childers, op. cit., p. 115.

quarrel is not with Egypt, it is with Colonel Nasser . . ."[15] This fact was also recognized by a *Washington Post* editor who wrote,

> Britain and France moved nominally to protect the Suez Canal but actually to restore it to international operation after Nasser had nationalized it — and if possible to topple Nasser himself.[16]

The Suez Canal Company's concession was not due to expire until November 17, 1968. The British government owned 44 percent of the Company's shares and over 25 percent of the remainder was owned by private shareholders in France. The Canal was a vitally strategic link in Britain's communication with her empire and almost all of Europe was heavily dependent upon the oil transported through the Canal from the Middle East. The interested parties, therefore, were not prepared to let a change in the status quo go unchallenged.

At London, a conference of twenty-four nations most directly concerned was held during August 16-23 without Egyptian participation. At the conference, Mr. John Foster Dulles, United States Secretary of State, presented a plan for an international board to operate the Suez Canal Company. Eighteen nations voted for the American plan, but Egypt rejected it, as did the Soviet Union, India, Indonesia and Ceylon.[17] Egypt, in fact, considered an international management board, on which it would be only one voice among many, "collective colonialism."

Going one step further, the United Kingdom and France

---

15 Maurice Harari, *Government and Politics of the Middle East* (N.J.: Englewood Cliffs, Prentice-Hall, Inc., 1962), p. 881.

16 *The Washington Post* (August 14, 1966).

17 *New York Times* (August 22, 1956). India proposed that operation of the Canal remain in the hands of an Egyptian board of control, advised by an international body; see also U.S.A. Documents, op. cit., p. 55 et seq.

organized on September 12, 1956, the so-called "Suez Canal Users Association." If Egypt, said Sir Eden, refused to cooperate, the "Users Association" would "be to take such further steps as seem to be required, whether through the United Nations or by other means."[18] Despite Nasser's rejection of the idea as "an association for waging war," a second London conference was held from September 19-21 and on October 1, a "Suez Canal Users Association" was inaugurated.[19]

As all negotiations met with failure, the issue shifted to the United Nations' Security Council. A complaint against Egypt for terminating international control of the Suez Canal had been presented by Britain and France. Egypt, on the other hand, had asked the Security Council to consider British and French threats to the peace. More than ever now, the problem became a crisis for the world community to consider and to find a peaceful solution to serve the maintenance of peace and security in that area.

Finally, after informal talks between the parties and with the help of Mr. Hammarskjöld, the following "six requirements," which would govern a Suez settlement, were agreed upon:[20]

a. There should be free and open transit through the Canal without discrimination, overt or covert — this covers both political and technical aspects;

b. The sovereignty of Egypt should be respected;

---

[18] Parliamentary Debates: House of Commons Official Report, 5th Series. Vol. 558 (September 12, 1956), pp. 10-11.

[19] See Press Release 502, U.S. Department of State Bulletin XXXV (October 1, 1956), pp. 507-8; see also U.S.A. Documents, op. cit., p. 327 et seq.

[20] U.N. Doc. S/3671; SCOR, 11th Year, 742nd and 743rd meetings (October 13, 1956); p. 3 and pp. 17-18 respectively; see also the text in Documents on American Foreign Relations, 1956 (New York: Harper, for the Council on Foreign Relations, 1957), pp. 342-343.

c. The operation of the Canal should be insulated from the politics of any country;

d. The manner of fixing tolls and charges should be decided by agreement between Egypt and the users;

e. A fair proportion of the dues should be allotted to development;

f. In case of disputes, unresolved affairs between the Universal Suez Maritime Canal Company and the Egyptian Government should be settled by arbitration, with suitable terms of refference and suitable provisions for the payment of sums found to be due.·

In the Security Council, however, the Soviet Union vetoed a resolution suggesting the implementation of these principles.

The Military Invasion of Egypt

Since the beginning of the Suez crisis the connection between the Palestine question and the Suez case must have become apparent to the Western European Powers and to Israel, just as it had always existed in the minds of Arab leaders. Israel had already been shaken by the withdrawal of British military forces from Suez which gave Egypt a much freer hand for effective action in Palestine. The problem of Israeli ships and the insistence of Egypt to prevent them from passage through the Canal brought out more clearly, the obvious parallel between the interests of Israel and those of the United Kingdom and France in their common antagonism to Egypt.

The preparation for war began: France sent considerable military equipment, especially fighter aircraft, to Israel in September and October, 1956, and some officers with it; diplomatic and military contacts were multiplied.[21]

On Monday, October 29, 1956, the Israeli Government announced to the world that it had invaded Sinai "in order to destroy the bases from which the Fedayeen groups operate." A few hours later, on October 30, 1956, an Anglo-French ultimatum was issued to Israel and Egypt calling for cessation of fighting within twelve hours and withdrawal of all troops from a ten-mile radius of the Suez Canal area, the Israeli army on the east bank and the Egyptian army on the west. Furthermore, Egypt was asked to accept temporary British and French occupation of key positions at Port Said, Ismailia and Suez.[22] The ultimatum was forthrightly rejected by Egypt and accepted by Israel. President Eisenhower of the United States sent fretful messages to Eden and Mollet urging them to refrain from carrying out the terms of the ultimatum. President Eisenhower expressed "his earnest hope that the United Nations Organization would be given full opportunity to settle the items in the controversy by peaceful means instead of by forceful ones."[23] The Anglo-French ultimatum, however, turned the situation from a local Middle Eastern war into a Western invasion of Egypt. There was no other way to interpret it despite the reasons that were given: to stop the war and to protect British and French subjects, British and French shipping, and the canal. The United States, however, was not informed in advance of this crucial decision because, as Mr. Mollet later admitted, they feared Washington would not approve their action and might upset their schedule.[24]

---

[21] See the report of James Morris in the *Manchester Guardian* (November 20, 1956).

[22] U.N. Doc. S/3712 (October 30, 1956).

[23] U.S. Department of State, United States Policy in the Middle East (1959), p. 142.

[24] Interview, *New York Times* (December 10, 1956).

130

There was a secret agreement between the United Kingdom, France and Israel prior to the Suez invasion. This was recently confirmed for the first time by the British Prime Minister, Harold Wilson, on August 10, 1966, following the disclosure by Christian Pineau, then French Foreign Minister, that a secret agreement was signed between the three invading states. Mr. Wilson said,

> All I can say is prima facie evidence, including that of the then French Foreign Minister, now suggests there was a clear agreement in advance and that there was a joint plan of invasion.[25]

He went on to say that the British Parliament was kept in ignorance and "so I believe were three quarters of the then Cabinet."[26]

Earlier in an interview on the British Broadcasting Corporation TV (BBC), Christian Pineau, former French Foreign Minister, confirmed that on October 24, 1956, he met at a private villa in France and signed what he called "the Anglo-French-Israelian treaty."[27] The former French Foreign Minister went on to say that this treaty

> was necessarily secret because the circumstances were very difficult, and I think maybe after ten years it would be possible to say more. If my English friends after this period accept to say all the truths about this question I should agree.[28]

Furthermore, Israeli General Moshe Dayan confirmed the agreement when he stated that "his country would not

---

25 *The Washington Post* (August 10, 1966).
26 Ibid.
27 Ibid.
28 Ibid.

have acted if it had not been assured of a simultaneous British and French effort."[29]

In any case, the invasion occurred. On October 30, the United States representative called for an immediate meeting of the Security Council to consider "The Palestine Question: steps for the immediate cessation of the military action of Israel in Egypt."[30] On the same day, a United States-sponsored resolution calling upon Israel to leave Egypt without delay and asking all Member States to "refrain from the use of force or threat of force" and "from giving any military, economic or financial assistance to Israel so long as it has not complied with this resolution," was defeated by Anglo-French veto. Similarly, another cease-fire resolution sponsored by the Soviet Union met the same fate in the Security Council.[31]

On October 31, British and French bombers began to raid military targets in Egypt. The Anglo-French attack on the Egyptian air force was in progress less than twenty-four hours after the votes in the United Nations Security Council. In justifying this military action against Egypt, Prime Minister Eden told the British House of Commons that:

> It is really not tolerable that the greatest sea highway in the world, one on which our Western life, so largely depends, should be subject to the dangers of an explosive situation in the Middle East which, it must be admitted, has been largely created by the Egyptian Government along familiar lines. . . .[32]

---

29 Ibid., (August 14, 1966).

30 U.N. Doc. S/3706 (October 30, 1956).

31 SCOR, 11th Year, 749th meeting (October 30, 1956), p. 31.

32 Parliamentary Debates, House of Commons Official Report, 5th Series, Vol. 558 (October 31, 1956), p. 1450.

Indeed, the British and French motive, the real motive, was not, as it seemed, to protect the waterway and separate the fighting armies, but to force President Nasser's hand into compromising on the Canal dispute. They may also have hoped to prevent Nasser, or at least to weaken his prestige, from being able to lead a united Arab movement not only against Israel but also against the United Kingdom and France in the Arab World and Africa.

A fundamental difference, however, had developed between the traditional Western allies in regard to their Middle Eastern policy and their attitude towards President Nasser. Britain and France considered Nasser as a belligerent anti-Western, and his fall from political power would be a triumph for the anticommunist alliance.[33] Secretary of State Dulles, on the other hand, hoped to bring down Nasser, but preferred to achieve this motive by economic pressure. The United States Government believed, however, that the Anglo-French military intervention in Egypt had seriously weakened Western denunciations of Soviet "imperialism" at the very time when some states in Eastern Europe were rising up against Soviet policy. "The British and French Governments are taking action against Egypt not only in opposition to United States policy but in defiance of the principles of the United Nations."[34]

What, then did the invasion accomplish? It probably brought some "military security" to Israel. But for the United Kingdom, and to a lesser extent for France, it was a disaster. It caused the premature end of Anthony Eden's political career and the shrinking of British power in the Middle East. On the other hand, because of his political victory, President Nasser emerged after the Suez crisis as the very center of power in the Arab World and the champion of Arab Nationalism. As such, the Suez crisis had marked a turning point in the entire Middle Eastern affairs.

[33] *New York Times* (November 1, 1956).
[34] Ibid.

Furthermore, the crisis grew out of not only resentment and obsession, but also from a rupture of effective diplomatic understanding and communication between the United States and its Western allies. The United Kingdom and France conspired in secret, for their leaders believed that the United States might not take sufficient account of their vital interests in the area. Had they consulted the United States, this crisis might not have occurred.

II. CREATION OF THE MACHINERY OF PEACE-KEEPING

In Egypt the impact of the war was very severe. Israeli forces had penetrated into Sinai and had occupied the Gaza Strip and the Gulf of Aqaba. On the other side, the Anglo-French troops had landed and occupied Port Said. At New York, the Security Council, because of the Anglo-French veto, was unable to work or take any effective action towards its "primary" responsibility in the maintenance of international peace and security. A third world war was likely to occur; a general war seemed inevitable. At the United Nations the Soviet Union proposed that the Security Council, acting under Article 42 of the Charter, authorize the U.S.S.R. and the United States to send "naval and air forces, military units, volunteers, military instructors and other forms of assistance" to Egypt.[35] Also the Soviet Union threatened that the United Kingdom and France might face "some stronger power" if they did not halt their invasion.[36] The Soviet Union, furthermore, informed the United States that fighting in Egypt "contains danger of turning into a third world war."[37] The United States, on the other hand, made it clear that any move by the Soviet

---

[35] This proposal was rejected by the Council on November 5, 1956; see SCOR, 11th Year, 755th meeting (November 5, 1956), pp. 4-14.

[36] *New York Times* (November 6, 1956).

[37] Ibid.

134

Union to intervene in the Middle East by force, would meet American opposition and resistance.[38]

From a pragmatic point of view, however, the United States did not believe that the Western Powers, even if temporarily successful in using force against Egypt, could make such a victory, if achieved, "stick" over a long period of time. This had been the lesson of the earlier occupation of Egypt, and the lesson of Syria, Palestine and North Africa. The leading Western State, furthermore, was unwilling to let the leading Eastern State reap all the benefits of acting on behalf of the Arabs in such a case, in which the aggression was clear.

As the Security Council was barred from acting by the Anglo-French veto, Yugoslavia, supported by both the United States and the Soviet Union, proposed on October 31, 1956, convoking an emergency special session of the General Assembly, under the "Uniting for Peace" resolution in order "to deal with the deepening crisis," and submitted a draft resolution to the Security Council.[39] The representative of the United Kingdom questioned the constitutionality of the move and maintained that the procedure proposed in the Yugoslav draft was out of order and was not in accordance with the terms of the "Uniting for Peace" resolution. The United States representative supported the Yugoslav draft resolution when he stated that it was "relevant and clearly applicable under the present circumstances."[40] When the vote was taken on the British motion, it was defeated by 6 to 4 (Australia, Belgium, France and the United Kingdom), with one abstention (China). In fact, the United States achieved a great victory in "persuading other delegations to write letters to the Secretary-General, saying they noted the decision of

---

38 White House news release, U.S. Department of State, United States Policy in the Middle East, p. 182.

39 U.N. Doc. S/3719.

40 GAOR, Twelfth Session, Supplement No. 2 (1957), p. 38.

the Security Council to convene an emergency session and concurred in it."[41] The Yugoslav draft resolution, therefore, was adopted by 7 votes in favor, 2 against (France and the United Kingdom), with 2 abstentions (Australia and Belgium).

At New York the United Nations General Assembly convened and began to consider the matter on November 1, 1956. The situation before the General Assembly was in many ways unique, for past crises afforded little precedence. In some respects the Korean case in June, 1950, one might say, seemed to contain elements similar to those prevalent in the Suez crisis. In both cases there was open military attack: Israel invaded Egyptian territory in Sinai, and North Korea crossed the thirty-eighth parallel into South Korea. In 1956, as in 1950, there were no organized international police forces ready to restore international peace and security. The World Organization, in both crises, was called upon to deal with a situation in which the idea of peace-observation and peace-keeping machinery was presented. Finally, the Great Powers were involved in both cases. However, different from the Korean situation was the diplomatic rupture between the Western allies in the Suez crisis of 1956. "It was embarrassing to the United States to find itself in the company of the Soviet Union in condemning its traditional allies and threatening them with chastisement."[42]

In the General Assembly several of the Afro-Asian states, together with the communist bloc, favored direct condemnation of Israel, the United Kingdom, and France as aggressors, and described their military action against Egypt as "a continuation of the tradition of colonialism."[43]

---

41 Joseph P. Lash, op. cit., p. 82.

42 John C. Campbell, *Defense of the Middle East: Problems of American Policy* (New York: Frederick A. Praeger, 1960), p. 112.

43 GAOR, The First Emergency Special Session, 561st meeting (November 1, 1956), p. 34. The words quoted are those of the representative of Ceylon.

136

What kind of policy should the General Assembly pursue, and what was the most workable solution that would effectively bring about a real peace and strengthen the prestige of the United Nations? No doubt the extreme policy of enforcement was hazardous especially if the invaders, two of whom were Great Powers, refused to obey. On the other hand, conciliation was not the appropriate measure since the principles of the United Nations Charter were clearly violated when the territorial integrity and political independence of Egypt were impaired. So, the General Assembly had no choice except to follow a middle course between the paths of coercion and conciliation.

To stop the fighting, Secretary of State Dulles presented a United States draft resolution which was adopted as the November 2 cease-fire resolution. The American move was approved in a vote of 64 in favor, 5 against (Australia, France, Israel, New Zealand and the United Kingdom) and 6 abstentions (Belgium, Canada, Laos, the Netherlands, Portugal and the Union of South Africa).[44] This resolution called for an immediate cease-fire and a halt to the movement of military forces and arms into the area. It urged the parties to withdraw behind the armistice lines, desist from raids across those lines, and observe scrupulously the Armistice Agreements. Furthermore, it recommended to all Member States that they refrain from introducing military material into that area of tension. The resolution also urged that steps be taken to reopen the Suez Canal and restore freedom of navigation. Finally, it gave the Secretary-General the responsibility of observing and reporting on compliance to the Security Council and the General Assembly "for such further action as they may deem appropriate."

Mr. Lester Pearson, then Canadian Minister for External Affairs, told the delegations that the cease-fire resolu-

---

44 U.N. Doc. A/3256 (November 1, 1956); it subsequently became resolution 997 (ES-I), GAOR, 1st Emergency Special Session, Suppl. No. 1, A/3354 (November 2, 1956), p. 2.

tion of November 2 did not provide for any steps to be taken by the United Nations for a final peace settlement.

> Allowing the armed forces of Egypt and Israel to resume their old positions confronting each other in fear and hatred would lead again to incidents, bloodshed, and ultimately another explosion.[45]

The Canadian Foreign Minister then suggested the creation of a vehicle for peace-keeping and the development of an approach for peacemaking: a policy of "preventive diplomacy." He requested that the Secretary-General be authorized

> . . . to make arrangements with Member States for a United Nations force large enough to keep these borders at peace while a political settlement is being worked out — a truly international peace and police force.[46]

In fact, four draft resolutions were before the General Assembly. An Afro-Asian draft renewed the call for a cease-fire and set a twelve-hour deadline for compliance. There were two United States draft resolutions concerning the establishment of United Nations commissions to work out new approaches to the Palestine and Suez problems. A fourth draft was presented by Mr. Pearson of Canada to establish a United Nations peace-keeping machinery by which compliance could be secured with the Afro-Asian cease-fire proposal.

The Canadian and the 19 power draft resolutions were put to vote on November 4, 1956. The former was adopted by 57 votes to none, with 19 abstentions, as resolution 998

---

45 GAOR, First Emergency Special Session (November 1-November 10, 1956), p. 36.

46 Ibid.

(ES-I);[47] the latter was adopted by 59 votes to 5, with 12 abstentions, as resolution 999 (ES-I).[48] It was a real turning point for it provided the birth of the United Nations' pioneering force for international peace-observation and peace-keeping.

The General Assembly's resolution had directed the Secretary-General to submit a plan within forty-eight hours for the setting up, with the consent of the nations concerned, "of an emergency international force to secure and supervise the cessation of hostilities" in accordance with the terms of the November 2, resolution.[49]

On November 4, the Secretary-General reported that only Egypt had accepted the cease-fire resolution. Mr. Hammarskjöld also reported that the Chief-of-Staff of UNTSO had advised that Israel had informed him, on 4 November, that the General Armistice Agreement with Egypt no longer had any validity and that he had been asked by the Israeli authorities to order the United Nations Truce Supervision Organization out of the Gaza area.[50] He then proposed establishment without delay of a United Nations Command, and that Gen. E. L. Burns, Commander-in-Chief of the United Nations Truce Supervision Organization, be Chief of the new command. The Secretary-General further requested that he be quickly authorized to recruit

---

47 Ibid., p. 71. The abstaining states were: Czechoslovakia, Egypt, France, Hungary, Israel, Laos, New Zealand, Poland, Portugal, Romania, Ukrainian Soviet Socialist Republic, Union of South Africa, Union of Soviet Socialist Republics, United Kingdom of Great Britain and Northern Ireland, Albania, Australia, Austria, Bulgaria, Byelorussian Soviet Socialist Republic.

48 Ibid. Against: Australia, France, Israel, New Zealand, United Kingdom. Abstaining: Belgium, Denmark, Dominican Republic, Finland, Iceland, Laos, Luxembourg, Netherlands, Norway, Portugal, Sweden, Union of South Africa.

49 Ibid.

50 See in this point, Yearbook of the United Nations (New York: U.N., 1956), p. 29.

officers "drawn from countries which are not permanent members of the Security Council."[51]

Accordingly, on November 5, 1956, the General Assembly adopted a resolution establishing a United Nations Command for an emergency international police force to supervise and secure the cessation of hostilities in accordance with all the terms of the General Assembly resolution 997 (ES-I) of November 2, 1956.[52] This resolution had urged "that all parties now involved in hostilities in the area agree to an immediate cease-fire, and as part thereof, halt the movement of military forces and arms into the area." It had also urged Egypt and Israel

> . . . promptly to withdraw all forces behind the armistice lines, to desist from raids across the armistice lines into neighboring territory, and to observe scrupulously the provisions of the armistice agreements.

Further recommendations were that no military goods be introduced into the area by any Member State, and "that, upon the cease-fire being effective, steps be taken to reopen Suez Canal and restore freedom of navigation." These resolutions of November 2 and November 5, really furnished both the constitutional and the functional bases for the United Nations Emergency Force. However, the philosophical rationalization for the creation of the international police force was the realization by the international community that

---

[51] U.N. Doc. A/3289 (November 4, 1956). First report of the Secretary-General on the plan for an emergency international United Nations Force, requested in resolution 998 (ES-I), adopted by the General Assembly on 4 November 1956.

[52] GAOR, 1st Emergency Special Session, 565th meeting (November 4, 1956), p. 89; it subsequently became Resolution 1000 (ES-I). The draft resolution was adopted by 57 votes in favor, none opposed, and 19 abstentions. Abstaining were New Zealand, Poland, Portugal, Romania, Turkey, Ukraine, Union of South Africa, U.S.S.R., the United Kingdom, Albania, Australia, Bulgaria, Byelorussia, Czechoslovakia, Egypt, France, Hungary, Israel and Laos.

in order to re-examine this problem, to find a new approach to it and to arrive at a comprehensive solution, the first requirement is the restoration of peace; there can be no kind of conciliation and no kind of settlement while there is war. As means of restoring peace we have suggested two basic principles. The first is that we offer Israel a guarantee, the guarantee of an international force which will be able to forestall real or illusory dangers and at all events the dangers which according to Israel existed along its borders. Secondly, in return for this guarantee, we ask Israel that when the United Nations forces arrive it should withdraw its forces to the territory where it has lawful jurisdiction or, in other words, from territories which are outside Israel's jurisdiction and have, for one reason or another, been occupied by Israel's forces.[53]

In the General Assembly, great differences showed themselves as to the nature and responsibilities of the proposed international police force, and it was essential for Mr. Hammarskjöld to take these differences into consideration in all of his decisions regarding the nature, size and functions of the peace-keeping force as well as its status.

To France, Israel, and the United Kingdom, supported by Australia and New Zealand, the new international organ should be an instrument of pressure on the Egyptian Government. The United Nations police force, these States felt, should stay in Egypt until desirable political settlements had been achieved. The invading States further hoped that the presence of their forces in Egypt would represent a bargaining power for them in any potential discussions with President Nasser over Suez and Palestine problems. With their troops occupying the Suez Canal and Sinai, the invaders felt that they would be in a better position to

---

53 Ibid., p. 87.

extract from the Egyptian President a settlement favorable to their interests. A political price, they thought, would be paid by Nasser for the withdrawal of their forces, and in their eyes, the price would be equally high if the occupation troops were made up of United Nations soldiers or of their own forces.[54]

To Egypt, on the other hand, supported by other Arab States and others including the two super-powers, the United States and the U.S.S.R., the approach of the invading States was unacceptable. Egypt and its supporters felt that, constitutionally and in terms of reference, the proposed international force was merely a temporary measure to insure observance of a cease-fire and peaceful withdrawal of the Anglo-French-Israeli troops from the Egyptian soil. An occupation force was certainly not to be envisaged, and the tasks of the United Nations forces would have to be very different from those of the invading armies. Furthermore, the bargaining positions of the British, French and Israeli governments in their disputes with Egypt were not to be improved by their use of force in violations of the principles of international law and the United Nations Charter.

Indeed, not only had the General Assembly stipulated that "consent of the Nations concerned" was essentially needed to create the force, thus giving Egypt veto power over the United Nations entry into Egyptian soil, but also the two super-powers, the United States and the U.S.S.R., were fundamentally, though for different reasons, in agreement with Egypt. It was believed that any show of sympathy on the part of the United States for its traditional Western allies and Israel would decidedly turn the Arab World against the American interests, the only Western power that was then still commanding some respect in the area. These political attitudes, however, had an unmistak-

---

54 William Frye, *A United Nations Peace Force* (New York: Oceana for the Carnegie Endowment for International Peace, 1957), p. 3.

able influence on the concept, the functions and the status of the United Nations Emergency Force.

Basing his analysis on the General Assembly resolutions and opinion, the Secretary-General submitted on November 6, 1956, his second and final report in which he set forth the fundamental principles that govern the International Force, its functions, size, organization, financing and recruitment. It was on the basis of principles presented in his report that Britain, France, Israel and Egypt unconditionally accepted a cease-fire.[55] In his report, Mr. Hammarskjöld described a temporary international police force, "the length of its assignment being determined by the needs arising out of the present conflict," with a chief officer appointed by the United Nations and ultimately responsible to the General Assembly or the Security Council or both. The full determination of UNEF's tasks and its legal status was left open, but it was clearly stated in that report that "there is no intent in the establishment of the Force to influence the military balance in the present conflict and, thereby, the political balance affecting efforts to settle the conflict." Accordingly, positive neutrality was the law describing the character of the Force and governing its functions. As such, UNEF was not established to be used as a military or political tool that would strengthen the position of any party to the conflict.

Although paramilitary in nature, UNEF was not to have military objectives, but only to work on the basis of consent of the states concerned. Mr. Hammarskjöld, therefore, pointed out that, in his conception of the nature of the Force, the elements of conciliation and enforcement were to be fundamentally and practically combined. Although political consent was an essential feature of the entire scheme, UNEF itself was functionally responsible to the United Nations. Enforcement actions were not planned,

---

55 Secretary-General Second Report, U.N. Doc. A/3302 (November 6, 1956).

yet the Force was to be more than an observers' corps and its essential function, to secure the cessation of hostilities and a withdrawal of forces, was decidedly military in character. It was created and supervised by the international community and "the basic political decisions of the Assembly, of course, constitute the fundamental law of this whole operation."[56]

On November 7, 1956, the General Assembly adopted the second report of the Secretary-General and asked him to continue discussions with Governments of Member States concerning offers of participation in the United Nations Force.[57] Later on the same day, Mr. Hammarskjöld informed the Egyptian Government that the Force was ready. But before giving its permission for the entry of UNEF into its soil, the Egyptian Government asked for clarification as to the nature and character of the new international organ. After one week of deliberations, Egypt, the Host State, finally agreed to the entry of the Force into the Egyptian territory. Immediately, on November 15, the first group of United Nations troops landed in Egypt, and by mid-December it was operating in the Suez Canal area. By early February 1957, UNEF had been virtually brought to its full strength of some 6,000 men from ten Member States: Brazil, Canada, Colombia, Denmark, Finland, India, Indonesia, Norway, Sweden and Yugoslavia.

The General Assembly's constitutional competence to establish an international peace-keeping force to be stationed on a sovereign territory was challenged by some Member States, notably the Soviet Union and other members of the Socialist Bloc. In explaining its attitude towards Resolution 1001, in the vote upon which the Soviet Union abstained, the Soviet delegate declared that the creation

---

[56] GAOR, 1st Emergency Special Session, 567th meeting (November 7, 1956), p. 119.

[57] Ibid., p. 126. The vote was: 64 in favor, none opposed, and 12 abstentions (abstaining were members of the Soviet Bloc, Egypt, Israel, and the Union of South Africa.)

144

of UNEF constituted a violation of the principles of the United Nations Chárter, for only the Security Council is "exclusively" authorized, under Chapter VII of the Charter, to create an international armed force. The only reason for a Soviet abstention, rather than a negative vote, was that Egypt, the victim of aggression,[58] had accepted the presence of the Force on its territory.[59]

This interpretation was adopted by the Soviet Union in spite of the fact that the Soviet delegate had voted for the transfer of the question to the General Assembly under the "Uniting for Peace" resolution. Perhaps the most significant result of the Soviet attitude was a refusal to pay assessed contributions to the cost of the Force, which led the General Assembly ultimately to request an Advisory Opinion from the International Court of Justice.

However, it was never disputed that the creation of an international force such as UNEF was beyond the competence of the United Nations as a whole; what was in issue was whether the Organization's acts were undertaken by the proper organ; if not, it was contended that the peace-keeping actions initiated by the General Assembly should be considered unconstitutional.

In its Advisory Opinion, to which this writer subscribes, the International Court ruled that the establishment of UNEF was in accordance with the provisions of the Charter and within the purposes of the Organization; for the opera-

---

58 It may be noted that although none of the three invading States, Israel, France, or the United Kingdom was qualified by any organ of the U.N. as an "aggressor," this qualification was clearly understood and upon this understanding the U.N. acted.

59 Off. Rec. G.A., 1st Emergency Special Sess., paras. 291-297. That the Soviet Union was not prepared to abandon its view that only the Security Council could establish an international armed force is clear from the statement of the Soviet delegate, Kuznetsov; Ibid., **567 Mtg.** (7 November 1956), pp. 127-128.

tions were undertaken to promote and maintain international peace and security.[60]

TABLE I
THE MANPOWER SIZE OF UNEF ON
SEPTEMBER 15, 1957[61]

Contingents	Officers	Other Ranks	Total
Brazil	44	501	545
Canada	113	1059	1172
Colombia	31	491	522
Denmark	25	399	424
Finland	15	240	255
India	27	930	957
Indonesia	37	545	582
Norway	71	427	498
Sweden	27	322	349
Yugoslavia	55	618	673
TOTAL	445	5532	5977

60 I.C.J. Reports (1962), p. 151 et seq. Also for the various opinions given in this case, see R. Y. Jennings (1962), II International and Comparative Law Quarterly, p. 1170 et seq.

61 U.N. Doc. A/3694 and Add. 1, p. 2.

TABLE II
THE MANPOWER SIZE OF UNEF ON
AUGUST 22, 1962[62]

Contingents	Officers	Other Ranks	Total
Brazil	40	590	630
Canada	82	863	945
Denmark	45	517	562
India	80	1169	1249
Norway	84	529	613
Sweden	33	391	424
Yugoslavia	68	642	710
TOTAL	432	4701	5133

62 U.N. Doc. A/5172, p. 5. The Indonesian contingent withdrew on September 12, 1957; the Finnish withdrew on December 5, 1957; the Colombian unit withdrew on October 28, 1958.

147

TABLE III
THE MANPOWER SIZE OF UNEF ON JULY 31, 1966

Country	Contingent	All Ranks	Total
BRAZIL	Infantry battalion (including 4 military police)	600	
	Headquarters staff	5	605
$\underline{a}$ /			
CANADA	Service units	692	
	Headquarters staff	5	
	Military police	18	
	Air transport unit	89	804
$\underline{b}$ /			
DENMARK	Infantry battalion	320	
	Headquarters staff	5	
	Headquarters medical staff	15	
	UNEF hospital	69	
	Military police	8	417
INDIA	Infantry battalion	962	
	Brass band	34	
	Headquarters staff	12	
	Service units	114	
	Military police	16	1,138
$\underline{b}$ /			
NORWAY	Infantry battalion	280	
	Headquarters staff	3	
	Military police	6	289
$\underline{c}$ /			

SWEDEN	Headquarters staff	1	1
YUGOSLAVIA	Reconnaissance battalion (including 13 military police)	700	
	Headquarters staff	5	705
	GRAND TOTAL:		3,959

a / The Canadian Reconnaissance Squadron was withdrawn on 20 February 1966.

b / The Norwegian and Danish units were placed under a single battalion and the structure of command was mixed. Commanding officers were alternately Danish and Norwegian. The authorized total strength of the "Danor" Battalion was 600 all ranks.

c / The Swedish Battalion returned to Sweden on 10 March 1966.

Source: U.N. Doc. A/6406 (September 7, 1966), p. 3.

Obviously, however, although the General Assembly was authorized under the "Uniting for Peace" resolution to establish an international police force, it could not, from a practical point of view, give life to its decision without cooperation from Member States and their contributions to the Force. In his second report on UNEF, Mr. Hammarskjöld made it clear that the proposed international force "would be limited in its operations to the extent that consent of the parties concerned is required under generally recognized international law."[63] Mr. Arthur Lall, the delegate from India, understood these words to mean "with the consent of the nations which will contribute to an emergency international United Nations force" and that "countries which are engaged in hostilities will not be members of the emergency force."[64] The sponsor of the

---

63 U.N. Doc. A/3302, p. 20.

64 GAOR, 1st Emergency Special Session, 563rd meeting (November 5, 1956), p. 70.

resolution, Lester Pearson, pointed out the same idea when he said:

> What we had in mind was that the Secretary-General, in submitting a plan to the United Nations, should not include in that plan for an international force the name of any country without the consent of that particular country.[65]

Accordingly, members of the United Nations were reaffirming that although the General Assembly could "recommend" to its Member States that they contribute to UNEF, it could not bind a state to comply with its request. But, on the other hand, Member States have already pledged not only "to fulfill in good faith the obligations assumed by them in accordance with [the United Nations Charter]," but also to "give the United Nations every assistance in any action it takes in accordance with the present Charter. . . ."[66] Member States, therefore, must give great consideration to all General Assembly recommendations, that is at least on moral grounds.

The great powers were deliberately excluded from participating in the composition of the Force.

> The primary reason for excluding the great powers was to make clear that Britain and France were not to be deputized as U.N. policemen; a secondary, but scarcely less important reason, was to keep Soviet troops out of the Middle East.[67]

Indeed, the exclusion of the Big Four was essential not only because it would facilitate the peaceful settlement of the local dispute, but also because it would exclude from the

---

65 Ibid., p. 71.

66 Article 2, Paragraphs 2 and 5 of the United Nations Charter.

67 William R. Frye, op. cit., p. 12.

area a possible confrontation between the United States and the Soviet Union. By so doing, the World Organization recognized the need to insulate the Arab-Israeli dispute from the cold war.[68] For the containment of the cold war, the international community decided not only to force the invaders out, but also to keep the super-powers out. This preventive diplomacy approach to world peace had to be carried out by UNEF.

On the other hand, the States which agreed to participate in the United Nations Force made their offers of aid conditioned by expressed reservations. One of the reservations stated by the Finnish Government was that the assignment of its unit would be for a limited time only and "therefore determined exclusively by the needs arising out of the present conflict in the area in question."[69]

To Indonesia,

> it was on this clear understanding of the temporary, emergency nature of the United Nations Emergency Force that my Government participated in it. . . . However, if the functions of the Force should be broadened or enlarged beyond its original purpose, such as linking it indefinitely with the Truce Supervision Organization, then my Government certainly would have to reserve its right to reconsider its continued participation.[70]

To India,

> a. UNEF is set up with the understanding that Anglo-French troops should withdraw from

---

[68] Robert C. Good, "The United States and the Colonial Debate," in Arnold Wolfers, ed., *Alliance Policy in the Cold War* (Baltimore: Johns Hopkins, 1959), pp. 257-258.

[69] U.N. Doc. A/3302/Add. 21.

[70] GAOR, 11th Session, Plenary meeting 649 (February 1, 1957), Vols. II-III, p. 1043.

Egypt and that Israel should withdraw behind
the armistice lines;

b. the United Nations Force is not, and must not
be, in any sense a successor to the invading
Anglo-French forces, or in any sense to take
over its functions;

c. the Force may have to function through Egyptian territory. Therefore, Egyptian consent is
required;

d. UNEF is a temporary force for an emergency;
and

e. the Force must be balanced in its composition.

Furthermore, it was understood that the participating
state was entitled to withdraw its forces on condition that
"adequate prior notification" should be given in order to
avoid any difficulty that might affect the functions of the
Force. However, it was also understood that the participating states would, in good faith, leave to the General Assembly the decision on whether the mandate of the Force has
been fulfilled.[71]

Egypt: The Host State

While the General Assembly was authorized to establish
UNEF with the consent of the states which contribute units
to the Force, it could not, without violating the generally
recognized principles of the law of nations and the United
Nations Charter, request the international police force to
be stationed or to operate on the soil of a sovereign country
without its free consent. A state's sovereignty and territorial integrity would, therefore, forbid the entry of foreign forces, even if international in composition and char-

---

71 L. B. Sohn, "The Authority of the United Nations to Establish and
Maintain a Permanent United Nations Force," *American Journal of International Law*, LII (1958), p. 237.

acter, into its territory without its voluntary approval unless such forces were dispatched by the Security Council for enforcement actions taken under Chapter VII of the United Nations Charter. With this understanding, the voluntary Egyptian consent to the stationing of a United Nations Force on the Egyptian soil had not been denied at any time. In an Aide-mémoire, approved by the General Assembly on November 24, 1956, Secretary-General Hammarskjöld had agreed with Egypt on the guiding principles that govern the presence and functioning of UNEF on its soil. In this document, two principles are of particular importance:

a. The Government of Egypt declares that, when exercising its sovereign rights on any matter concerning the presence and functioning of UNEF, it will be guided in good faith by its acceptance of General Assembly resolution 1000 (ES-I) of November 5, 1956.

b. The United Nations takes note of this declaration of the Government of Egypt and declares that the activities of UNEF will be guided, in good faith, by the task established for the Force in the aforementioned resolutions (resolutions 997, 1000 [ES-I]). With this understanding, however, the United Nations reaffirms its willingness to maintain UNEF until its task is completed.[72]

On February 8, 1957 Hammarskjöld negotiated and concluded an Agreement on the Status of the Force with the Egyptian Government. Both the Aide-mémoire and the Agreement are particularly significant in the making of the Force and in determining its nature and functions.

---

[72] GAOR, 11th Session, Annexes, Vols. II-III, Agenda Item 66, pp. 9-10; see also General Assembly Resolution 1121 (XI) (November 24, 1956), GAOR, 11th Session, Suppl. No. 17 (A/3572), p. 61.

Perhaps the most important question that was raised in connection with the Egyptian consent was whether Egypt, the Host State, did have a veto power over the composition of the Force, its size and the length of its mandate.[73] Although a political question the answer of which would have to be determined by political factors, Egypt was consulted, and its consent was secured, in regard to all matters pertaining to the Force. On the question of withdrawal of consent, however, Egypt clearly stated that the Force must leave its territory whenever the Egyptian Government so requests:

> . . . as must be abundantly clear, this Force has gone to Egypt to help Egypt, with Egypt's consent; and no one here or elsewhere can reasonably or fairly say that a fire brigade, after putting out a fire, would be entitled or expected to claim the right of deciding not to leave the house.[74]

Both Egypt and the United Nations were guided by what they mutually agreed upon in the Aide-mémoire of November 20, 1956, as the basis for consultation on all

---

73 Charles P. Noyes, "The Problem of 'Consent' in Relation to a U.N. Force," in Frye, op. cit., pp. 151-152.

74 GAOR, 11th Session, Plenary meeting 597th (November 27, 1956), Vol. I, p. 348. This viewpoint was shared by the Soviet Union. It goes without saying that the United Nations forces must also withdraw from the demarcation line and from Egyptian territory in general as soon as the Republic of Egypt should consider it necessary, Ibid., 589th meeting (November 22, 1956), pp. 223-224. The government of India also concurred with this interpretation, Ibid., 596th meeting (November 26, 1956), p. 333. Israel was adamantly opposed to the above views: "if we were to accept one of the proposals made here — namely, that the Force should separate Egyptian and Israeli troops for as long as Egypt thought it convenient and should then be withdrawn on Egypt's unilateral request, we would reach a reduction to absurdity. Egypt would then be in a position to build up, behind the screen of this Force, its full military preparations and, when it felt that those military preparations had reached their desired climax, to dismiss the United Nations Emergency Force and to stand again in close contact and proximity with the territory of Israel. . . ." Ibid., 592nd meeting (November 23, 1956), p. 275.

154

important matters such as withdrawal of consent. This Aide-mémoire, one may say, has the character of an international agreement, and, as such, could be terminated by:

a. a withdrawal of consent of the "Host State" since the very presence of the international force was based on a consent that was voluntarily given by that State;
b. a decision of the Secretary-General of the United Nations since the very presence of the Force was based on the Aide-mémoire of November 20, 1956, between the Secretary-General and the Egyptian Government. This decision may be taken especially when the "Host State" withdraws its consent to the presence of UNEF on its soil; for, at the moment the Government of the United Arab Republic withdraws its consent, the participating states would no doubt withdraw their troops. On the other hand, and as a practical matter, the Secretary-General could not assume responsibility for ordering the United Nations troops to withstand military action on the part of the sovereign soil of the "Host State";
c. a General Assembly decision;
d. agreement between Egypt and the United Nations wherein specific stipulations regarding withdrawal of the Force would be enunciated; or
e. denunciation of the constituted agreement by the other party.

On the other hand, was the consent of the invading states required for the creation of the United Nations Emergency Force as well as for determining its mandate? Secretary-General Hammarskjöld pointed out that "UNEF as a practical operation was made possible only by the concurrence, in one form or another, of the parties to the conflict in its establishment by the General Assembly."[75] However, he stated, "the General Assembly did not make the cease-fire dependent upon the creation or the functioning of UNEF."[76] It was said, furthermore, that "Israel's consent was in no legal sense a requisite to the establishment or operation on Egyptian territory of UNEF. Nor was the consent of the United Kingdom or France."[77] The State of Israel declared on November 8, 1956, that it "will willingly withdraw its forces from Egypt immediately upon the conclusion of satisfactory arrangements with the United Nations in connection with the emergency international force."[78]

However, it is only realistic to conclude that because of the very nature of the United Nations' enforcement capability and the limitations imposed thereon, principally by Great Powers' politics, the consent of the invading states furnished the pragmatic basis for the law of UNEF.

In fact, Israeli attitude toward the Force was that of refusing to accept any international police force on Israeli soil. It maintained that "in a certain sense, Israel is a military state: there isn't room on her territory for armed forces . . . other than her own."[79] Israel, furthermore, had no faith in UNEF's ability to stop the "fedayeen" activities. The Zionist State, moreover, seemed afraid to accept such an international force on its land, for world opinion may one

---

75 U.N. Doc. A/3943, p. 12.

76 GAOR, 12th Session, Annexes, Agenda Item 65, p. 11.

77 Charles P. Noyes, op. cit., p. 152.

78 U.N. Doc. A/3320, p. 32.

79 Chaumont, "La situation Juridique des Etat Membres à l'égard de la Force d'Urgence des Nations-Unies," Annuaire Français de Droit International, IV (1958), p. 430. "Israel est, dans un certain sens, un Etat militaire; il n'y a pas sur son territoire, place pour d'autres forces armées . . . que les siennes"; see also Aide-Mémoire of Ben-Gurion (January 23, 1957).

day try to impose a peace settlement with reduced boundaries. Also, the fear of the emergent Arab Nationalism; the potential Arab unity; the uncertainty of its status; the uncertainty of Great Powers' support; and the determination of the Arab States not to recognize Israel, made Israel gravely sensitive to "its territorial and military sovereignty."

III. THE NATURE OF THE UNITED NATIONS EMERGENCY FORCE

The General Assembly resolutions of November 2 and November 5, 1956, not only provided a birth certificate for UNEF, but the Force's nature and responsibilities were also generally delineated in these resolutions. However, Secretary-General Hammarskjöld, in his First Report, conceptualized the role of the Force in these words:

> It would be more than an observers' corps, but in no way a military force temporarily controlling the territory in which it is stationed; nor, moreover, should the Force have military functions exceeding those necessary to secure peaceful conditions on the assumption that the parties to the conflict take all necessary steps for compliance with the recommendations of the General Assembly.[80]

In his Second Report to the General Assembly, Secretary-General Hammarskjöld described the Force as a "paramilitary" body.[81] In disagreeing with Hammarskjöld's characterization of the nature of the Force, General Burns made the following comment:[82]

> I objected to the use of the term "paramilitary" to describe UNEF or its functions. The Oxford English

---

80 U.N. Doc. A/3302, p. 21.
81 Ibid., para. 10.
82 Burns, op. cit., p. 313.

157

Dictionary defines "paramilitary" as "having a status or function ancillary to that of military forces." Examples are constabularies or gendarmeries organized more or less on military lines and having functions of maintaining order in turbulent areas, with a regular military force behind them. But UNEF was and is unquestionably formed of military units, from the regular forces of the nations contributing. It is not ancillary to any "other" military force.

This inappropriate (in my view) use of the term "paramilitary" perhaps arises from a misapprehension that a military force in all situations invariably and necessarily uses all the arms and means at its disposal to achieve its object. This, of course, is not so, as an army can give "aid to the civil power" under great restrictions as to its use of arms. In my view, UNEF is certainly a military force, but with a strictly limited and defined task and mode of action prescribed for it.

Possibly "paramilitary" in the text was used to allay the doubts of some supporters of the Resolution.

Following, however, are some important principles which underlined the very nature of the Force an determined its functions and mandate:

a. UNEF was a temporary operation, set up on an "emergency" basis and, as such, the Force was not to be viewed as a permanent United Nations peace-keeping machinery.

b. UNEF was a subsidiary organ of the United Nations and, as such, the authority of its officers was fully independent of the policies of any one state. Functionally, furthermore, the Force was to remain positively neutral in the Arab-Israeli impasse.

c. Since UNEF was established by a General Assembly "recommendation" and not a Security

158

Council "decision," the Force could not be used for an enforcement action.

d. The responsibility entrusted to UNEF "could not be achieved through an organization similar in kind to UNTSO or to the Egyptian-Israel Mixed Armistice Commission. . . ."[83]

Nevertheless, the Force itself was not only a peace observation unit patrolling the already established Armistice Demarcation Line between Egypt and Israel, but it was also a peace-keeping machinery and a preventive diplomacy tool aimed at securing the cessation of the hostilities of the 1956 Suez campaign and ensuring the withdrawal of the invading troops from the Egyptian territory.

IV. THE THRUST OF UNEF

As has been indicated, UNEF did not replace the already existing truce supervision machinery (the MACs, UNTSO, the Chief-of-Staff), which continued to operate on the Lebanese, Jordanian and Syrian Armistice Demarcation Lines. Only along the Egyptian-Israeli Armistice Demarcation Line, UNEF was stationed and continued to operate, theoretically, in cooperation with the Egyptian-Israeli MAC. In his report, Secretary-General Hammarskjöld defined UNEF's peace-observation and peace-keeping functions as follows:[84]

In the General Assembly resolution the terms of reference are . . . "to secure the cessation of hostilities in accordance with all the terms" of the resolution of 2 November, 1956. This resolution urges that "all parties now involved in hostilities in the area agree to

---

83 U.N. Doc. A/3943, p. 10.

84 E. Lauterpacht, The U.N. Emergency Force: Basic Documents (New York; Praeger, 1960), p. 2.

159

an immediate cease-fire and as part thereof halt the movement of military forces and arms into the area"; and also "urges the parties to the Armistice Agreements promptly to withdraw all forces behind the armistice lines, to desist from raids across armistice lines into neighboring territory, and to observe scrupulously the provisions of the Armistice Agreements." These two provisions combined indicate that the functions of the United Nations force would be, when a cease-fire is being established, to enter Egyptian territory with the consent of the Egyptian Government, in order to help maintain quiet during and after the withdrawal of non-Egyptian troops, and to secure compliance with the other terms established in the resolution of 2 November, 1956. The force obviously should have no rights other than those necessary for the execution of its functions, in cooperation with local authorities. It would be more than an observers corps, but in no way a military force temporarily controlling the territory in which it is stationed; nor, moreover, should the force have military functions exceeding those necessary to secure peaceful conditions on the assumption that the parties to the conflict take all necessary steps for compliance with the recommendations of the General Assembly. Its functions can, on this basis, be assumed to cover an area extending roughly from the Suez Canal to the armistice demarcation lines, established in the Armistice Agreement between Egypt and Israel.[85]

One could, therefore, summarize the principal thrust of the Force as follows:

(a) Urgent Thrust:

(1) Reopening of the Suez Canal.

(2) Securing the withdrawal of the invading

---

85 Ibid., pp. 14-15.

forces from the Suez Canal, Gaza Strip, and Sharm el-Sheikh areas.

(b) Continuing Thrust:
(1) Maintaining quiet in the area during and after the withdrawal of the invading troops.

The Reopening of the Suez Canal

On December 22, 1956, the Anglo-French forces completed their withdrawal with UNEF contingents moving in and taking up positions. Meanwhile, in response to the resolution of November 2, in which the General Assembly had urged that "upon the cease-fire being effective steps be taken to reopen the Suez Canal," Mr. Hammarskjöld made the necessary arrangements for clearing the Suez Canal for international navigation. On December 27, 1956, clearance operations began, and by April 10, 1957, the first commercial vessel was able to pass through the waterway.

On April 24, 1957, the Republic of Egypt deposited and registered with the United Nations Secretariat a Declaration on the Suez Canal whereby the Egyptian Government declared that:[86]

a. Free and uninterrupted navigation for all nations within the limits of and in accordance with the provisions of the Constantinople Convention of 1888 would be afforded and maintained;

b. Any increase beyond one percent in the current rate of tolls within any twelve months would be the result of negotiations and, failing agreement, would be settled by arbitration;

86 United Nations Treaty Series, CCIXV (1957), pp. 300-308.

161

c. The Canal would be operated and managed by the autonomous Suez Canal Authority established by the Egyptian Government on July 26, 1956; all tolls would be payable in advance to this Authority;

d. Complaints of discrimination or violation of the Canal code would be referred first to the Canal Authority and, if not resolved, to an arbitration tribunal composed of one nominee chosen by the complainant, one chosen by the Authority and a third to be chosen by both; in the event of disagreement on the third arbitrator, the selection would be made by the President of the International Court of Justice, upon the application of either party; and

e. The Egyptian Government would pledge to take the necessary steps to accept the compulsory jurisdiction of the International Court of Justice.

At the end of April 1957, debate on the Egyptian Declaration took place in the Security Council. The point of discussion was that Egypt had not formally accepted the compulsory jurisdiction of the International Court of Justice and the fear that it might amend or withdraw the obligations assumed in its Declaration. Mr. Henry Cabot Lodge, the United States representative to the United Nations, pointed out that "there is no assurance that the six requirements will in fact be implemented. . . ." Therefore, he said, "any de facto acquiescence by the United States must be provisional. . . . United States vessels will be authorized to pay Egypt only under protest. . . ."[87] Consequently, on July 22, 1957, Egypt supplemented its Declaration of April 24 by accepting the compulsory juris-

---

[87] *New York Times* (April 27, 1957).

162

diction of the International Court of Justice in all legal disputes that might arise between the parties to the Constantinople Convention of 1888 regarding the interpretation or the applicability of its provisions.

On April 29, 1958, under the good offices of the International Bank for Reconstruction and Development, the United Arab Republic and the Suez Canal Company's stockholders signed a Head of Agreement whereby the former undertook to pay $81 million as compensation and to leave all the external assets to the latter. The Final Agreement, which confirmed the Head of Agreement, was signed at Geneva on July 13, 1958. All compensations have been paid and the Agreement has been fully implemented in good faith.

Gaza Strip

Under the terms of the Armistice Agreement between Egypt and Israel on February 24, 1949, the Strip fell under the jurisdiction of Egypt, and as a result, Egypt had administered Gaza since that time. However, the Armistice Agreement, realizing its temporary and unique nature, did not define the sovereign status of the Strip. In November, 1956, Israel occupied Gaza, denounced the Armistice Agreement with Egypt, and declared that the Egyptian administration of the Strip had ended.[88]

On January 24, 1957, Israel proposed that it withdraw its military forces from Gaza but continue to supply administrative services in the Strip.[89] This Israeli scheme was rejected by Secretary-General Hammarskjöld in his report to the General Assembly on the same day. Furthermore, the Israeli demand for guarantees before withdrawing forces from Gaza and Sharm el-Sheikh was also declared inad-

---

[88] GAOR, 11th Session, Plenary meeting 638 (January 17, 1957), Vols. II-III. p. 890.

[89] U.N. Doc. A/3511 (January 24, 1957), GAOR, 11th Session, Annexes, Vols. II-III, Agenda Item 66, p. 46.

missible. Referring specifically to the situation in Gaza, Hammarskjöld recalled the provisions of the General Armistice Agreement between Egypt and Israel which delineated the line beyond which the armed forces of the two parties were not to move and which left Gaza under the Egyptian control and administration. Moreover, the Secretary-General emphasized the fact that the United Nations was not permitted to lend assistance for securing a de facto situation contrary to the one created by the general Armistice Agreement. Hammarskjöld hereby decisively excluded the possibility of administrative control by Israel over the Gaza area.[90] Upon withdrawal of Israeli forces, the Secretary-General planned deployment of the United Nations Emergency Force in Gaza exactly as the Force had done in the Sinai Peninsula.

In the General Assembly, great differences showed themselves with respect to the Secretary-General's report of January 24. A number of Western delegates expressed considerable sympathy with the Israeli demand for guarantees. They maintained that the basis for Israeli compliance might well be UNEF's indefinite deployment in the Strip and elsewhere in order to "hold the scales between the parties and to prevent any recurrence of trouble."[91] Norway was convinced that it was clearly within the competence of the Force to prevent a breach of the 1956 cease-fire, and accordingly, of the 1948 cease-fire.[92] This, also, was the principal view of the United States.[93] India was concerned above all that the Force should not be used as a foreign army of occupation.[94] Indonesia also stressed the temporary nature of UNEF.[95] Colombia was convinced that the United

---

90 U.N. Doc. A/3512, p. 48.
91 GAOR, 11th Session, Plenary meeting 638, op. cit., p. 882.
92 Ibid., 651st meeting (February 2, 1957), p. 1084.
93 Ibid., 639th meeting (January 17, 1957), p. 898; and 650th meeting (February 2, 1957), p. 1050.
94 Ibid., 641st meeting (January 18, 1957), p. 930; and 651st meeting (February 2, 1957), p. 1070.
95 Ibid., 649th meeting (February 1, 1957), p. 1043.

Nations "has never been entrusted with the administration of a territory."[96] The Soviet Union together with the States of the Socialist Camp, on the other hand, were totally opposed to all who advocated UNEF's deployment in Gaza, in Sharm el-Sheikh, or on the armistice lines. Any such action, the Soviet representative said, would "turn the United Nations Emergency Force into what would in effect be a permanent occupation force" and create "a dangerous precedent of interference in the domestic affairs of a sovereign State."[97] Therefore, he concluded, upon the withdrawal of Israeli troops, the operation of the Force should cease.

Finally, on February 2, 1957, the General Assembly adopted a resolution calling upon Israel to withdraw its forces "without delay," and asking both Egypt and Israel to observe scrupulously the provisions of the Armistice Agreement, and considered that:

> After full withdrawal of Israel from the Sharm el-Sheikh and Gaza areas, the scrupulous maintenance of the Armistice Agreement required the placing of the United Nations Emergency Force on the Egyptian-Israel armistice demarcation line and the implementation of other measures as proposed in the Secretary-General's report. . . .[98]

On February 22, 1957, Mr. Hammarskjöld informed the General Assembly of Egypt's "willingness and readiness to make special and helpful arrangements" in Gaza "with the United Nations and some of its auxiliary bodies, such as the United Nations Relief and Works Agency for Palestine Refugees and UNEF."[99] This, of course, clearly

---

96 Ibid., 638th meeting (January 17, 1957), pp. 892-893.

97 Ibid., 646th meeting (January 29, 1957), pp. 1002-3; and 652nd meeting (February 2, 1957), p. 1077.

98 A/RES. 1125-XI (February 2, 1957), GAOR, 11th Session Suppl. No. 17 (A/3572), p. 62.

99 GAOR, 11th Session, Plenary meeting 659 (February 22, 1957), op. cit., p. 1192.

implied that Egypt had agreed to United Nations presence in Gaza Strip.

As to Israel, on the other hand, it was not until President Eisenhower's letter to Prime Minister Ben-Gurion on March 2 that withdrawal of Israeli forces was finally effected; and by March 7, 1957, the United Nations Emergency Force was fully deployed in the Strip and Israel had completed its withdrawal from the Gaza area.[100]

On March 8, 1957, General Burns, Commander of UNEF, flew to Gaza. This was the picture he saw:

> The main street was filled with processions of demonstrators. While we had at first thought that the parades which had been taking place since the liberation of the Strip were more or less spontaneous manifestations of joy at being freed from the Israeli occupation, I observed that the banners they carried and the slogans they shouted were in favor of the return of the Egyptians, and acclaiming President Nasser. . . . However . . . I saw no cause to fear that UNEF could not fulfill its task of maintaining peaceful conditions. . . .[101]

On March 10, 1957, a great number of the population organized a demonstration and attempted to raise the Egyptian flag at the United Nations headquarters. The international police force was equipped with arms, yet no instructions had been issued from headquarters regarding their use. "I was forced to think," said General Burns, "what the situation of UNEF, some 5,000 in all, would be in a hostile population of 300,000. . . ." It was plainly impossible to think of UNEF's checking disorders as the Israelis had done. . . .[102] However, the attitude of the

---

100 U.S. Department of State, United States Policy in the Middle East, pp. 332-33; see also E. L. M. Burns, op. cit., p. 259.

101 E. L. M. Burns, op. cit., p. 260.

102 Ibid., p. 264.

166

people was perfectly clear. They did not want to be ruled by outsiders. The streets were spanned with banners bearing such announcements as "Egypt is our Mother. We will never be separated from Egypt."[103]

As the troubles exploded in the Strip, President Nasser, on March 12, accused UNEF of exceeding its authority, failure to maintain law and order in Gaza and, therefore, declared that Egyptian authorities would assume complete control of the Strip. In this way, President Nasser made it clear that the international police force should play only the role of supervision and observation of the demarcation line between Egypt and Israel. When Dr. Bunche visited President Nasser on March 13, he did not succeed in convincing the Egyptian President to cancel or at least delay sending Maj. Gen. Mohammed Abdel Latif, the Administrative Governor into the Strip. On the same day, the United States Ambassador to Egypt, Mr. Raymond Hare, met President Nasser, but he too did not succeed in accomplishing what Dr. Bunche had failed to achieve.[104] On March 14, 1957, Maj. Gen. Mohammed Abdel Latif entered the Strip as Egyptian Administrative Governor. The Israelis were greatly angered by the Egyptian move when they wrongly accused Dr. Bunche of "selling" the Strip to Egypt on his arrival in the area.[105]

The Gulf of Aqaba

The Gulf of Aqaba is a small body of water the coastline of which is shared by Israel, Jordan, Saudi Arabia, and the United Arab Republic, and leads to the Red Sea through the Strait of Tiran at its entrance. Since 1950, however, Egypt had maintained a blockade against Israeli shipping to and from the Port of Elath. Accordingly, the question of Israeli freedom of navigation in the Gulf has

---

103 Ibid.
104 Ibid., pp. 267-268.
105 Ibid., p. 271.

become an integral part of the Palestine problem. It has become a political question, determined by political factors and controlled by them.

The Arab States have always asserted their collective sovereignty over the Strait of Tiran and the Gulf of Aqaba on the grounds that both the Strait and the Gulf constitute an Arab "mare clausum" and not an international waterway. They consider its waters as "res nullius" rather than "res communis," and therefore the existence of historic waters is a self-evident truth, " it is a rule of law by itself."[106] It follows, then, that the historic waters have never been part of the high seas, nor are they a rival category.

In support of this view, the representative of Saudi Arabia to the United Nations pointed out that for fourteen centuries the Gulf of Aqaba has always been the historical route to the Holy Places of Mecca under Arab sovereignty. It is due to this undisputed fact he said, that no single international authority makes any mention whatsoever of the Gulf as an international waterway open for international navigation.[107] Furthermore, Saudi Arabia juridically based the historical character of the Gulf upon the Constantinople Treaty of 1888:

> . . . The territorial character of the Gulf, its waters, entrance and straits, was affirmed by the Treaty of Constantinople of 1888 concerning the Suez Canal. Article 10 (par. 3) of the said Treaty specified that the stipulations contained in that Treaty do not apply to the Arabic States lying on the Red Sea and the Gulf of Aqaba. The records of the negotiations leading to the said Treaty clearly reveal that the Gulf of Aqaba and its straits were intended to be excluded from the proposed freedom of international navigation in the Suez Canal, thus acknowledging that the waters of the Gulf, its entrance and the straits, are territorial

---

[106] U.N. Doc. A/3575 (April 15, 1957).
[107] GAOR, 12th Session, 697th Plenary meeting (October 2, 1957), p. 233.

and implying no freedom of international navigation through them.[108]

Moreover, the occupation of a strip of the Gulf of Aqaba by the State of Israel was "nothing but a military control without sovereignty whatsoever. Israel has no sovereign status in the Gulf of Aqaba."[109] Indeed, Israel's foothold on the Gulf was based on the General Armistice Agreements which, by their very nature and express provisions, vested no sovereignty.

Finally, Mr. Ahmed Shukairy, then Saudi Arabian representative to the United Nations, submitted the following as legal points that the Gulf has always been under Arab sovereignty:

a. The contents of the Sublime Porte Ministry of Foreign Affairs Circular Note Verbale of October 1, 1914, wherein omission of the Gulf of Aqaba is a clear indication that the Gulf was considered to be under Ottoman sovereignty. The west shore of the Gulf was in Egyptian territory, and Ottoman sovereignty over Egypt continued until December 18, 1914.

b. Omission of the Gulf of Aqaba in the International Sanitary Convention of 1912.

c. Article 10, Paragraph 3 of the Constantinople Convention of 1888 is an asserted recognition that the Gulf is a locked Arab Gulf without any international character.

It is a generally recognized rule of international law that straits connecting two open seas must be left free to the innocent commercial navigation of all states, even though

---

[108] U.N. Doc. A/3575 (April 15, 1957), p. 4.

[109] Statement by the representative of Saudi Arabia in the General Assembly. GAOR, 12th Session, 697th Plenary Meeting (October 2, 1957), p. 233.

both shores belong to the same country and the passage bay be so narrow that the waters are territorial. In support of this view, the International Court of Justice ruled that the decisive factor in determining the status of a strait is its geographical situation as connecting two parts of the high seas and the fact that it is being used for international navigation.

The legal question now is whether the Gulf of Aqaba is an open or a closed sea. The Gulf is open to the sea at one end; it merely gives access to a port at the other. Should this situation be legally considered as between two open seas? Dr. Boggs points out that:

> An additional category was originally planned: Zones of access to the high seas, by surface and air, for States apparently denied access from relatively short coasts on bay or gulf, because the usual delimitation techniques would pinch them off from the high seas. Problems would have been considered such as those of the Gulf of Aqaba, where both Israel and Jordan have very short coasts between those of Egypt and Saudi Arabia. . . .[110]

In 1955, during the discussion in the International Law Commission over the status of bays, the Government of Israel raised a question regarding the bay whose coastline is shared by more than one State. The Israeli Government pointed out that

> where access to a given port is only possible by traversing a strait, then it is quite immaterial whether that strait is or is not within the waters classed as territorial sea of one or more of the littoral States, or what is the legal nature of the waters on which the harbour is situated.[111]

---

[110] A.J.I.L. (1951), p. 246.
[111] U.N. Doc. A/CN. 4/99/Add. 1.

Realizing that this is a unique case, the International Law Commission made this comment on Article 17 of the law of the sea:

> The question was asked what would be the legal position of straits forming part of the territorial sea of one or more States and constituting the sole means of access to a part of another State. The Commission considers that this case could be assimilated to that of a bay whose inner part and entrance from the high seas belong to different States. As the Commission felt bound to confine itself to proposing rules applicable to bays, wholly belonging to a single coastal State, it also reserved consideration of the above-mentioned case.[112]

This comment, along with the Commission's draft of Article 17, was submitted to the Geneva Conference on the Territorial Sea and Contiguous Zone of 1958 which refused to adopt it. What the International Law Commission concluded can be summarized as follows:

1. The Straits of Tiran are not straits within the meaning of Article 17, paragraph 4, because they do not connect two parts of the high seas but a part of the high sea with a gulf or bay; therefore, Article 17, paragraph 4, prohibiting the suspension of innocent passage, does not apply.

2. The Straits of Tiran are comparable to a bay bordered by several States; therefore, Article 17, paragraph 4, does not apply.

3. States have a right of innocent passage through the territorial seas of other States under Article 16, but a coastal State was authorized by the Commission to suspend temporarily such pas-

---

112 GAOR, 11th Session, Supp. No. 9 (A/3159), p. 20.

sage "in definite areas of its territorial sea" under Article 17, paragraph 3.

4. Inasmuch as the only navigable channel in the Straits of Tiran and the Gulf of Aqaba to the Israeli port of Elath passes through territorial seas, access to that port could be suspended by the coastal States concerned under Article 17, paragraph 3.

5. Be that as it may, it was not the task of the Commission to lay down rules for particular or even unique cases.

During the war of October 1956 against Egypt, Israel had the opportunity to occupy Sharm el-Sheikh for the purpose of destroying the Egyptian blockade and opening the waterway to its navigation. It refused to withdraw its troops without satisfactory guarantees that the Egyptian blockade would not be restored, and asked of the United Nations "effective arrangements" and "special measures" to that end.[113] Accordingly, Israel was not satisfied with the mere entry of the United Nations Emergency Force into the Sharm el-Sheikh area to replace its forces, but needed to be certain, before withdrawal, of the special arrangements that should be taken to secure Israeli freedom of navigation in the waterway.

In this connection, Secretary-General Hammarskjöld pointed out that

the international significance of the Gulf of Aqaba may be considered to justify the right of innocent passage through the Straits of Tiran and the Gulf in accordance with recognized rules of International law.[114]

---

[113] GAOR, 11th Session, Plenary meeting 638 (January 17, 1957), Vols. II-III, p. 889.

[114] U.N. Doc. A/3512, p. 49.

172

However, the Secretary-General strongly maintained that, because of the principles guiding the United Nations, Israeli military action and its consequences should not be allowed to influence the matter.

In the General Assembly, great differences emerged as to whether the United Nations Emergency Force should play a role in securing the freedom of passage through the Straits until a final settlement between the parties could be reached:

To Australia: UNEF should secure the status of the Gulf as an international waterway. The Gulf serves no less than four littoral states . . . all of which should without discrimination be able to use this waterway for their own peaceful purposes.[115]

To India: Any enlargement of the functions of UNEF would require basic consideration, consultation and agreement by all the parties concerned.[116]

To the Arab States: Both the Suez and Aqaba questions were part of the entire Palestine problem, and therefore could not be resolved until Israel recognized the Arabs' rights to their own homes in Palestine. As Fadhil El-Jamali, then representative of Iraq to the United Nations, precisely put it in a speech before the General Assembly on January 29, 1957:

. . . the Suez Canal, the Gulf of Aqaba and that resolution (of the Security Council in 1951) are all tied to the state of war. If there were no state of war the freedom of passage would certainly be guaranteed. But there is a state of war because the rights of the Arabs of Palestine have been denied. . . . If you want

---

[115] GAOR, 11th Session, 638th meeting (January 17, 1957), p. 884.
[116] Ibid., 641st meeting (January 18, 1958), p. 930.

Egypt to observe the Security Council resolution of 1951 with respect to the Suez Canal why do you not observe the General Assembly resolutions of 1947, 1948, 1949 and onward, concerning the refugees and their right to return to their own homes?[117]

To Israel: The Israeli delegation suggested the possibility of entrusting UNEF with the task of guaranteeing the innocent passage of all ships through the Gulf of Aqaba.[118]

To the United States: UNEF should be stationed at Sharm el-Sheikh until it was clear that the Israelis' right to use the Gulf of Aqaba had been established in practice. She made it clear that the United States would exercise the right of free and innocent passage through the Gulf, and would join with others to secure general recognition of this right.[119]

In this atmosphere of contention, the General Assembly agreed on two points:

a. that the withdrawal of Israeli forces from the Sharm el-Sheikh area was to be accomplished immediately; and

b. that UNEF should not be used so as to prejudge the solution of the controversial questions involved; the Force was not to be deployed in such a way as to protect any special position on these questions.[120]

---

117 Ibid., 639th meeting (January 17, 1957), p. 906; GAOR, 11th Session (January 29, 1957); and see Burns, op. cit., p. 308.

118 Ibid., 638th meeting (January 17, 1957), p. 892.

119 *New York Times* (March 17, 1957).

120 U.N. Doc. A/3512, p. 50.

174

The role of the Force then was to secure the withdrawal of Israeli troops, to replace them, and to "assist in maintaining quiet in the area." Accordingly, on March 2, 1957, Israel withdrew its forces from the Sharm el-Sheikh area, and UNEF took over. Mrs. Golda Meir, then Israeli Foreign Minister, explained her country's decision to withdraw as follows:

> Our sole purpose has been to ensure that, on the withdrawal of Israeli forces, continued freedom of navigation will exist for Israel and international shipping in the Gulf of Aqaba and the Straits of Tiran.[121]

V. EVALUATION

Undoubtedly, the establishment and presence of the United Nations Emergency Force was a manifestation of the late Secretary-General Dag Hammarskjöld's preventive diplomacy which aimed at providing for a cooling-off period during which the United Nations and the good offices of the peace-loving states might find a more favorable atmosphere for peacemaking. As such, the Force marked the beginning of a new approach to international peace: the peace-keeping approach whereby troops from the Great Powers were excluded, and the United Nations was called upon to intervene in areas outside the Great Powers' traditional peripheries for the filling of security "vacuums" in such a way as to "prevent" East-West military confrontation. Indeed, the creation of UNEF has constituted one of the most significant de facto revisions in the United Nations Charter: a shift from Collective Security through Peace-Enforcement to Preventive Diplomacy through Peace-Keeping.

> Here we have a record of strong, swift actions which, without doubt in my mind, headed off a third world

---

[121] Bloomfield, op. cit., p. 219.

war. If the United Nations had done only this one thing in its short life, it would have more than justified its existence.[122]

Although it succeeded in maintaining reasonable quiet along the demarcation lines between Israel and the United Arab Republic, UNEF was not to be used as a machinery to secure the status quo in the Arab-Israeli impasse. It was of a particular importance for the world community not to forget the temporary nature of the force that represented it. The Force was not, by any means, a solution to the Arab-Israeli conflict. Instead, UNEF represented just one-half of the dual responsibility of the World Organization for the maintenance of world peace — the peace-keeping responsibility. Thus, its greatest responsibility of "making peace" remains unfulfilled. Indeed, the peace-keeping machinery that was planned to be temporary should not have been left without a supplementary peacemaking body to deal with the humanitarian, political, and territorial problems. The absence of such a supplementary organ, however, changed the temporary character of the Force to one which was neither temporary nor permanent. The Force lost its transitional nature because it stayed in the area for more than ten years and the making of peace was still lacking. On the other hand, UNEF was not a permanent Force and was never planned to become such because:

(a) Had UNEF continued indefinitely, it would have violated the law of its creation.

(b) As was mentioned, the very presence of the Force was based on the consent of Egypt.

(c) The United Nations has not yet established a permanent force of its own.

(d) The problem of financing the Force.

---

[122] Inis L. Claude, Jr., *Swords into Plowshares*, 3rd, rev. ed. (New York: Random House, 1964), p. 290.

Part Three

The Third War...
And After....

The world is a stupendous machine, composed of innumerable parts, each of which being a free agent, has a volition and action of its own; and on this ground arises the difficulty of assuring success in any enterprise depending on the volition of numerous agents. We may set the machine in motion, and dispose every wheel to one certain end; but when it depends on the volition of any one wheel, and the correspondent action of every wheel, the result is uncertain.

NICCOLO MACHIAVELLI,
"On Fortune, Chance"

Chapter VI

The Third War: The Diplomacy of "Peace" through Conquest

I. A POLITICAL BACKGROUND

The Suez invasion of 1956 had not only added a new dimension to the "Palestine Question" by "Arabizing" it, but it had also marked a turning point in the Middle Eastern internal as well as external affairs in two principal ways: (a) The Arab nationalist movements took anti-Western trends; and (b) Radiated from and centered around the Arab-Israeli impasse, the American-Soviet cold war diplomacy entered into the Middle East.

With regard to the United Nations, on the other hand, the Suez crisis marked a de facto change in the nature and functions of the World Organization for the maintenance of international peace and security: a shift from collective security through peace-enforcement to peace-keeping through preventive diplomacy.

179

To control the cold war, the two super-powers had to stay militarily out, and to enable the United Nations to undertake a peace-keeping mission, the super-powers had to step in politically. UNEF was the by-product of those two realistically inseparable principles.

Unfortunately, however, the international peace-keeping force turned out to be a new form of an "occupation force," though unique in its nature and functions. The force was established by the General Assembly to secure the withdrawal of the invading troops and to station temporarily with the "consent of the nations concerned" until a just and lasting peace would be secured. It was understood, therefore, that the United Nations should proceed in a reasonable period of time, if not immediately, toward the peacemaking actions for solving the principal issues underlying the Arab-Israeli impasse. The Organization, however, failed to pursue that role. Furthermore, because of the internal and external problems mentioned in Chapter V, UNEF failed even to secure its limited objectives.

To the Arab World, Israel has become a living energetic threat to the Arab's very existence. They have rightfully become impatient due to the fact that the United Nations resolutions pertaining to Palestine have remained unfulfilled. To the United Arab Republic, moreover, UNEF turned out to be a "unique occupation force," an idea that was rejected in 1956, securing the remaining de facto situation resulting from the 1956 tripartite aggression against Egypt. Furthermore, President Nasser felt that although UNEF had a deterrent and restraining influence along the U.A.R.-Israeli frontiers, its presence had allowed the World Organization to ignore the hard realities of the underlying conflict for more than ten years.

Considering all these factors, the Government of the United Arab Republic sent on May 16, 1967, a message to the Commander of UNEF, Major General Rikhye, requesting withdrawal of "all UN Troops which install OPS along our borders."[1] On May 18, 1967, the United Nations Secretary-General received the following message from Mr. Mahmoud Riad, Minister of Foreign Affairs of the United Arab Republic:

> The Government of the United Arab Republic has the honour to inform Your Excellency that it has decided to terminate the presence of the United Nations Emergency Force from the territory of the United Arab Republic and Gaza Strip. Therefore, I request that the necessary steps be taken for the withdrawal of the Force as soon as possible.

> I avail myself of this opportunity to express to Your Excellency my gratitude and warm regards.[2]

To the United Arab Republic, any attempt to exert pressure to reconsider its decision would not only be contrary to the "Law of the Force" but also a violation of the U.A.R. sovereign rights and an invitation to making UNEF an "occupation force."

To Israel, the withdrawal of UNEF "should not be achieved by a unilateral United Arab Republic's request alone" and that Israel should have "a voice in the matter."[3]

Indeed, the United Nations Secretary-General had no choice but to comply with the legitimate request of the U.A.R., the Host State. On May 18, 1967, he met with the Permanent Representatives of the states providing the Force; then with the Advisory Committee on UNEF, set up under the terms of resolution 1001 (ES-I) of November 7, 1956, for consultation on the situation. Two principles were clearly understood: (a) that UNEF was constitutionally based on the free consent of the U.A.R., and that the Force could not possibly work effectively, or even exist,

---

[1] A/6730, Para. 6, sub - para. 3 (a).
[2] U.N. Doc. Report of the Secretary-General on the withdrawal of the United Nations Emergency Force (UNEF), (May 18, 1967), p. 6.
[3] Ibid., p. 5.

181

without the consent and cooperation of the Host State; and (b) that Israel could not claim to have "a voice in the matter" since Israel, contrary to the General Assembly's resolution 1125 (XI) of February 2, 1957, which envisaged that UNEF would be stationed on both sides of the Armistice Demarcation Line, had always refused the presence of the international Force on its soil. Moreover, Mr. U Thant believed that

> the decision for withdrawal of the Force, on the request of the host Government, rested with the Secretary-General after consultation with the Advisory Committee on UNEF which is the organ established by the General Assembly for consultation regarding such matters.[4]

The Secretary-General did not find it constitutionally necessary, politically convenient, or even practical to request, either by himself or through the Advisory Committee, the convening of the General Assembly to consider the matter. Mr. U Thant reported the situation to the Security Council on May 19, 1967. In his report he told the Council that the situation in the Near East was "extremely menacing."[5] The Council met for the first time after this report on 24 May 1967, but took no action.

As a result of all considerations, explored through different meetings and channels of consultation, the Secretary-General decided to comply with the request of the Government of the U.A.R. regarding the withdrawal of the UNEF from its soil. This decision was transmitted on May 18, 1967, to the Foreign Minister of the U.A.R. It said in part:

> . . . In view of the message now received from you, therefore, your Government's request will be com-

---

4 Ibid., p. 11; see also GAOR, Eleventh Session, annexes, agenda item 66, U.N. Doc. A/3563, annex 1, B, 2.

5 Ibid., p. 13; see also U.N. Doc. S/7896.

plied with and I am proceeding to issue instructions for the necessary arrangements to be put in train without delay for the orderly withdrawal of the Force. . . .[6]

As was indicated in Chapter V,[7] both Egypt and the United Nations were guided by what they agreed upon in the Aide-mémoire of November 20, 1956 — the "Good Faith" regarding any matter concerning the presence and the functioning of UNEF. This "Good Faith" Aide-mémoire clearly meant:

a. To Egypt: no limitation on its inherent and declared right to withdraw its consent to the presence of the Force on its soil. Speaking before the General Assembly on November 27, 1956, three days after the approval of the "Good Faith" Aide-mémoire by the General Assembly, Dr. Mahmoud Fawzi, then the Egyptian Foreign Minister, told the representatives of the international community that:

> . . . the General Assembly could not request the United Nations Emergency Force to be stationed or to operate on the territory of a given country without the consent of the Government of the country. . . .[8]

b. To the United Nations: the "Good Faith" Aide-mémoire meant that the Organization should respect the wishes of the Government of Egypt.

---

6 See the full text of this message in Ibid., pp. 7-8.

7 See supra., pp. 153-155.

8 GAOR, Eleventh Session, plenary Meetings, 587th meeting, paras. 48-50.

The Question of the Gulf of Aqaba

As was mentioned in Chapter V,[9] the Strait of Tiran, the entrance of the Gulf of Aqaba, has always been exclusively Arab territorial waters under the generally recognized rules of international law. The tripartite aggression of 1956 did not change this fact, though it did create a de facto situation contrary to the rule of law. With the withdrawal of UNEF, however, it was natural that the de facto situation which was guarded by the Force should be changed in order to go back to the normal situation prevailing before the Suez crisis of 1956.

Furthermore, because of the very nature of the Arab-Israeli General Armistice Agreements of 1949, and the refusal of Israel to comply with the United Nations resolutions pertaining to Palestine, a state of war has always been in existence between the Arab States and Israel. Under international law, an armistice does not end the state of belligerency. Consequently, the belligerents are entitled to certain rights such as the right to boycott, to blockade and to capture neutral vessels attempting to break a blockade, and the right to seize contraband of war.

Accordingly, on May 22, 1967, President Nasser announced that Israeli ships and ships carrying strategic materials to Israel would be prevented from passing through the Strait of Tiran. The President of the United Arab Republic declared that:

> today our forces occupy Sharm el-Sheikh. By this action we mean to enforce our right and sovereignty over the Aqaba Straits, which are the territorial waters of Egypt, and under no circumstances shall we allow the Israeli flag to pass through these Straits.[10]

---

9 See supra. pp. 167-175.

10 Press Release, Press Department, Embassy of the United Arab Republic, Washington, D.C., U.S.A. (May 26, 1967), p. 2; see also the text of President Nasser's statement at the press conference held in Cairo on May 28, 1967.

On May 23, 1967, the Secretary-General flew to Cairo, in order to discuss the situation with the U.A.R. Government. While Mr. U Thant was still in Cairo, Canada and Denmark requested an urgent meeting of the Security Council to consider the grave situation in the Middle East. They felt that the meeting of the Council might reinforce the efforts of the Secretary-General being made at Cairo.

On May 24, 1967, the Security Council met to consider the situation in the Middle East. During the discussion the Council invited the representatives of Iraq, Israel, Jordan, Kuwait, Lebanon, Libya, Morocco, Pakistan, Saudi Arabia, Syria, Tunisia and the United Arab Republic to participate in the debate, without vote. At the Security Council meeting, a draft resolution was submitted by Canada and Denmark whereby the Council would: (a) express full support for the efforts of the Secretary-General to pacify the situation; (b) request all Member States to refrain from any step which might worsen the situation; and (c) invite the Secretary-General to report to the Council upon his return to enable it to continue its consideration of the matter. In the Security Council, however, great differences showed themselves as to the practicability and the usefulness of its meeting while the Secretary-General was still in Cairo: To the United States, such an urgent meeting was a necessity and "the Council would be burying its head in the sand if it did not recognize the threat to peace in developments in the Middle East since the Secretary-General's departure for Cairo."[11]

To the United Kingdom, it was necessary for the Council to reinforce the efforts of the Secretary-General to preserve peace in the area, and the Council's "first aim [would] be to counsel restraint and to keep the peace until new plans for peace-keeping could be worked out."[12]

---

[11] GAOR, Twenty-Second Session, Supplement No. 1 (A/6701), Annual Report of the Secretary-General on the Work of the Organization, 16 June 1966-15 June 1967, p. 2.

[12] Ibid.

To the U.S.S.R., "the situation in the Middle East was being dramatized by certain Western Powers for reasons other than a true concern for peace in the area."[13]

The United Arab Republic, together with Mali and India, considered the meeting of the Security Council untimely. The U.A.R. representative told the Council that the focus should be made on the tragedy of Palestine, and its lawful inhabitants whom Israel had deprived of their homes and properties and who had been living in refugee camps on international charity. It was regrettable that the United Nations had been kept silent and powerless while Israel had been refusing to comply with its resolutions concerning Palestine. "It was regrettable," furthermore, "that Canada and Denmark had seen fit to act on behalf of the United States and the United Kingdom; they were making the situation far worse by deliberately ignoring the repeated provocations by Israel." The representative of the United Arab Republic maintained that "Israel could not have committed its many acts of aggression without outside encouragement and support; in the present case, that came from the United Kingdom and the United States." Finally, Mr. Mohammed Awad El-Kony declared that the proposed draft resolution "was an attempt to sabotage the mission of the Secretary-General."[14]

Israel, on the other hand, claimed that there were "threats against the territorial integrity, the political independence and the very existence of Israel."[15] Its representative denied that his State had concentrated large forces along the Israeli-Syrian frontiers. This, however, came contrary to what the Secretary-General had stated in his report to the Security Council on May 19, 1967, in which Mr. U Thant asserted that "there had been in the past few days

---

13 Ibid., p. 3.
14 Ibid.
15 Ibid.

186

reports of troop movements and concentrations, particularly on the Israel side of the Syrian border."[16]

France was more practical and realistic when its representative told the Security Council that:

> As long as the major powers were not in agreement, the Security Council could take no action and must limit itself to addressing an appeal to the parties to refrain from any initiatives that might jeopardize peace.[17]

As a result of all these differences, particularly between the Soviet Union and the United States, the Council adjourned without taking any action.

Upon his return from his mission to Cairo, Mr. U Thant submitted on May 26, 1967, a report to the Security Council. In this report, the Secretary-General emphasized the following points:[18]

a. The situation in the Middle East was at present more disturbing, indeed more menacing, than at any time since the Suez crisis of 1956.

b. The allegation that the withdrawal of UNEF was the primary cause of the crisis in the Middle East ignored the fact that the underlying basis for this and other crisis situations in the area was the continuing Arab-Israeli conflict, which had been present all along.

c. That a legal controversy had existed prior to 1956 as to the extent of the right of innocent passage by commercial vessels through the Strait of Tiran and the Gulf of Aqaba. The Secretary-

---

16 Ibid., p. 1.
17 Ibid., p. 3.
18 Ibid., pp. 3-4.

General would not, however, go into the legal aspects of that controversy.

d. That a peaceful outcome of the present crisis would depend upon a breathing spell which would allow tension to subside from its present explosive level.

e. That the Egyptian-Israeli and the Israeli-Syrian Mixed Armistice Commissions were to be reactivated.

f. That the United Nations, and the Security Council in particular, must search and eventually find peaceful and just solutions to the Arab-Israeli impasse.

On May 27, 1967, the representative of the United Arab Republic sent a letter to the President of the Security Council requesting the inclusion in the agenda of the Council of an item entitled "Israel's aggressive policy, its repeated aggression threatening peace and security in the Middle East and endangering international peace and security." The United Kingdom, on the other hand, requested the inclusion of the Secretary-General's report of May 26, 1967.

Consequently, the Security Council met on May 29, 1967. The principal debate which took place at that meeting focused on the status of the Gulf of Aqaba after the Government of the United Arab Republic had announced a blockade of Israeli ships and other ships carrying strategic materials to Israel. Again, great differences showed themselves: To the United Arab Republic,

The Gulf of Aqaba had always been a national inland waterway subject to Arab sovereignty. Since the Gulf's only three legitimate littoral States — Saudi Arabia, Jordan and the United Arab Republic — were all in a state of war with Israel, their right to bar enemy vessels was recognized under international law. The claim that Israel had a port on the Gulf had no validity, as Israel had illegally occupied seven miles of coastline on the Gulf, including Umm Rashrash in violation of Security Council resolutions of 1948 and the Egyptian-Israel General Armistice Agreement. The Armistice Agreements did not vitiate [its] rights to impose restrictions on navigation in the Strait; nor had the 1956 aggression changed the legal status of the Gulf of Aqaba or the United Arab Republic's rights over its territorial waters. Furthermore, the Secretary-General had stated in his report of 26 February 1957 that the stationing of UNEF could not be used to impose a solution for a political or legal question that was controversial, since its function was to prevent hostilities. Nothing that had been said in the General Assembly by Israel or some other delegations could affect the lawful rights of the United Arab Republic.[19]

The Government of Israel, on the other hand, declared that it would consider the blockade of the Gulf of Aqaba as an attack. Its representative told the Security Council that "interference with the freedom of navigation in the Gulf of Aqaba and the Strait of Tiran was an offensive action against Israel. . . ."[20] He stated, furthermore, that Israel would not permit a return to the conditions prevailing prior to 1956.

To the United States, the Gulf of Aqaba was considered as an "international" waterway. Confirming a televised statement made earlier by the President of the United States on May 23, 1967, Mr. Arthur Goldberg told the Security Council that "a blockade of Israel shipping was illegal and potentially dangerous to the cause of peace." The United States representative then suggested that "effec-

---

19 Ibid., p. 5. See also supra. pp. 167-175.
20 Ibid.

tive steps must be taken by the Security Council to reaffirm the General Armistice Agreements and revitalize the armistice machinery."[21]

To the Soviet Union, the closure of the Gulf of Aqaba to Israeli ships was not only legally valid, but it was also an essential self-defense measure to prevent Israeli attacks on Arab States. The representative of the U.S.S.R. told the Security Council that Israel "did not wish to abandon its policy of provocation and military adventures against the neighboring Arab States. . . ." Mr. Nikolai Fedorenko then attacked the United States for "showing partiality" and "defending the extremist circles in Israel that it so generously assisted, while making pious appeals to both sides." Finally, the U.S.S.R. representative told the Security Council that it should "decisively condemn Israel's provocations and threats against the Arab States."[22]

Indeed, the Soviet Union took the occasion to reaffirm its interest in the Middle East. It warned the Western Powers, and more particularly the United States, that the security and stability in the Middle East, a region adjacent to its shores, was so vital to the security and interest of the Soviets. This clearly meant that the U.S.S.R. would not allow the United States' policy in the Middle East to go unchallenged.

Furthermore, one of the leading Soviet international lawyers, Prof. I. Blishchenko, defended the Arab's right in the Gulf of Aqaba when he wrote in the Army newspaper *Red Star* that there were no international agreements on the Gulf or the Strait of Tiran at its mouth. Therefore, he said, it was quite legal for the United Arab Republic to be guided by the 1958 Geneva Convention on Territorial Waters, which gives seagoing nations the right of passage as long as this does not threaten the security of the shoreline states.

---

21 Ibid., p. 4.
22 Ibid., p. 5.

190

To India, the action of the United Arab Republic was understood to be "defensive in nature." The Gulf of Aqaba, however, was considered "an inland sea and entry into it lay within the territorial waters of the United Arab Republic." Accordingly, the representative of India told the Security Council, "no State or group of States should attempt to challenge by force the sovereignty of the United Arab Republic over the Strait of Tiran." He then suggested a modus vivendi, but "any arrangement worked out must be within the framework of the sovereignty of the United Arab Republic."[23]

As was the case of the Suez crisis of 1956, the connection between the Palestine Question and the Aqaba crisis became apparent to the Western Powers and to Israel, just as it had always existed in the minds of the Arabs. Also, similar to the situation before the Suez crisis of 1956 when Israel had been shaken by the withdrawal of the British troops from Suez, Israel was shaken by the withdrawal of UNEF which worked as a vital buffer against major war between Israel and the United Arab Republic for more than ten years.

With the debate taking place at the United Nations, some very significant diplomatic moves were carried out outside the World Organization:

a. To insure Western Powers' support, Mr. Abba Eban, the Israeli Foreign Minister, visited Washington, London, Paris and Canada. Also, for adopting a unified policy on the Middle Eastern crisis, a meeting was held between President Johnson, Mr. Pearson, the Canadian Prime Minister, and Mr. Wilson, the British Prime Minister.

b. Unlike the Suez crisis, the two super-powers were not in agreement as to how to settle the

_____
[23] Ibid., pp. 5-6.

Aqaba crisis. For this reason, however, they realized that they were directly involved. Therefore, and in order to avoid any misunderstanding or miscalculation, they used the Hot Line between the White House and the Kremlin. Indeed, neither the United States nor the Soviet Union was willing to be dragged into a military confrontation in the Middle East — a region outside their traditional peripheries. Instead, they appealed to both Israel and the United Arab Republic to avoid hostilities and not to start war. The Soviet Union warned Israel and asked President Nasser not to fire the first shot. The United States, on the other hand, declared through its President on May 23, 1967, that "the United States strongly opposes aggression by anyone in the area, in any form, overt or clandestine." President Johnson further maintained "that the United States is firmly committed to the support of the political independence and the territorial integrity of all the nations of the area."

c. Moreover, on the same day, May 23, 1967, the President of the United States sent a message to President Nasser in which Mr. Johnson said, "I do urge you to set as your first duty to your own people, to your region, and to the World Community this transcendent objective: the avoidance of hostilities." He further suggested to send the United States' Vice-President to Cairo for discussion with the U.A.R. officials. On June 2, 1967, President Nasser responded by stating that the United Arab Republic had never started any aggression but should continue its policy to defend itself and any other Arab country against any aggression. President Nasser further suggested to send Vice-President Zakaria Mohieddin for discussion with the American officials. Mr. Mohieddin was scheduled to arrive in Washington on Wednesday, June 7, 1967.

At this point, one may conclude that the dynamic diplomacy carried out cautiously by the United States and the Soviet Union principally aiming at controlling, not fighting, their cold war over the Middle East, was the most important contributing factor to the state of confusion and illusion which prevailed not only at the United Nations but also, and to be sure most important, in the Arab World during the two weeks prior to June 5, 1967.

II. THE WAR . . . AND THE SEARCH FOR PEACE

In the morning of Monday, June 5, 1967, the Third War between the Arab States and Israel occurred. A few hours after the outbreak of hostilities, the Security Council met in an emergency session. The following was the picture before the Council as presented by the Secretary-General:

> Gen. Indar Jit Rikhye, the Commander of UNEF, had reported that violations of the United Arab Republic air space by two Israel aircraft had occurred over Gaza and El-Arish . . . UNEF personnel in Rafah camp had reported heavy fighting between United Arab Republic and Israel forces across the frontier . . . large-scale air raids throughout the United Arab Republic and . . . attacks by Israel forces on EL-Qusaima in Sinai . . . General Rikhye had also reported that Israel aircraft had strafed a UNEF convoy south of Khan Yunis . . . killing three Indian soldiers and wounding several others.

General Odd Bull, Chief of Staff of UNTSO, had
reported that firing in Jerusalem had started . . .
United Nations observers on the Syrian border had
reported air battles between Israel and Syrian planes
. . . The Chief of Staff of UNTSO had reported that
Israel troops had forcibly occupied Government House.
. . .[24]

On June 6, the Secretary-General reported to the Security Council further information which he had received
from the United Nations observers in the field. Mr. U
Thant told the Council that

UNEF headquarters in Gaza had come under direct
Israeli artillery fire . . . forcing the Commander of
UNEF to re-establish headquarters at Tre Kroner Camp
near the beach in Gaza. During the shelling three
Indian soldiers had been killed and another three
wounded.[25]

It was clear to the Security Council that Israel started
the Third War in the Middle East. There was no other
interpretation to the report of the Secretary-General. The
representative of the United Arab Republic told the council that "Israel had once again committed a treacherous
aggression against his country." Mr. El-Kony then maintained that "in the face of aggression his country had no
choice but to defend itself in accordance with Article 51
of the Charter." He called on the Security Council "to
condemn vigorously the Israeli aggression."[26]

For the third time in two decades, the United Nations
found itself face-to-face with an Arab-Israeli war. The
war had to be contained and peace had to be restored in

[24] GAOR, Twenty-Second Session, Supplement No. 1 (A/6701), op. cit.,
pp. 7-8.

[25] Ibid., p. 8.

[26] Ibid.

the area. To do this, the Great Powers had to stay out and the Israeli invading troops had to go out. In other words, a cease-fire resolution and a withdrawal of the Israeli forces to the positions they held prior to June 5, 1967, were the most urgent actions to be taken by the World Organization.

a. The Question of Cease-Fire

At the Security Council's meeting on June 6, 1967, the Council adopted unanimously, as resolution 233, a draft resolution presented by its President in which the Council[27]

1. Calls upon the Governments concerned as a first step to take forthwith all measures for an immediate cease-fire and for a cessation of all military activities in the area;

2. Requests the Secretary-General to keep the Council promptly and currently informed on the situation.

At the Council's meeting, the representative of the Soviet Union declared that his Government "resolutely supported the Governments and peoples of the Arab States in their just struggle for independence and sovereign rights." He further demanded the unconditional withdrawal of the Israeli forces behind the armistice demarcation line. "The United Nations," Mr. Fedorenko told the Council, "must condemn the actions of the Government of Israel and take urgent measures to restore peace in the Middle East."[28]

The United States, on the other hand, considered that the cease-fire resolution was "the first step towards peace in the Middle East." Mr. Goldberg denied that the United

---

27 U.N. Doc. S/RES/233 (1967), the 1348th Meeting (June 6, 1967).
28 GAOR, Twenty-Second Session, op. cit., p. 8.

States aircraft had participated on the side of Israel in the Middle East war. He further asked for "an immediate impartial investigation by the United Nations of the charges."[29] The representative of the United Kingdom took a similar position and denied the same charges.[30]

In spite of the Security Council's appeal to the Governments concerned to cease fire, military activities in the area were still continuing on June 7, 1967. On the same day the representative of the Soviet Union requested the meeting of the Security Council. He told the Council that "the forces of aggression continued to engage in military operations, paying no heed to Security Council resolution 233 (1967) of 6 June." He presented a draft resolution whereby the Council[31]

1. Demands that the Governments concerned should, as a first step, cease fire and discontinue all military activities at 2000 hours GMT on 7 June 1967;

2. Requests the Secretary-General to keep the Council promptly and currently informed on the situation.

This draft resolution was unanimously adopted, as resolution 234 (1967).

On June 7, the Government of Jordan informed the Security Council of its compliance with the Council's cease-fire resolution. At the same time, Jordan complained to the Council of Israel's non-observance of the cease-fire.

Disregarding the Security Council's two cease-fire resolutions of June 6 and 7, Israel not only had not stopped fighting but it had also made use of the time elapsed to occupy

---

29 Ibid.

30 Ibid.

31 U.N. Doc. S/RES/234 (1967), the 1350th Meeting (June 7, 1967).

additional Arab territory. It was this situation which carried both the United States and the U.S.S.R. to request a meeting of the Security Council on June 8.

The representative of the United States introduced a draft resolution: ". . . its purpose was to stop the fighting and to provide for movement towards the final settlement of all outstanding questions between the parties." According to the American draft resolution the Security Council would[32]

1. . . .

2. . . .

3. Call for discussions promptly thereafter among the parties concerned, using such third party or United Nations assistance as they might wish looking toward the establishment of viable arrangements encompassing the withdrawal and disengagement of armed personnel, the renunciation of force regardless of its nature, the maintenance of vital international rights and the establishment of a stable and durable peace in the Middle East;

4. . . .

5. . . .

The representative of the Soviet Union, on the other hand, presented a draft resolution whereby the Security Council would[33]

1. vigorously condemn Israel's aggressive activities and its violations of Council resolutions 233 (1967) and 234 (1967), of the United Nations

---

32 GAOR, Twenty-Second Session, op. cit., p. 10.
33 Ibid.

Charter and of United Nations principles; and
2. demand that Israel immediately halt its military activities against neighboring Arab States, remove all its troops from the territory of those States and withdraw them behind the armistice lines.

From the two draft resolutions, one may draw two very significant, yet remarkably different, lines of thinking. On one side, the United States had linked the withdrawal of the Israeli forces with a "discussion" among the parties concerned aiming at the end of the state of war between them. This attitude would in fact amount to legalizing the aggression for political and territorial gains. The Soviet Union, on the other hand, had demanded the immediate unconditional withdrawal of the Israeli troops from occupied Arab territories to their positions before the June war. Indeed, these two opposing stands were the heart of the whole political crisis of the Middle Eastern war.

At that meeting of June 8, the Government of Israel informed the Security Council of its acceptance of the Council's call for an immediate cease-fire, provided that the other parties accepted. On the same day, the Government of the United Arab Republic informed the Council of its compliance with the cease-fire as prescribed in June 6 and 7 resolutions, if the other party also ceased fire. Indeed, the acceptance of the cease-fire by both Israel and the United Arab Republic raised the immediate prospect of the end of hostilities. Finally, on June 9, the Government of Syria announced its acceptance of the cease-fire resolutions, provided that the other party accepted.

It seemed at this point of development that all parties concerned had accepted the Council's appeals for a cease-fire. However, on the whole length of the Israeli-Syrian armistice demarcation line, Israel continued its hostilities. On June 9, Syria requested an urgent meeting of the Security Council to deal with the situation. The Chairman of the Israeli-Syrian Mixed Armistice Commission "had confirmed later that Israel aircraft had bombed north and east of Lake Tiberias on the morning of 9 June."[34] After some charges and counter-charges, the Council unanimously adopted its third resolution, as resolution 235 (1967), in which the Council (1) confirms its previous resolutions; (2) demands the cessation of all hostilities; and (3) requests the Secretary-General to report to the Council in two hours about the immediate compliance with the Council's cease-fire resolutions.

On June 10, the situation was seriously deteriorating; the Israeli forces had occupied the Syrian town of Kuneitra and were moving towards the Syrian capital. At the request of Syria, the Security Council held a pre-dawn emergency meeting. Reporting on the developing military situation in the area, the Secretary-General told the Council that

> United Nations observers had reported bombing and hostilities continuing in Syria, along the ridges overlooking the eastern shores of Lake Tiberias, and on the eastern bank of the Jordan River, and that Damascus airport and suburbs had been bombed by the Israeli air force.[35]

At the meeting, the representative of the Soviet Union warned that if Israel did not immediately cease its military operations "the Soviet Union, together with all peace-loving states, would have to apply sanctions against Israel." Mr. Fedorenko further told the Council that in view of the continuing Israeli aggression against the Arab States, "the Soviet Government had decided to break off diplomatic relations with Israel."[36]

---

[34] Ibid., p. 11.
[35] Ibid., p. 12.
[36] Ibid.

The representative of the United States told the Council that his Government's single goal had been "to quench the flames of war in the Middle East and begin to move towards peace in the area." He introduced a draft resolution in which the Council would (1) condemn any and all violations of the cease-fire; (2) request the Secretary-General to investigate and report on any violation; (3) demand the respect of the Council's cease-fire resolutions by all the parties concerned; and (4) call upon the Governments concerned to cease all military activities.

On June 11, the situation was still deteriorating as a result of the continuing Israeli military activities against Syria. The Syrian representative, therefore, requested the convening of the Security Council. Based upon the American draft, the President of the Council introduced a draft resolution which was unanimously adopted, as resolution 236 (1967), whereby the Council (1) condemns any and all violations of the cease-fire; (2) requests the Secretary-General to investigate and report on any violation; (3) affirms the prohibition of any forward military movements subsequent to the cease-fire; (4) calls for the prompt return to the cease-fire positions of any troops which may have moved forward subsequent to 1630 hours GMT, June 10; and (5) calls for full cooperation with the United Nations observers.

Finally, in a supplemental report, the Secretary-General informed the Security Council that both Israel and Syria had accepted the cease-fire arrangements proposed by the Chief-of-Staff of UNTSO, whereby

> all firing and troop movements would cease at 1630 hours GMT on 10 June, and on the morning of 11 June, United Nations observers would be deployed from Kuneitra on the Syrian side and from Tiberias on the Israeli side.[37]

---

37 Ibid., p. 13.

b. The Question of Withdrawal: The Diplomacy of Peacemaking

It was clear from the very beginning of the Aqaba crisis that whoever starts the war would have a better chance to win or at least to avoid serious destructions and losses. The military victory of Israel, however, surprised even the most optimistic Israelis. In six days, Israel militarily occupied the West Bank of the Jordan River (Jordan), Gaza and Sinai (U.A.R.) and Golan Heights (Syria).

To Israel and its supporters, principally the United States, the military conquest of the Arab territories and the presence of the Israeli forces therein had given them a real bargaining power in any potential discussions over the whole Arab-Israeli problem. With its troops in occupation of the Arab lands, and the closure of the Suez Canal as a result, Israel felt that it would be in a better position to extract from the Arabs a settlement favorable to its interest. Again, as in the case of the Suez crisis of 1956, Israel thought that a political price would be paid for the withdrawal of its troops. As the representative of Israel put it, "it was now the task of the Governments concerned to elaborate among themselves a new system of relationships based on the acceptance of Israel's statehood. . . ."[38]

To the Arab States and their supporters, principally the Soviet Union, the Israeli approach was unacceptable. Indeed, to let this policy to go unchallenged, the United Nations would be creating a very serious precedent whereby any country that feels confident of its power or has the support of any other power, could undertake aggressive acts in order to impose by force its political will and secure some political gains.

Between the two opposing approaches, however, there was a general "consensus" among most of the Member

---

[38] Ibid., p. 9.

Map II — Further Expansion by War

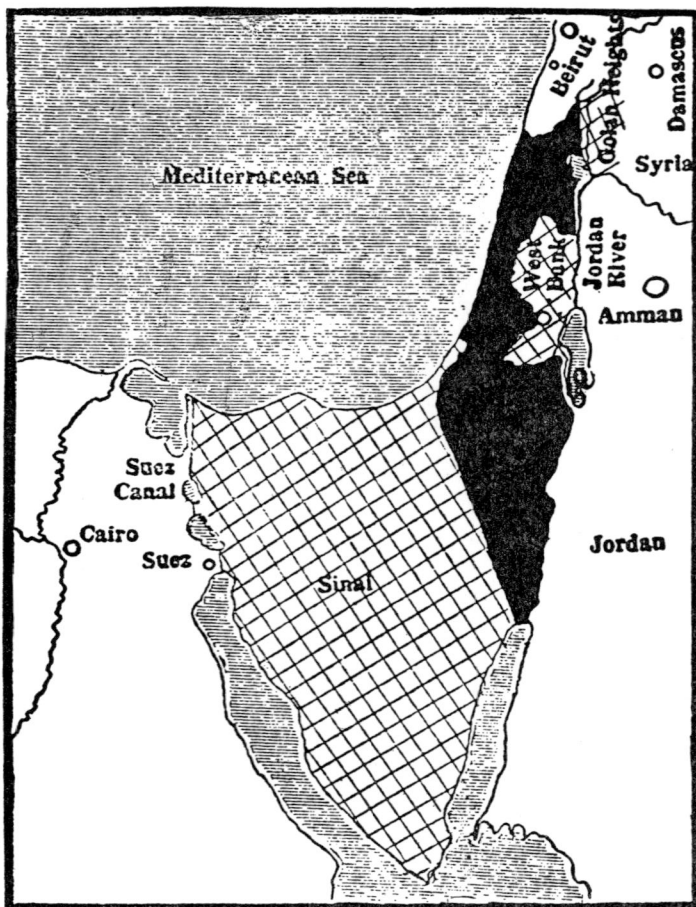

Expanded Israel prior to June 5, 1967 (20,700 sq. kilometres and a population of 2.7 million)

Arab Territories occupied by Israeli forces in the June War of 1967. Israel has expanded to 87,000 sq. kilometres, and its population has increased to include 1.5 million Arabs.

States at the United Nations which could be summarized as follows:

a. That occupation or acquisition of territory by military conquest is inadmissible under the United Nations Charter, and consequently Israel's troops should withdraw from "all" the territories occupied in the June war;

b. There should be a just settlement of the whole question of Palestine; and

c. That "every" State in the Middle East has the right to exist free from any threats or acts of war, and consequently the territorial integrity and political independence of "all" the States in the area shall be secured and respected.

Accordingly, the question of withdrawal of the Israeli forces became the principal subject of the grand debate which was carried out through three main diplomatic forums: (1) The General Assembly Emergency Special Session; (2) The American-Soviet Summit Meeting at Glassboro; and (3) The Security Council.

1.   The General Assembly Emergency Special Session

As had been done in the Suez crisis of 1956, and in order to avoid the American veto in the Security Council, the Government of the Soviet Union, using the rules of the "Uniting for Peace" resolution of November 1950, requested a special emergency meeting of the General Assembly to consider the grave situation in the Middle East and to order the withdrawal of Israeli forces from those parts of the territory of the United Arab Republic, Syria and Jordan which they had seized in the June war.

On June 17, 1967, the General Assembly met in its

Fifth Emergency Special Session. Premier Kosygin presented his case in person to the United Nations General Assembly. He strongly demanded: (1) that the United Nations condemn Israel as the aggressor; (2) that Israel be compelled to withdraw behind the lines established by the 1949 General Armistice — thus giving up all Arab territories which it had seized in the June war; and (3) that Israel be responsible for paying full compensation for war damages done to the Arab States.

The United States representative, on the other hand, presented his Government's position confirming a policy statement made earlier by President Johnson in an address to a group of educators in Washington whereby the President of the United States called for settlement of the Middle East crisis on what he called "five great principles of peace":

1. Every Middle East nation has a right to live, and that right must be respected by its neighbors.

2. Arabs and Israelis must work together to solve the problem of refugees from their three wars.

3. All nations must be assured free passage through international waterways.

4. All nations should take responsibility for ending the arms race in the Middle East. The United Nations should require reports of all arms shipments.

5. There must be respect for the political independence and territorial integrity of all Middle East nations, plus "recognition of the special interest of three great religions in the holy places of Jerusalem."

For nearly three weeks, the General Assembly debated

the crisis in the Middle East. The Assembly had before it two main draft resolutions to consider: (a) The Yugoslav draft resolution, backed by the Soviet Union, demanding the immediate withdrawal of the Israeli troops to their positions prior to June 5, 1967. (b) The Latin American draft resolution, supported by the United States, linking an Israeli withdrawal to an end of belligerency in the area.

Instead of a rush to adopt any resolution, the General Assembly meeting turned into a days-long debate. As the two draft resolutions indicated, the two main issues, inherently inseparable, were whether Israel should be condemned as the aggressor, and whether it should be forced back to the 1949 demarcation lines. Both issues pitted Soviet against American views.

However, as has always been the case, while the representatives of the Member States were debating the matter on the Assembly's floor, the important diplomatic aspects of the session went on behind the scenes through what may be called a "corridor diplomacy," between the United States and the Soviet Union. There was a movement by representatives of some states to work out a compromise between the American and Soviet positions. Some supported the idea of a third party acting as a mediator between the Arab States and Israel — perhaps the United Nations itself. But the Israeli Government refused the idea and insisted on a "direct negotiation" with the Arabs without intervention by the United Nations or any state.

The two Great Powers, however, agreed on a proposed, but unpublicized, resolution that virtually included everything in the original United States "five great principles of peace" in the Middle East, except the fourth point regarding the control of the arms race in the area. This could be rated as an interim tactical shift of Soviet position, rather than pervasive evidence of any sound American-Soviet "concert" on the Middle East. However, when it ventured to try getting the Arab States to accept the pro-

205

posed draft resolution, the Soviet Union seriously miscalculated the rebuff it received.

In the showdown, when each of the two draft resolutions was put into vote, neither the Soviet-backed draft demanding the unconditional withdrawal of the Israeli forces from all Arab territories they occupied during the six-day war, nor the American-supported draft resolution trying to link withdrawal to an end by the Arab States of the state of war with Israel, won the required two-thirds majority of the General Assembly's 122 members.

Indeed, debate of the Arab-Israeli Third War in the General Assembly was not an edifying spectacle. It must have been disillusioning to hopeful idealists who still think of the United Nation's capability to challenge the arrogance of national power for securing international peace through the rule of world law and the principles of human justice. In two decades, and under the presence of the United Nations in the area, Israel was able to occupy by force the whole of Palestine, Sinai and part of Syria, depriving about one and one-half million Arabs of their homes and properties to live, under the United Nations auspices, in camps on international charity. Yet, the World Organization has been unable to put its own resolutions into force. Indeed, at the United Nations the facts were twisted, logic was distorted, and tortured semantics were confusing.

The General Assembly, however, adopted two important resolutions concerning the measures taken by Israel to change the status of the City of Jerusalem. In the first resolution (2253-ES-V) adopted on July 4, 1967, the Assembly declared "invalid" all measures taken by Israel to change the status of the Holy City. It further called upon Israel "to rescind all measures already taken and to desist forthwith from taking any action which would alter the status of Jerusalem."[39] The other resolution concerning

39 The resolution was adopted by 99 in favor, none against, with 20 abstentions one of which was the United States.

206

Jerusalem (2254-ES-V) was adopted by the General Assembly on July 14, 1967, whereby the Assembly expressed "the deepest regret and concern of the non-compliance by Israel with resolution 2253 (ES-V)," and its "failure" to implement it.[40] This resolution, however, remains unimplemented.

On the critical question of withdrawal, the General Assembly was faced by what seemed like complete deadlock. The most obvious reason behind the Assembly's failure was that, unlike the 1956 emergency special session, the United States and the Soviet Union were not in agreement. The Soviet Union blamed the United States for the Assembly's failure to act. "The position of the United States Government," said Foreign Minister Andrei Gromyko, "blocked recommendations in favor of the immediate withdrawal of Israeli troops." Similarly, the Soviet Government newspaper Izvestia accused the United States of using "all kinds of political pressure" to block resolutions demanding withdrawal of Israeli troops.

On July 21, 1967, therefore, the General Assembly decided to adjourn temporarily its fifth emergency special session. The Assembly requested the Secretary-General to forward the records of its session to the Security Council "in order to facilitate the resumption by the Council, as a matter of urgency, of its consideration of the tense situation in the Middle East."[41]

2. The Glassboro Summit Meeting

Before discussing and evaluating the work done and the results achieved at Glassboro, it may be useful to touch upon the American-Soviet "political spirit" which prevailed prior to the Meeting, during its discussions, and still com-

---

40 The resolution was adopted by 99 in favor, none against, with 18 abstentions one of which was the United States.

41 U.N. Doc. A/RES/2256 (ES-V). The resolution was adopted by 63 in favor, 26 against, with 27 abstentions.

manding the two Great Powers' relations. This "political spirit" could be briefly weighed as follows:

In the late 1950s, and more particularly ever since the Berlin crisis of 1961, the two Great Powers found themselves facing a challenge of a nontraditional world which required a new system of relationships, new strategies and certain valves of security. Indeed, the nuclear proliferation, the general development in the weaponry system; the new centers of power; and the developing rift in each of the two main traditional blocs (the Sino-Soviet dispute in the East and the American-European problem in the West), have not only required a new Great Powers' diplomacy but they have also imposed very definite limitations on Great Powers' actions, reactions and interactions.

To both the United States and the Soviet Union, the world of the 1960s has outgrown the cold war, and to attempt to translate the issues of the 1950s into the conditions of the 1960s is to produce irrelevancy and nonsense. Realistically, therefore, the cold war concept has become functionally limited. Consequently each side carefully avoided pressing the other inescapably into a corner and developed negotiating positions carefully calculated to allow the other some legitimate room in which to make countermoves. This has developed a new pattern of response to each other: a response to the change in their relations from conceptual crisis to revisionism, and from political tension to more flexible strategy suitable to the new needs and the living and changing realities of our times.

Therefore, the two Great Powers have been eagerly searching for ways to control their cold war struggle. This means identifying boundary lines of conflict within which they could fight their battles safely. Moscow and Washington, in other words, since they cannot again control the entire world political process and are further impaired in their capability by their continuing disagreement, must search out and begin to exploit areas in which they could concert their policies and their power. To them, this is the way to restore their great-power status in a changing world. Accordingly, they have developed a mutual consensus on two principal safety limits: (a) A procedural safety limit which means arms control and nuclear non-proliferation. (b) A geographic safety limit which means: (1) mutual recognition of each other's "sphere of influence"; (2) establishment of "buffer zones"; and (3) unwillingness to confront each other militarily in areas outside their traditional peripheries.

With this understanding and these limitations of the post-cold war and the post-bipolar era in mind, President Johnson and Chairman Aleksei Kosygin marched to Glassboro on June 23, 1967.

Primarily, the Soviet Chairman came to New York to attend the General Assembly Emergency Special Session which was held at the request of the Soviet Union. As the General Assembly's debate droned on, the summit meeting was finally arranged. Realistically speaking, it became apparent that the United Nations dropped into the background.

The Glassboro Summit was the seventh between the American and Soviet Chiefs of State since 1943, when President Roosevelt met with Soviet Premier Stalin at Tehran. The others were the following: Yalta, 1945; Potsdam, 1945; Geneva, 1955; Camp David, 1959; and Vienna, 1961. At Glassboro, however, they were able to discuss some of the world's biggest problems: The Middle East, Vietnam and the proliferation of nuclear weapons.

On the Middle Eastern crisis, however, the two Big Powers were limited by many factors in their decision-making processes. On one hand, the Soviet Premier could hardly promise to let the Arabs down or to take any less active a stand in the Middle East crisis. Indeed, Mr. Kosygin could risk no gesture in the United States that would arouse suspicion in the Arab World. President Johnson, on the other hand, could hardly promise to let Israel down, or to take any less active a stand in a part of the world that holds the oil on which many Western countries depend, and real estate of strategic importance.

The Big Two held two meetings on June 23 and 25 after which each side merely confirmed his Government's position on the Middle East problem. On the important issue of withdrawal of Israeli forces from occupied Arab territories, the Summit Meeting was a complete failure. President Johnson again declared

> that every State has a right to live, that there should be an end to the war in the Middle East — and that in the right circumstances there should be withdrawal of troops. This is a long way from agreement — but it is a long way also from total difference.[42]

The position of the Soviet Union, on the other hand, was clearly stated by Premier Kosygin in a statement on the Summit and also at a news conference held at the United Nations on June 25, 1967. The Soviet Chairman said

> the main thing now is to achieve a prompt withdrawal behind the armistice lines of the forces of Israel which has perpetrated aggression against the Arab States. This question is of signal importance for the restoration of peace in the Middle East . . . Regarding the limitation of arms shipments to the Middle East areas, this is a question that should be resolved after the withdrawal of forces behind the armistice lines.[43]

To conclude, however, one may say that the "Spirit of Glassboro" on the Middle East could be understood only in terms of a tacit agreement that neither the United States nor the Soviet Union would permit itself to be drawn into a Middle East shooting war, but otherwise to disagree.

---

[42] *The Washington Post* (June 26, 1967), p. A 10.
[43] Ibid.

3. The Security Council

As has been indicated, the General Assembly decided on July 21, 1967, to adjourn and requested the Secretary-General to forward the records of the Fifth Emergency Special Session to the Security Council. By this action the Assembly actually threw the Middle East problem back again to the Council where the Great Powers enjoy a special status. It was also understood that the Security Council should consider, "as a matter of urgency," the tense situation in the area which involved the withdrawal of the Israeli invading troops from the occupied Arab territories.

On the urgent question of withdrawal, three main draft resolutions were presented before the Security Council:

a. India, Mali, and Nigeria's joint draft resolution of November 7, 1967, which suggested a just and lasting peace in the Middle East based on the following principles: (1) that occupation by military conquest is inadmissible under the United Nations Charter; (2) that Israeli forces should withdraw from occupied Arab territories; (3) that every state in the area has the right to live in peace and consequently the state of belligerency should be terminated; (4) that the problem of Palestine refugees should be justly settled; and (5) that freedom of navigation through international waterways in the area should be guaranteed.

b. The United States' draft resolution of November 7, 1967, whereby the Security Council would affirm that just and lasting peace in the Middle East requires: (1) "withdrawal of armed forces from occupied territories"; (2) termination of the state of war in the area; (3) "mutual recognition and respect for the right of every

211

State in the area to sovereign existence"; (4) a guarantee of freedom of navigation through international waterways; (5) "a just settlement of the refugee problem"; (6) the establishment of demilitarized zones; and (7) a limitation of the arms race in the area.

c. The Soviet Union's draft resolution of November 20, 1967, whereby the Security Council would urge that for the achievement of a just peace in the Middle East, the following steps should be taken: (1) the Israeli armed forces should immediately withdraw to the positions they held prior to June 5, 1967; (2) the States in the area should immediately recognize that each of them has the right to live in peace and consequently "all States in the area should put an end to the state of belligerency"; (3) the Palestine refugee problem should be justly solved; and (4) there should be a guarantee of "innocent passage through international waterways in the area in accordance with international agreements."

Indeed, both the Indian and the Soviet draft resolutions marked a turning point in the traditional stand of the two countries on the crisis. In consultation with the Arab States, both India and the Soviet Union agreed with their friends that in the interest of peace such a shift seemed to be the only way out in the face of the very strong American attitude on the matter. This flexible trend, however, opened a door for the United Kingdom to do a little compromise between the Indian and Soviet drafts on one hand, and the United States' draft on the other. Britain was eager for a settlement principally because closure of the Suez Canal was proving costly in terms of shipping as well as domestic gasoline prices, with a threat of permanent shifts in trade patterns.

The British-sponsored draft resolution was unanimously adopted by the Security Council on November 22, 1967.[44] This resolution has become the keystone in the process of seeking a peaceful settlement of the Middle East dispute. The Great Powers agreed to "the inadmissibility of the acquisition of territory by war." They emphasized "the need to work for a just and lasting peace in which every State in the area can live in security." The resolution further affirmed that a just and lasting peace in the area should include the application of these principles: (1) "withdrawal of Israeli armed forces from territories occupied in the recent conflict"; (2) "termination of all claims or states of belligerency"; (3) every State in the area has the right to live in peace "within secure and recognized boundaries free from threats or acts of force"; (4) a guarantee of freedom of navigation through international waterways; (5) "a just settlement of the refugee problem"; and (6) the establishment of demilitarized zones. The Security Council further requested the Secretary-General "to designate a Special Representative to proceed to the Middle East . . . to achieve a peaceful and accepted settlement in accordance with the provisions and principles in this resolution." Dr. Gunnar Jarring, the Ambassador of Sweden to the Soviet Union, was chosen to be Mr. U Thant's Special Envoy to the Middle East.

Because of the very nature of the United Nations authority and the limitations imposed thereon, it was clearly understood from the very beginning that the implementation of the principles envisaged in the Security Council's resolution on the peaceful settlement of the Middle East crisis would depend primarily on the attitudes of the parties directly involved, the Arab States and Israel, and exclusively

---

44 U.N. Doc. S/RES/242 (November 22, 1967); see the full text of this resolution in Appendix H.

on the policies of the two major parties indirectly involved, the United States and the Soviet Union.

Although very vague, the Arab States declared their acceptance of the Security Council's resolution of November 22, 1967. To them, the basic principle in this resolution was the withdrawal of the Israeli forces to the positions they had held prior to June 5, 1967. As stated in the Council's resolution, this provision was given the first priority. Consequently, the literal interpretation of the resolution would mean that there would be no application before the implementation of this provision of single importance — the withdrawal. In other words, the whole resolution was based primarily upon the principle of withdrawal of the invading troops, the noncompliance with which would certainly destroy the whole structure. Indeed, any other interpretation would not only be contrary to the letter and the spirit of the resolution, but it would also be an invitation to legalizing war for territorial and political gains.

In an interview made by two editors of *Time*, President Nasser summarized the position of the United Arab Republic as follows:[45]

> . . . We have agreed to a peaceful solution, implementing the 1967 Security Council resolution. Until now, Israel has not accepted it. She says she will not leave the occupied areas until we sit down with her to talk peace. But we refuse to sit. It is not called for in the Security Council resolution. If we sit now, we sit as defeated people, sitting only to capitulate. This we cannot do.

> . . . If Israel agrees on two main points, this will solve the problem. The points are land — withdrawal from all occupied territory — and people — the Palestinians must have the choice of returning to their homes.

---

45 *Time* (May 16, 1969), p. 31; see also Ibid., pp. 29-39.

. . . We could not accept the international occupation of Sinai. . . . Israel wants to have Sinai demilitarized. We could agree to such a situation with the Security Council, with Dr. Gunnar Jarring — something like that — for a short period. But on the permanent demilitarization of Sinai, we refuse.

. . . If there were a solution to all problems, this (a nonaggression pact with Israel) would be something to think about. (Also in this case), the Canal (Suez Canal) would be no problem.

I accept the reality of Israel, and so will my people, if there is a humanitarian solution. Call it Israel, or whatever they want to call it, and I will recognize it.

. . . We are for complete withdrawal from Arab Jerusalem. Without that, there can be no peace. We were not planning for war in 1967, but we must plan for war now in case everything else fails.

During his official visit to the United States in April 1969, King Hussein of Jordan clearly stated his position, which he confirmed to be the position of President Nasser as well, in a speech at the National Press Club in Washington, D.C. The Jordanian monarch declared that "Israel must withdraw from all the territory it occupied during the 1967 war, and must also concede the right of the 1.5 million Palestinian refugees to either repatriation or compensation." On the other hand, "the Arabs," he maintained, "would put an end to their 21-year-old state of belligerency against Israel and guarantee Israel's right to live in peace." Furthermore, the King promised that "free navigation through the Suez Canal and the Gulf of Aqaba would be guaranteed 'for all'."[46]

Actually, the Arab States' acceptance of the Security

---

46 *Newsweek* (April 21, 1969), p. 42.

Council's resolution may be correctly viewed as a turning point in the whole Middle East crisis. This new Arab policy could only be interpreted in two inseparable ways: (a) Arab interest in a just peace; (b) Arab new strategy based upon: (1) the realization of some new realities in the area; (2) a shift from a policy of "total victory or nothing" to what may be called a doctrine of "flexible response." This new doctrine might open room for certain alternatives short of a total victory for either side to the conflict.

In this connection of Arab strategy, it may be useful to point out that instead of adopting a strategy of tactical initiatives, the entire Arab strategic concept in their conflict with Israel was founded on the notion of "response," in a sense of "defensive" strategy. But "response" as a focus makes sense only if it were admitted to be preparatory to some later day when the Arab States would deal noncoercively with Israel on a give-and-take basis. Accordingly, and since this assumption was certainly ruled out, "military victory" for Israel did not necessarily mean "political defeat" for the Arabs.

To Israel, on the other hand, the Security Council's resolution was only a "working paper" or a "guideline" with no other validity. As such, the Israeli Government had first refused to comply with the resolution and to discuss its provisions with the Secretary-General's Special Envoy. She insisted, instead, on "direct negotiations" with the Arab States with the Council's resolution being the focus of their discussions.

The principal thesis of Israeli leaders was that peace could only be achieved through "direct" negotiations with the Arab States. "As long as the Arabs won't sit down with us," declared the Israeli Prime Minister, "that means they don't accept our existence."[47] Mr. Abba Eban, Israeli Foreign Minister, stated that as far as the Security Coun-

---

47 *The Washington Post* (March 5, 1969); See also *The Washington Post* (June 16, 1969).

cil's resolution is concerned, "we've made so many statements on the acceptance of the resolution as the framework of a negotiated settlement. . . . The word 'agreement' is the very essence of our position."[48]

Regarding the two principal issues, held firmly by the Arab States as declared by President Nasser, the land and the people, the Israelis made it plain that for spiritual and security reasons they would not, under any circumstances, give up "all" the Arab territories they won in 1967. Israel claimed that the Security Council's resolution speaks of the Israeli withdrawal from "territories" it occupied, but does not use the word "all." As such, Israel interpreted the resolution as justifying its claim that the Old City of Jerusalem, taken from Jordan, the Golan Heights, captured from Syria, and Sharm el-Sheik, taken from the United Arab Republic, are "not negotiable." Indeed, the Israelis determined to cling to the military advantage brought to them by the new geography gained as a result of the Third War. Unable to win the peace after winning three wars, the Israelis decided to expand their territorial power to what they considered a new "security" line far away from the heart of Israel. They rationalized this policy as follows:

> We [the Israelis] thought after June, 1967, that we had a situation like that at the end of the 1956 Sinai war when the victory bought security in the form of time. It would take a decade, we calculated — in 1957 correctly, as it turned out — for the enemy to build back his capacity to hit us again. So, with that security, we could afford to go back to our pre-war borders.
>
> But now we see that there is no parallel. In less than two years, thanks to Russia, the Arab countries have restored their war potential to where it was. Time can no longer be our 'demilitarization factor' and so we must hold the other security we have, space between us and the heart of the enemies and military force.

---

48 *The Washington Post* (March 6, 1969).

Geography — Sinai and the West Bank — is our security factor now.[49]

With regard to the Arab refugee problem, on the other hand, "the awkward fact is that the Israelis — as they privately admit — do not even want to discuss the matter."[50]

To conclude, however, one should point out that the Arab-Israeli differences on the Security Council's resolution of November 22, 1967, centered around two basic matters: (a) interpretation; and (b) procedure. These views on the terms of peace were further reaffirmed in the official reply of each of the United Arab Republic, Jordan and Israel to a 14-point questionnaire sent to them in March 1969 by Dr. Gunnar V. Jarring, the Secretary-General's Special Representative for Peace in the Middle East. Ambassador Jarring's mission, it was understood, should remain within the realm of quiet diplomacy and strictly confidential due to the unique nature of the Middle East conflict which has brought a great controversy among the Arabs, especially after the June War, on the strategy and the terms of peace. However, Mr. Darius S. Jhabvala, U.N. Correspondent of *The Boston Globe*, successfully obtained the document and published it.[51]

Accordingly, the kind of peace settlement that Israel sketched for itself during the Six-Day War, and shortly after it, became impossible to achieve. To Israel, the "real" peace is one in which its existence enjoys the "consent" of the Arabs. This "consent," if ever materialized, certainly depends on terms Israel seems unwilling to make, on grounds that they would undermine its defensive security. Furthermore, the Arabs' "consent," if ever given, would not reflect the "consensus" of the Arab masses, and certainly would

---

49 *The Washington Post* (May 4, 1969).

50 *Newsweek* (April 21, 1969), p. 42.

51 *The Boston Globe* (April 22, 1969), pp. 1-2; see also Appendix J for full text of Dr. Jarring's questions and the replies to them.

218

not be agreeable to those Arabs who have suffered the most, the Palestinian refugees. There has been no doubt, for instance, that King Hussein of Jordan is willing to accord that "consent" and would have, had he been able to effectively control the Palestinians who comprise more than two-thirds of the population in Jordan. President Nasser, on the other hand, could not agree to a peaceful settlement that would undermine the rights of the Arab refugees. However, the other side of the dilemma is that in the absence of progress towards a settlement for a just peace, the prospect for a political solution becomes dim indeed, and a fourth Arab-Israeli round would be inevitable.

Realizing the basic differences between the Arab States and Israel on the nature and the binding effect of the Security Council's resolution, and aware of their involvement and the limitations imposed therein, the four Great Powers, the principal political sponsors of the Council's action, "liberalized" their own original views on the matters and developed in June, 1969, a general consensus on the guiding principles for securing a just and lasting peace in the Middle East. While the constitutional base of the Great Powers' consensus was the Security Council's resolution of November 22, 1967; its central theme was "withdrawal and the nature of the peace agreement"; and its main political directions were:[52]

> (a) That any "contractual agreement" must be a package deal in which no section would be implemented until the entire package was accepted by all sides;
>
> (b) That the objective is the establishment of a just and lasting peace, not merely a new armistice between Arab States and Israel;
>
> (c) That any territorial adjustment in the June,

---

[52] *The New York Times* (June 13, 1969), pp. 1-2.

1967, cease-fire lines must not reflect the weight of conquest; and

(d) That the settlement should not be imposed but rather peacefully secured through the United Nations go-between, Gunnar Jarring.

Indeed, the Great Powers' general consensus on the guiding principles for peace in the Middle East was a compromised formula on both the interpretation of the Security Council's resolution and the procedures for its implementation. For more than a year, however, the two Great Powers principally involved in the area, the United States and the Soviet Union, failed in persuading the warring parties of the credibility of the new formula for peace. While the Arab States had insisted on a strict interpretation of the Security Council's resolution which has built its entire structure on the principles of "Withdrawal" and "Mediation," Israel had insistingly declared that no compliance before "a direct negotiation" on all aspects of the Arab-Israeli crisis.

Perhaps the most important pressuring factor in the whole process of peaceful settlement has been the growing Palestinian Revolutionary Movements principally led by Al-Fatah's leader Yasser Arafat. To them, a return to the 1967 status quo, even if achieved, would be a continuation of a refugee status. It would only take the Palestinian refugees back to the same alienating conditions on the West Bank of the Jordan River and in the Gaza Strip without being able to become self-ruled in their own home. Since the Six-Day War, the fedayeen movements have emerged not only as a manifestation of Palestinian Nationalism, the principal aspiration of which is the revival of the Palestine State, but also as independent entities that pay allegiance only to their revolting state-of-mind. These growing movement have certainly added a very dynamic dimension to the conflict to the extent that no peace arrangements would

220

come to pass without a satisfactory solution to the refugee problem. "Without our consent," said Dr. George Habash, leader of the Popular Front for the Liberation of Palestine, "the other Arabs can do nothing, and we will never agree to a peaceful settlement."[53]

The Turning Points

Based on the Great Powers' general political consensus of June 1969, the United States' Secretary of State, William P. Rogers, proposed on June 19, 1970, a 90-day standstill cease-fire along the Suez Canal between Israel and the United Arab Republic; he also suggested that Dr. Gunnar Jarring's Mission be reactivated to seek implementation of the Security Council's resolution of November 22, 1967. Although the precise terms of the cease-fire proposal were kept secret by mutual consensus, following are points of that proposal's general focus:

a. That all military activities would be barred in a zone at least 50 kilometers (32 miles) deep on each side of the Canal. Military forces in this zone could hold their positions but any buildup or movement of men or weapons would be a violation of mutual understanding. Israel and the United Arab Republic themselves would not only have primary roles in enforcing the standstill limited cease-fire, but they could also use their own means in checking each other's activities in the cease-fire area;

b. That the United Nations Truce Supervision Organization's roughly 100 observers would continue to patrol both sides of the Canal and report any cease-fire violations. Also each side

---

53 *Time* (August 10, 1970), p. 22.

could report violations to the observers, to the United Nations' Secretary-General, or to the Security Council;

c. That American and Soviet intelligence means, including orbiting photo-reconnaissance satellites and electronic monitoring ships in the Mediterranean, would back up the policing arrangements by providing data on enemy activities to Israel and the U.A.R., respectively; and

d. That indirect talks for peace would start under the auspices of Ambassador Gunnar Jarring within the framework of the Security Council's resolution of November 22, 1967.

It was further understood that the proposed limited cease-fire would apply only to the United Arab Republic — the only Arab country which, in April 1969, formally declared the postwar cease-fires void. On the Jordanian, Syrian, and Lebanese fronts, the cease-fires originally instituted at the conclusion of the Arab-Israeli war of June 1967, and never formally abrogated by those countries, were understood to be still in effect. On the Jordanian-Israeli cease-fire front, however, Jordan should not only continue to avoid cease-fire violations by its army regulars, but it would also be legally obligated to prevent cease-fire violations from its territory by the Palestinian fedayeen. In responding to these latter violations, it was understood, Israel should not give anyone the right to void the cease-fire.

Accordingly, the very essence of the United States' proposal was that during a cease-fire of at least 90 days, Israel, Jordan and the U.A.R. — working through United Nations go-between Gunnar Jarring — would hold "indirect" talks aimed at the implementation of the Security Council's resolution of November 1967. This stop-shooting-start-talking formula is a "quiet diplomacy" approach whereby one might achieve what arms and conquest have failed to bring into the Middle East. To the American diplomacy, time was running short and if the drive for peace in the Middle East fails, the United States could face the following consequences:

a. A fourth round between the Arab States and Israel that could lead to a military confrontation between the United States and the Soviet Union at a time when the American people are trying to get out of South Vietnam and do not have the heart to go into another war, hoping to reduce the United States military presence in Western Europe and to give up the role of policing the international political system, all in response to the living and changing realities that have shaped the diplomacy of the nuclear age.

b. Increase of Soviet influence in a strategic area stretching from the Eastern Mediterranean to the Arab Gulf and into the Indian Ocean.

c. Loss of about 2 billion dollars in direct American investments in the Middle East, and a cut in American exports to the Arab World which totaled more than 845 million dollars in 1969.

d. Exclusion of the United States from Middle East oil supplies which would eventually not only increase oil prices but would also seriously affect American oil investments in the area.

The United States further realized that the traditional ways of trying to separate the belligerents by means of corridors and to keep them apart with an international peace force without dealing realistically with the very roots of the belligerency, had failed in the Arab-Israeli case. Moreover, to prevent war by maintaining a military balance of power in the area, would be an invitation for an arms race which would eventually lead to an arms explosion and inevitably to war.

Finally, the United States' proposal for a limited cease-fire was dictated by a mutual American-Soviet diplomatic concert aimed at controlling, not fighting, a cold war in the Middle East. The American policy on the Middle East realized that the Soviet Union had become a decisive power in the area, and if the United States' attitude towards the Arab-Israeli conflict had facilitated a very threatening Soviet presence therein, a new American approach to that conflict had to be initiated, should the Soviet influence be contained. Therefore, one should say, the American proposal for peace in the Arab-Israeli crisis not only grew out of a real concern about an area of key political, economic and strategic interests, but it was also a manifestation of President Nixon's "Era of Negotiation" in international affairs.

Key in the American cease-fire proposal was the response of President Gamal Abdel Nasser of the United Arab Republic who was given the first option to accept or reject the American initiative. On July 22, 1970, Nasser declared the United Arab Republic's acceptance of the United States' proposal. In the past, President Nasser had repeatedly rebuffed appeals by the United States and other Western powers for a return to the 1967 cease-fire agreement, asserting that a cessation of shooting would be an acceptance of a de facto status quo and a surrender to Israeli occupation of the Sinai peninsula and the other occupied Arab territories. However, the Arab leader felt that a limited cease-fire aimed at giving the quiet diplomacy a try within the framework of the Security Council's resolution (a resolution the U.A.R. had accepted) might offer a new opportunity for peace. Knowing that its chances of success were very slight, and fully aware of the implications of his decision — a decision that was very hard to make — Nasser decided not to ignore the American peace proposal for tactical, political, and military reasons:

    a. Departing from the traditional Arab diplomatic strategy of "response," Nasser thought fit to take the "initiative" in accepting the notion of peacemaking for implementing the principles and the provisions of the Security Council's resolution of November 22, 1967. By doing this, the U.A.R.'s President aimed at not only testing the real American intentions and placing pressure on the United States to change its policy of arming Israel, but he also intended to appeal to the world public opinion with a declared quest for peace.

    b. A silent Suez front would indeed provide an opportunity for the U.A.R. to strengthen its defense.

However, the United Arab Republic's acceptance of the American proposal was clearly tied to the principal issue of Israeli withdrawal from the Arab territories seized in 1967. In his letter of July 22, 1970, to Secretary of State Rogers, the U.A.R.'s Foreign Minister Mahmoud Riad stated, "we are prepared to accept a cease-fire for a limited period of three months . . . though we believe the correct procedure to start in this case is to begin drawing up a timetable for withdrawal of the Israeli forces from the occupied territories."[54]

Israel, on the other hand, found it extremely difficult to oppose the United States' proposal, especially after the United Arab Republic had accepted it. The Israelis wanted some ironclad guarantees from the Nixon Adminis-

---

54 *The Washington Post* (August 8, 1970).

tration on the general circumstances surrounding the cease-fire and the proposed peace talks. They were principally interested in an unlimited cease-fire to be policed by a peace-keeping force other than the United Nations'. To them a 90-day cease-fire might be sufficient only to give the Arab States, particularly the U.A.R., an opportunity to strengthen their military positions. Israel was further uncertain of one basic issue around which Israeli policy has been centered — the United States' real intentions. During the Suez crisis of 1956, the United States threatened to vote for United Nations sanctions against Israel unless the Israeli troops withdrew from the Egyptian territories seized in the fighting. With that in mind, the Israelis were worried that once talks started, the Americans, who had exerted pressure to withdraw in the 1956 war and to stop shooting and start talking in the 1967 war, would inevitably exert pressure on Israel for making major concessions.

However, the Israelis realized, though subconsciously, that the winning of three wars brought no security to them, and the relatively quiet cease-fire lines they thought had been achieved by military victory became military targets and constant reminders of an indefinite state of war. As such, they felt less sure of their forecasts today than they were in the year immediately following the 1967 war. This feeling, coupled with the growing psychological, political and military presence of the Palestine liberation groups symbolized through Al-Fatah, overshadowed Israel's intangible uncertainties and were decisive factors in Mrs. Golda Meir's decision on August 7, 1970, to accept the United States' proposal. The Israeli Prime Minister declared that Israel had accepted the truce "after we had reached the convictions that the cease-fire would become effective on conditions which would prevent its being abused." Mrs. Meir further said that Israel "would like to regard the cease-fire as a natural stage to be observed

226

on the road to a contractual peace established on defensible, agreed borders between us and Egypt."[55]

Indeed, achieving a truce was relatively easier on the Suez Canal front than on Israel's northern and eastern war lines. In Jordan, King Hussein's power had been considerably diminished by the Palestinian liberation organizations centered therein. Therefore, to expect a silent truce with Israel was too unrealistic and impossible to be attained. However, no formal declaration was considered necessary for Jordan to adhere to the United States' proposed limited cease-fire since Jordan had not formally declared the 1967 truce void. Realizing his internal problems, therefore, the Jordanian monarch was unable to formally take a unilateral stand on the United States' peace proposal. Instead, King Hussein decided to ally himself with President Nasser to whom he cabled, "we accept what you accept and reject what you reject."[56]

With the U.A.R. and Israel accepting the American proposal, a standstill limited cease-fire went into effect along the Suez Canal war front at 2200 hours GMT on August 7, 1970, until at least 2200 hours GMT on November 5, 1970. This also meant that steps had to be taken to start the peace talks between Israel, Jordan and the U.A.R. through the peacemaking mission of Dr. Gunnar Jarring. Reporting to the Security Council on the whole situation and the reactivation of Jarring's mission, Secretary-General U Thant said in his message of August 7, 1970:

> In accordance with that proposal [the American proposal] and in the light of these acceptances [Israel, Jordan and the U.A.R.], Ambassador Jarring has addressed to me on August 7 the following letter:
>
> "The United Arab Republic, Jordan and Israel advise me that they agree:

---

55 *The New York Times* (August 8, 1970).
56 *Time* (August 10, 1970).

227

"That having accepted and indicated their willingness to carry out [Security Council] Resolution 242 [of Nov. 22, 1967] in all its parts, they will designate representatives to discussions to be held under my auspices, according to such procedure and at such places and times as I may recommend, taking into account as appropriate each side's preference as to method of procedure and previous experience between the parties;

"That the purpose of the aforementioned discussions is to reach agreement on the establishment of a just and lasting peace between them based on (1) mutual acknowledgement by the United Arab Republic, Jordan and Israel of each other's sovereignty, territorial integrity and political independence; and (2) Israel's withdrawal from territories occupied in the 1967 conflict both in accordance with Resolution 242. . . ."[57]

Perhaps the most significant developments brought about by the American peace initiative and which have considerably affected both the psychological and the political environment of the Arab-Israeli crisis, could be summarized as follows:

a. For the Arab States:

1. Israel "dropped" its long-standing insistence on the principle of "direct negotiations" with the Arab States as a precondition for "relating to" or "accepting" the Security Council's resolution of November 22, 1967.

b. For Israel:

1. The United Arab Republic, the major fighting force among the Arab States and the central

---

[57] *The New York Times* (August 8, 1970).

focus of Israel's policy, accepted a standstill cease-fire. Although limited, it would require a drastic change in its military strategy for any party to resume fighting — a change from a defensive to an offensive strategy. Unless miscalculating the other party's intentions, neither side would be willing to give the other an excuse for declaring the truce void on a defensive basis; and to start all-out-war would require, considering the involvement of the two super-powers, more than local military capabilities.

2. The Arab States dropped their long-standing insistence on the procedural priorities in implementing the Security Council's resolution according to which the principle of withdrawal from the occupied Arab territories should be the first to be carried out. Instead, they consented to the concept of a "package deal" whereby the resolution would be carried out in all its parts at the same time.

The Palestinian nationalist movements, however, strongly opposed the American initiative and rejected the whole idea of peacemaking with Israel. The ten major groups of the Palestine liberation movement, although ideologically different, opposed any recognition of Israeli sovereignty. "The Palestinian Arab people," declares the Palestinian National Covenant, "reject every solution that is a substitute for a complete liberation of Palestine."

Moreover, the Palestinians were particularly uncertain of the real intentions of some Arab governments. They feared a focus of attention on recovery of the captured lands and an erosion of support for the refugee problem. In his meeting with Nasser shortly after the cease-fire had gone into effect, Al-Fatah's leader Yasser Arafat was reassured of the principal thrust of the United Arab Republic's peace-seeking diplomacy: withdrawal of Israeli forces from the Arab territories seized in the June 1967 war and a just solution of the Arab refugee problem.

Indeed, the fedayeen military units, approximately 50,000 strong, operating in Jordan, Lebanon and Syria, would certainly negate any peace efforts that might undermine their cause. Should they become alarmed in the process, they could wage an inter-Arab armed struggle aimed at forcing the peacemaking advocates into a position that would diminish any prospect for a peaceful settlement. The Civil War in Jordan erupted between the Jordanian army and the Palestinians even before the proposed peace talks got underway, had shown the real capabilities of the Palestinian movements and their role in the course of peace and the course of war in the Middle East.

The Jordanian Civil War, a rebellion against King Hussein's acceptance of the American peace proposal, did not only take the lives of several thousands, Palestinians and Jordanians, but it also raised the possibility of American intervention in the Middle East — an action that would not have been tolerated by the Soviet Union. Furthermore, the Jordanian Civil War has not only strengthened the fedayeen line in the Arab World, but it has also revived a world concern about the Palestinian refugee problem as an integral part of the Middle East crisis that can no longer be ignored.

At this point, one should not hesitate saying, the Civil War in Jordan overshadowed the American peace initiative and undermined its basic hypotheses. In particular, the war has enhanced the growing conviction that no peace arrangements would ever be feasible without the Palestinian consent being represented. Any peacemaking approach, therefore, should seriously seek to bring the Palestinian refugee communities within the ambit of diplomacy, otherwise it would be uprooting itself from a basic reality in the Arab-Israeli impasse. Indeed, from the point of view of pragmatic diplomacy, one should admit that the Palestinian

230

Arabs have been deprived of their country and are fighting for one; they have a government without a state and are determined to institute one. While these realities have continued to present themselves in the area, the United States' "quiet diplomacy" approach to peace failed to relate to them.

The prospects for peace, however, were further complicated as a result of Israel's attitude towards the proposed indirect peace talks. Shortly after the initial meeting with Ambassador Jarring on August 25, 1970, Israel declared a boycott of the talks, charging that the United Arab Republic had violated the terms of the cease-fire by moving antiaircraft SAM-3 missiles into the Suez Canal standstill zone. The Israeli cabinet, therefore, decided not to resume participation in the peace talks until the pre-August 7 status quo be restored. On September 3, 1970, the United States confirmed the Israeli allegation and requested "rectification" of the missile situation. The American "quiet diplomacy" further responded by authorizing selling Israel more Phantom F-4E fighter-bombers, Skyhawks, and the highly sophisticated electronic radar-jamming gear basically designed to negate the effect of SAM missiles.

The United Arab Republic, on the other hand, refused to accept these allegations and maintained that these missiles had existed in the area long before the cease-fire and were the primary cause of Israeli Phantoms' being shot down before August 7, 1970. The U.A.R. Government further accused Israel of violating the cease-fire by not only flying on the west side of the Canal, but also by building new bunkers and putting equipment in places where it was not before. Moreover, Foreign Minister Mahmoud Riad declared that the United States had undermined its own peace initiative when she had decided to sell more weapons to Israel in violation of a commitment previously made not to introduce weapons into the area.

Undoubtedly, the principal objective behind the Israeli diplomatic boycott was to enter upon "negotiations" or

231

"discussions" from a position of military supremacy to be secured by increasing American economic support and military supplies at least during the months of hesitation and maneuver. After it had successfully accomplished its objective, Israel decided in early January 1971, to return to the indirect peace discussions through tht United Nations mediator Gunnar Jarring. It was understood, however, that the Israeli Government would be less responsive to making any major concessions as long as the United States was willing to strengthen the Israeli offensive capabilities.

It should be concluded, therefore, that the American peace proposal was paralyzed by positive actions from within, inconsistent with the diplomacy of peacemaking, and negative responses from without consistent with the diplomacy of war. A foreign policy decision to arm Israel, not for securing a national existence but for maintaining a military superiority, at a time when the same foreign policy maker was mediating for peace, can only suggest that the United States' policy in the Middle East has no clearly defined directions. This further suggests that instead of isolating itself from that region's living and changing realities, the Americans would need to develop evenhanded policies on the Middle East, should this Great Power's national interests be secured in that strategic area of the world.

In response to the Israeli attitude towards the peace talks, on the other hand, the United Arab Republic found it necessary to condition the extension of the cease-fire beyond the expiration date on November 5, 1970, upon Israeli positive return to the peace talks and a declaration of readiness to abide by the Security Council's resolution of November 22, 1967. To the peacemaking advocates among the Arabs, a "quiet diplomacy" which permits Israel to boycott the talks for peace and, at the same time, strengthens Israeli military offensive capabilities, would turn out to be a "quiet surrender." In accepting, in early February 1971, the extension of the limited cease-fire along

232

the Suez Canal, the leaders in Cairo further urged a time-table for an Israeli withdrawal from all the territories occupied in the Third War, and the enforcement of the Security Council's resolution of November 22, 1967. To the United Arab Republic, a cease-fire which was planned to be limited in order to facilitate a new environment conductive to the making of peace, should remain in fact limited; otherwise it would, if unreasonably and fruitlessly prolonged, facilitate a new status quo conducive to the making of war.

The Sudden Death of Nasser and Sadat's Approach to Peace

As was mentioned, President Gamal Abdel Nasser was the principal pillar upon which any prospect for peace, either through enforcement or through pacific settlement, in the Middle East had rested. His unique leadership and great standing in the Arab World made neither peace nor war possible without him. As such, Nasser's acceptance of the American proposal on July 22, 1970, was central in the entire process without which it would not have been possible for the move to see the light. Guided by his enlightened pragmatic diplomacy and skillful political tactics, President Nasser had seen fit to accept the American peace initiative. In essence, Nasser's decision was consistent with his policy directions ever since the Security Council's resolution of November 22, 1967.

A few hours after he had signed a cease-fire agreement which put an end to the Civil War in Jordan, and the conclusion of an Arab Summit Meeting held at his request for that purpose, President Nasser died in Cairo on Monday, September 28, 1970, of a massive heart attack at the age of 52. His death was a political earthquake in the Middle East that would create vacuums, the filling of which would eventually determine the national and political face of the Middle East, with unforeseeable consequences

233

for the stability of the area and its future relations with the Eastern Powers, the Western Powers, and the Nonaligned States.

Indeed, Nasser's departure from the scene deprived the Arab World of its major leader and the champion of Arab Nationalism whose death spelled uncertainty for the future cohesion of the Arab States, and unpredictable developments in the Great Powers' play for influence in the area and in the Arab-Israeli conflict.

However, there is no reason to predict that the Nasserite philosophies and institutions, Nasser's instituted legacy, will be altered either internally in the United Arab Republic, or with regard to the Arab World and the Middle East, Africa, the Moslem World, or the Arab-Israeli war. In his first major policy speech before the National Assembly, President Anwar Sadat, Nasser's successor, declared on October 17, 1970, a pledge to follow Nasser's objective of struggling to liberate all Arab lands, occupied by Israel in the 1967 war and to achieve a settlement for the Palestinian refugees. President Sadat further announced that Nasser's legacy requires adherence to the following goals:

1. The dream of Nasser to unite the Arab countries.

2. Defining the enemies of our nation.

3. Maintaining a position of nonalignment between the major world power blocs.

4. Supporting the national liberation movements.

5. Defending the socialist gains in the U.A.R.

On the Arab-Israeli crisis, the most urgent challenge that the new leader had to place at the very top of his working agenda, President Sadat clearly spelled out his policy directions in the following terms, the understanding of which would justify a cease-fire and a positive response to which would eventually lead to a just and lasting peace in the area:[58]

a. That it would be difficult for the U.A.R. to discuss a peaceful arrangement of the Middle Eastern impasse while part of its territory was still under Israeli military occupation. "Can peace be induced," declared President Sadat, "while one of the parties [Israel] occupies one-seventh of the land of the other [the U.A.R.]? The occupying power automatically has a veto. . . ." Israel should, therefore, declare its readiness to abide by the Security Council's resolution of November 22, 1967, which emphasized the principle of total withdrawal from "all" Arab territories occupied in the 1967 war.

b. That "the problem is not cease-fire but how to dismantle the Israeli occupation in return for a lasting settlement. . . . But a permanent cease-fire will automatically lead to a permanent status quo and permanent occupation."

c. That a partial withdrawal of the Israeli troops "to a line behind El Arish [Sinai]" would not only "test Israel's alleged good intentions . . ." but also in return, the President pledged,

> I would guarantee to reopen the canal in six months to international trade. I would prolong the cease-fire to a fixed date to give Jarring time to work out the details. I would guarantee free passage in the Strait of Tiran with an international force at Sharm el-Sheikh. Its composition doesn't matter; the Big Four or other nations — it's immaterial to us. It would be guaranteed by the Security Council and could not be removed without all four agreeing. We would finally

---

58 *Newsweek* (February 22, 1971), pp. 40-41.

be grappling with fundamentals and a final settlement would at least be in sight. We are open-minded and open-hearted about the rest of the program. We will be flexible and willing to discuss anything that could lead to lasting peace in this part of the world. But mark this. It must be an over-all settlement for all territories occupied in 1967, not just Sinai.

d. That upon the implementation of the Security Council's resolution of November 22, 1967, in all of its parts, the United Arab Republic would agree to "the inviolability and political independence of every state in the area, including Israel. We pledge our solemn word on this. We have no designs on Israel, it is Israel that has designs on us. . . ."

Indeed, President Sadat's approach to peace in the Middle East could be best understood as a functional manifestation of a new political strategy which, while it recognizes the living and the changing realities in the conflict as well as its dimensions, aims at showing a maximum flexibility on both the procedural and the substantive issues. This Arab diplomacy would eventually push Israel into a situation in which the choice would be either to positively and flexibly respond or to reveal its "real intentions" before the world public opinion. It is calculated, furthermore, that this tactical shift in Arab diplomacy, from a "rigid response" to a "flexible initiative," might eventually make the United States re-examine its policy directions on the Middle East and hopefully reconsider its armament policy as well as other aids to Israel.

The Israeli Government, on the other hand, did not positively respond to President Sadat's approach to peace and, instead, reiterated its traditional position that it would not accept the border lines which existed before the 1967 war, and insisted on "secure, recognized and agreed borders"[59] that would have to be instituted in a

---

[59] *Newsweek* (March 8, 1971), pp. 66-67 and 70.

peace treaty with the Arab States. In keeping with this policy direction, Israel further failed to give "prior commitments" which had been requested on February 8, 1971, by Ambassador Gunnar Jarring from both Israel and the U.A.R. as inevitable declarations of good intentions and prerequisites of an eventual peace settlement between them. The United Nations mediator was seeking parallel commitments whereby (1) Israel would withdraw its forces from occupied U.A.R. territory to the former international boundary between Egypt and the British Mandate for Palestine; (2) the U.A.R. would enter into a peace agreement with Israel; and (3) both Israel and the U.A.R. would pledge the full implementation of the Security Council's resolution of November 22, 1967.

Although Jarring's initiative had left the status of the Gaza Strip undetermined, the U.A.R. gave a positive reply to the mediator's questions. Israel, however, questioned the constitutionality of the move and challenged Jarring's authority to take the initiative on substantive issues.

To conclude, however, it became undoubtedly clear that neither the Security Council's resolution of November 22, 1967, nor the United States' proposal of June 19, 1970, or Ambassador Jarring's initiative of February 8, 1971, or President Sadat's peacemaking approach, were able to peacefully produce any substantive changes in the Israeli position on the terms of peace in the Middle East. Failure of the peacemaking efforts would, therefore, inevitably leave no alternative but a collapse of the limited cease-fire and a resumption of war in which the United States and the Soviet Union might find themselves unwillingly dragged into an undesirable risky confrontation. Although it might not be a decisive war for either side, it would diminish for decades any chances for peace and uproot for years American presence and influence in the Middle East.

III. CONCLUSION: The Twilight Zone

At the very roots of the Middle Eastern crisis are psychological, humanitarian, territorial, political and organizational problems. While the psychological problem requires a sense of confidence, the humanitarian problem demands a sense of justice; the territorial problem rejects the weight of conquest; the political problem condemns the arrogance of power and requires a rational political behavior; and the organizational problem is the incapability of the United Nations to enforce its own resolutions. Failure to deal with these problems, however, has been due to crises from within and policies from without to which references have been made throughout this study, but could still be briefly summarized as follows:

    a. A deep division over the existence of Israel: in less than two decades, Israel had militarily won three wars with territorial gains seized in each war. The insistence of Israel on gradually changing the status quo by war and expanding its territorial boundaries by conquest has seriously alarmed the Arab States and raised questions about Israel's "real ambitions" in the area. This political and psychological fact will continue to prevail in spite of (1) the Security Council's resolution of November 22, 1967, which was accepted by some Arab States including the U.A.R., Jordan and Lebanon, could, if implemented by all parties to the conflict, be considered an international treaty which, among other things, envisaged a recognition of the existence of the State of Israel; and (2) the process of peacemaking implied attempts by Arab diplomacy to live with a nonaggressive and nonexpansionist Israel, and efforts to institute a system of guarantees conducive to the principle of peaceful coexistence. This system, if articulated, would be guaranteed by the Great Powers possibly within the framework of the United Nations.

b. The Arab refugee problem: for 23 years the Arabs of Palestine have been living in a refugee status with no serious efforts made to implement the United Nations resolutions pertaining to them. After the 1967 war, the Palestinians became highly alarmed at their increasing number (approximately one and one-half million) and greatly concerned about the Arab States' real intentions in view of the newly developing Arab "conciliatory diplomacy" aimed at a peaceful settlement with Israel. The Arab refugees have decided, therefore, to revolt against the entire process of alienation for determining their own destiny. Indeed, the fedayeen warfare has not only challanged the traditional political institutions in the Arab World, but it has also sparked a strong movement among all refugees and students for revenge against Israel to wipe out the stain of the humiliating Arab defeats. Accordingly, the Israelis have found the fedayeen movements potentially more dangerous than some of the Arab regular armies.

Indeed, a revival and implementation of the General Assembly's resolution (194-III) of December 11, 1948, which has given the uprooted Palestinian Arabs a choice between repatriation, that is a return to their homes in what is now Israel, or resettlement with compensation, would perhaps be the only practicable solution to the refugee problem. Israel,

239

however, has refused to comply with the Assembly's resolution and claimed that it could not absorb over one and one-half million Moslem and Christian Arab refugees, and retain essentially its fundamental character as a Zionist State. Furthermore, and particularly because of the Israeli attitude on the matter, it would be necessary to facilitate the establishment of a Palestinian State to include those parts of Palestine which Israel occupied in the 1967 war — the West Bank and Gaza. This creation could be undertaken by a referendum whereby the Palestinian people would determine their future and decide on their constitutional relationship, if any, with Jordan.

c. The territorial problem: there has been a great difference between what Israel seems prepared to give up from the territories it occupied in the June 1967 war and what the Arabs consider essential to get back in order to talk about "peace with honor." Israel, on the one hand, has shifted its security strategy from the element of "time" to the element of "space," and, as such, has insisted on new security guarantees through a territorial adjustment aimed at establishing what Israel considers "secure, recognized and agreed borders." The Arab States, on the other hand, have demanded that Israel abide by the Security Council's resolution of November 22, 1967, and withdraw from "all" the territories occupied in the 1967 war, and that any peaceful settlement should not reflect the weight of conquest. Between these two opposing policies is the dilemma of peace in the Middle East; and to reconcile these two approaches would require an American-Soviet concert on the entire Middle Eastern problem.

d. The American-Soviet cold war on the Middle East: as was stated, the Aqaba crisis of 1967 reinforced and widened cleavages that had existed between the Arab States and the Western Powers, particularly the United States, ever since the first Arab-Israeli war of 1948-1949. To the Arabs, Israel has been the most unfortunate kind of the remaining legacies of Western imperialism; the legacy of an expansive and aggressive nationalism — Zionism. As such, the Arabs have really viewed Zionism as the Americans have viewed Communism.

Accurately describing the Arab feeling towards the West and Israel, Professor John S. Badeau, former United States Ambassador to the United Arab Republic, and director of the Middle East Institute of Columbia University, states:

The most basic cause is found in the intense Arab reaction against long-continued domination of their destinies by foreign countries. In the fading days of Ottoman rule, the Arab communities of the Middle East were stirred by nationalistic consciousness akin to that involved in the emergence of the Zionist ideal in Jewry. . . . Thwarted in their struggle, some of their principal leaders responded to British promises during the First World War and joined the Allies in the overthrow of the Ottoman rule. They did so on the understanding that their national aspirations would be recognized and some form of independent Arab rule achieved. . . . This was not done. . . . It was the Great Betrayal of their national cause. . . . [Israel] was for them a tactic of fading imperial power to continue its control of Arab destinies. . . . In the ensuing attack on the new state, the Arabs were

241

not so much responding to the existence of Israel per se as to a long history of foreign control, domination, and manipulation at the hands of the great powers.[60]

On the other hand, the third Arab-Israeli war has enhanced the Soviet Union's influence in the Middle East and the Mediterranean Sea. "True, the Arabs have suffered a defeat," observed a Soviet diplomat, "but this defeat has brought them closer to us — not driven them away."[61] As such, one could say, while the memories and the living realities of the Arab-Israeli impasse have widened the cleavages between the Arab States and the Western Powers, the Soviet diplomacy in the conflict has gradually brought about an effective Soviet economic, political and physical presence in the Middle East.

Consequently, and with the shrinking of the British and the French presence in the area, particularly after the Suez crisis of 1956, the two super-powers have become deeply involved in the Middle Eastern politics as centered around and radiated from the Arab-Israeli dilemma. However, aware of the limitations of the nuclear age and, at the same time, concerned about their national interests, in the strategic location and the natural resources of the "shatterbelt," both the United States and the Soviet Union have decided to fight a carefully calculated cold war in the Middle East. The principal concern of this diplomacy is the development of face-saving devices, escape routes, security valves, and preventive measures all aimed at accepting each other's status of influence and, at

---

60 John S. Badeau, "The Arabs 1967," *The Atlantic Monthly* (December, 1967) pp. 103-104.
61 *New York Times* (July 23, 1967), p. 23.

242

the same time, preventing the two super-powers from being dragged into a military confrontation. Between a show of great power and a show of great restraint, a super-power's tactical preventive diplomacy has been tacitly developed. This no-peace-no-war diplomacy has resulted in a no-lasting-peace-no-decisive-war in the Middle East crisis. Indeed, as long as the policymakers of some Great Powers remain incapable, by virtue of lack of imagination, of realizing the inhuman tragedy in the Arab-Israeli conflict, and the new realities therein, there should be no reason to believe that the arrogance of power and the anarchy of war would ever come to an end in the Middle East.

e. Paralyzed by the aforementioned political realities, the United Nations has allowed itself to be used as a stage for a power play to the extent that it has bobbled its own effectiveness. On the Arab-Israeli crisis, the World Organization has turned itself away from the complicated grays of the living realities by taking no action to enforce its own resolutions. In fact, the United Nations would not have to reach beyond these resolutions, including the Security Council's resolution of November 22, 1967, for the establishment of a just and lasting peace in the Middle East. However, in view of the Western Great Powers' attitudes, particularly that of the United States, it would be unrealistic to expect that the United Nations would ever be able to take enforcement actions, or even effective sanctions, against Israel for noncompliance with the Organization's resolutions.

To conclude, however, it would be only pragmatic to

say that because of these five realistically inseparable, politically interrelated problems, neither the United Nations' peacemaking approach to peace in the Middle East, a principle that has been instituted in the Security Council's resolution of November 22, 1967, nor the United States' proposal of June 19, 1970, would be capable of decisively changing the potentially explosive twilight of war in the Arab-Israeli impasse. For the attainment of a just and lasting peace, however, the international community, particularly the Great Powers, would not only have to continue developing conciliatory devices and security valves, but, and to be sure most important, they would also have to (1) reject the weight of military conquest in any peacemaking arrangement in the Middle Eastern conflict; (2) develop new devices whereby Israel's policy would be effectively contained and future stability in the area would be internationally guaranteed; and (3) implement the United Nations General Assembly's resolution (194-III) of December 11, 1948, which has given the Arab refugees a choice between repatriation and compensation, bring them into the realm of diplomacy, deal with them as indigenous partners, and facilitate the "rebirth" of a territorial Palestinian entity as the only feasible solution to the national aspirations of the revolutionary Palestinian Nationalism.

Bibliography

A. United Nations Official Records and Documents

United Nations, General Assembly Official Records. First Special Session, 1947.
————. Second Session, ad hoc Committee on the Palestine Question; Third, Fourth, Twelfth and Fifteenth Meeting, 1947.
————. Second Special Session, Annex to Volumes I and II, 1948.
————. Second Special Session, Vol. I, Plenary Meetings of the General Assembly, April 16-May 14, 1948.
————. Third Session, Supplement No. 1, 1948.
————. Third Session, Parts I and II, Supplements Nos. 11 and 11A, PROGRESS REPORT OF THE UNITED NATIONS MEDIATOR AND ACTING MEDIATOR ON PALESTINE, 1948.
————. Fourth Session, REPORT OF THE SECRETARY-GENERAL, "Assistance to Palestine Refugees," A/1060 and Add. 1, A/C5/366, 1949.
————. Fifth Session, Supplement No. 19, INTERIM RE-

PORT OF THE DIRECTOR OF THE UNITED NA-
TIONS RELIEF AND WORKS AGENCY FOR PALES-
TINE REFUGEES IN THE NEAR EAST, "Assistance to
Palestine Refugees," 1950.
————. Sixth Session, Supplement Nos. 16 and 16A, REPORT
OF THE DIRECTOR OF UNRWA, "Assistance to Pal-
estine Refugees," A/1905, and SPECIAL REPORT OF
THE DIRECTOR OF THE ADVISORY COMMISSION
OF UNRWA, "Assistance to Palestine Refugees," A/1905/
Add. 1, 1951.
————. Seventh Session, Supplement No. 13, ANNUAL RE-
PORT OF THE DIRECTOR OF UNRWA, A/2171, 1952.
————. Eighth Session, Supplement No. 12, ANNUAL RE-
PORT OF THE DIRECTOR OF UNRWA, A/2470, 1953.
————. Ninth Session, Supplement No. 17, ANNUAL RE-
PORT OF THE DIRECTOR OF UNRWA, A/2717, 1954.
————. Tenth Session, Supplement No. 15, ANNUAL RE-
PORT OF THE DIRECTOR OF UNRWA, A/2978, and
SPECIAL REPORT OF THE DIRECTOR CONCERN-
ING OTHER CLAIMANTS FOR RELIEF, A/2978/Add.
1, 1955.
————. Eleventh Session, Supplement No. 14, ANNUAL RE-
PORT OF THE DIRECTOR OF UNRWA, A/3212, 1956.
————. Twelfth Session, Supplement No. 14, ANNUAL RE-
PORT OF THE DIRECTOR OF UNRWA, A/3686, 1957.
————. Fourteenth Session, Supplement No. 14, ANNUAL
REPORT OF THE DIRECTOR OF UNRWA, A/4213,
1959.
————. Sixteenth Session, ANNUAL REPORT OF THE
DIRECTOR OF UNRWA, A/4861, 1961.
————. Eighteenth Session, Supplement No. 13, ANNUAL
REPORT OF THE DIRECTOR OF UNRWA, A/5513,
1963.
————. Nineteenth Session, Supplement No. 68, ANNUAL RE-
PORT OF THE DIRECTOR OF UNRWA, A/5806, 1964.
————. CONCILIATION COMMISSION FOR PALESTINE
PROGRESS REPORTS, A/819, 838, 927, 992, 1252, 1255,
1288, 1367/Rev. 1, 1793, 1985, 2121, 2216, 2216/Add. 1,
2629, 2897, 3199.
United Nations, Security Council Official Records. Third Year.

————. Fourth Year, Special Supplements Nos. 1-4.

General Assembly, Official Records, First Emergency Special Session (1956), Plenary Meetings, 561st-572nd Meetings (Nov. 1-Nov. 10, 1956).

————. Official Records, Eleventh Session (1956-57), Plenary Meetings, Vol. I, 581st-597th Meetings (Nov. 27, 1956); Vols., II-III, 624th-668th Meetings.

————. Official Records, Eleventh Session (1956-57), Fifth Committee, 538th Meeting (Nov. 27, 1956-Feb. 25, 1957).

————. Official Records, Twelfth Session (1957), Fifth Committee, 639th Meeting (Dec. 6, 1957) and 646th Meeting (Dec. 12, 1957).

————. Official Records, Twelfth Session (1957), Plenary Meetings, 720th-729th Meetings (Nov. 22-Dec. 6, 1957).

————. Official Records, Thirteenth Session (1958-59), Plenary Meetings, 780th Meeting (Nov. 14, 1958) and 790th Meeting (Dec. 13, 1958).

————. Official Records, Thirteenth Session (1958-59), Fifth Committee, 697th-705th Meetings (Dec. 2-Dec. 11, 1958).

————. Official Records, Thirteenth Session (1958-59), Special Political Committee, 96th-100th Meetings (Oct. 28-Nov. 5, 1958).

————. Official Records, Fourteenth Session (1959-60), Plenary Meetings, 804th-809th Meetings (Sept. 24-Sept. 25, 1959).

————. Official Records, Fourteenth Session (1959-60), Fifth Committee, 749th-759th Meetings (Nov. 24-Dec. 4, 1959).

————. Official Records, First Emergency Special Session (1956), Annexes, Agenda Item 5.

————. Official Records, Fifteenth Sesssion (1960-61), Sixteenth Session (1961-62), Seventeenth Session (1962-63), Eighteenth Session (1963-64), Nineteenth Session (1964-65), Twentieth Session (1965-66), and Twenty-First Session (1966-67), Annexes.

————. Official Records (1960-1966), "United Nations Emergency Force. Report of the Secretary-General."

A/3267, Nov. 3, 1956, "Report of the Secretary-General submitted in pursuance of resolution 997 (ES-I), par. 5, adopted by the General Assembly on 2 November 1956."

A/3268, Nov. 3, 1956, "Letter dated 3 November 1956 from

the Alternate Permanent Representative of France, addressed to the Secretary-General."

A/3270, Nov. 3, 1956, "Communication dated 3 November 1956 from the Permanent Representative of Egypt, addressed to the President of the General Assembly and to the Secretary-General."

A/3272, Nov. 3, 1956, "United States of America: draft resolution."

A/3277, Nov. 3, 1956, "Letter dated 3 November 1956 from the Permanent Representative of Israel, addressed to the President of the General Assembly."

A/3278, Nov. 4, 1956, "Letter dated 3 November 1956 from the Permanent Representative of Syria, addressed to the President of the General Assembly."

A/3279, Nov. 4, 1956, "Aide-mémoire dated 3 November 1956 from the Permanent Representative of Israel, addressed to the Secretary-General."

A/3284, Nov. 4, 1956, "Second report of the Secretary-General submitted in pursuance of resolution 997 (ES-I), par. 5, adopted by the General Assembly on 2 November 1956."

A/3287, Nov. 4, 1956, "Report of the Secretary-General on communication with the Governments of France, Egypt, Israel and the United Kingdom of Great Britain and Northern Ireland concerning implementation of General Assembly resolution 997 (ES-I) and 999 (ES-I) dated 2 and 4 November 1956."

A/3288, Nov. 4, 1956, "Letter dated 4 November 1956 from the Permanent Representative of Egypt, addressed to the Secretary-General."

A/3289, Nov. 4, 1956, "First report of the Secretary-General on the plan for an emergency international United Nations Force requested in resolution 998 (ES-I) adopted by the General Assembly on 4 November, 1956."

A/3291, Nov. 5, 1956, "Letter dated 4 November 1956 from the Permanent Representative of Israel, addressed to the Secretary-General."

A/3293, Nov. 5, 1956, "Letter dated 5 November 1956 from the Permanent Representative of Great Britain and Northern Ireland, addressed to the Secretary-General."

A/3296, Nov. 5, 1956, "Third Report of the Secretary-General submitted in pursuance of resolution 997 (ES-I), par. 5, adopted by the General Assembly on 2 November 1956."

A/3298, Nov. 5, 1956, "Letter dated 5 November 1956 from the Permanent Representative of the Union of Soviet Socialist Republics, addressed to the Secretary-General."

A/3302 and Add. 1 to 16, Nov. 6, 1956, "Second and final report of the Secretary-General on the plan for an emergency international United Nations Force requested in resolution 998 (ES-I), adopted by the General Assembly on 4 November 1956."

A/3310, Nov. 7, 1956, "Aide-mémoire dated 5 November 1956 from the Secretary-General, addressed to the Governments of France and the United Kingdom of Great Britain and Northern Ireland."

A/3313, Nov. 7, 1956, "Letter dated 7 November 1956 from the Secretary-General, addressed to the Minister of Foreign Affairs of France."

A/3317, Nov. 8, 1956, "Confirmation of the appointment of Major General, E. L. M. Burns as Chief of the United Nations Command for the emergency international force."

General Assembly, Official Records, Eleventh Session (1956-57), Annexes, Vols. II-III, Agenda Item 66.

A/3375, Nov. 20, 1956, "Report of the Secretary-General on basic points for the presence and functioning in Egypt of the United Nations Emergency Force."

A/3376, Nov. 20, 1956, "Report of the Secretary-General on the clearing of the Suez Canal."

A/3380, Nov. 21, 1956, "Letter dated 21 November 1956 from the Permanent Representative of Egypt, addressed to the Secretary-General."

A/3383 and Rev. I, Nov. 21, 1956, "Report of the Secretary-General on administrative and financial arrangements for the United Nations Emergency Force."

A/3384 and Add. 1 and 2, Nov. 21, 1956, "Report of the Secretary-General on compliance with General Assembly resolution 997 (ES-I)."

A/3395, Nov. 26, 1956, "Exchange of letters between the Minister for Foreign Affairs of Israel and the Secretary-General."

A/3402, Nov. 30, 1956, "Twenty-second report of the Advisory Committee on Administrative and Budgetary Questions:

administrative and financial arrangements for the United Nations Emergency Force."

A/3410, Dec. 1, 1956, "Letter dated 1 December 1956 from the Permanent Representative of Israel, addressed to the Secretary-General."

A/3425, Dec. 4, 1956, "Letter dated 4 December 1956 from the Permanent Representative of Israel, addressed to the Secretary-General."

A/3456, Dec. 14, 1956, "Thirty-fifth report of the Advisory Committee on Administrative and Budgetary Questions: possible claims in respect of death or disability attributable to service in the United Nations Emergency Force."

A/3466, Dec. 18, 1956, "Memorandum dated 17 December 1956 from Minister for Foreign Affairs of Egypt, addressed to the Secretary-General."

A/3479, Dec. 21, 1956, "Letter dated 18 December 1956 from the Permanent Representative of Israel, addressed to the Secretary-General."

A/3483, Dec. 31, 1956, "Letter dated 31 December 1956 from the Permanent Representative of Israel, addressed to the Secretary-General."

A/3491, Jan. 10, 1957, "Note by the Secretary-General, transmitting a report dated 3 December 1956 on the situation in the area."

A/3492, Jan. 10, 1957, "Second report of the Secretary-General on the clearing of the Suez Canal."

A/3500 and Add. 1, Jan. 15, 1957, "Report by the Secretary-General on compliance with General Assembly resolution calling for withdrawal of troops and other measures."

A/3511, Jan. 24, 1957, "Note by the Secretary-General transmitting an aide-mémoire on the Israel position on the Sharm el-Shiekh area and the Gaza Strip."

A/3512, Jan. 24, 1957, "Report of the Secretary-General in pursuance of General Assembly resolution 1123 (XI)."

A/3526, Feb. 9, 1957, "Report of the Secretary-General on arrangements concerning the status of the United Nations Emergency Force in Egypt."

A/3527, Feb. 11, 1957, "Report of the Secretary-General in pursuance of General Assembly resolution 1124 (XI)."

A/3568, March 8, 1957, "Second report of the Secretary-General in pursuance of General Assembly resolutions 1124 (XI) and 1125 (XI)."

General Assembly, Official Records, Twelfth and Thirteenth Sessions (1957) (1958-59), Annexes, Agenda Item 65.

A/3694 and Add. 1, Oct. 9, 1957, "Report of the Secretary-General."

A/3761, Dec. 3, 1957, "Twenty-sixth report of the Advisory Committee on Administrative and Budgetary Questions."

A/3899, Aug. 27, 1958, "Report of the Secretary-General."

A/3943, Oct. 9, 1958, "Summary study of the experience derived from the establishment and operation of the Force: report of the Secretary-General."

A/3989, Nov. 11, 1958, "Report of the Special Political Committee."

A/4002, Nov. 19, 1958, "Twenty-fifth report of the Advisory Committee on Administrative and Budgetary Questions. Budget estimates for the period 1 January to 31 December 1959."

General Assembly, Official Records, Fourteenth Session (1959), Annexes, Agenda Item 28.

A/4160, July 23, 1959, "Cost estimates for the maintenance of the Force: report of the Secretary-General."

A/4171, July 31, 1959, "Budget estimates for the maintenance of the Force: report of the Advisory Committee on Administrative and Budgetary Questions."

A/4176 and Add. 1 and 2, Sept. 10, 1959, "Manner of Financing the Force: report of the Secretary-General on consultations with Governments of Member States."

A/4210 and Add. 1, Sept. 10, 1959, "Progress report of the Secretary-General on the United Nations Emergency Force."

A/4396, July 8, 1960, "United Nations Emergency Force. Cost estimates for the Maintenance of the Force. Report of the Secretary-General. Budget estimates for the period 1 January to 31 December 1961."

A/4409, July 21, 1960, "United Nations Emergency Force: budget estimates for the period 1 January to 31 December 1961. Second report of the Advisory Committee on Administrative and Budgetary Questions to the General Assembly at its fifteenth session."

B. Memoirs

Azcarate, Pablo De. *Mission in Palestine 1948-1952*. Washington, D.C.: The Middle East Institute, 1966.

Burns, E. L. M. *Between Arab and Israeli*. New York: Ivan Obalensky, 1963.

Eden, Anthony. *The Memoirs of Anthony Eden*. Cambridge: Riverside, 1960.

Eytan, Walter. *The First Ten Years*. New York: Simon and Schuster, 1958.

Glubb, J. B. *A Soldier with the Arabs*. London: Hodder and Stoughton, 1957.

————. *The Story of the Arab Legion*. London: Hodder and Stoughton, 1948.

————. *War in the Desert*. London: Hodder and Stoughton, 1960.

Hutchison, E. H. *Violent Truce*. New York: The Devin-Adair Company, 1956.

James, MacDonald G. *My Mission in Israel 1948-1951*. New York: Simon and Schuster, 1951.

Morton, Geoffrey J. *Just the Job: Police, Palestine Mandate*. London: Hodder and Stoughton, 1957.

Von Horn, Major General Carl. *Soldiering for Peace*. New York: David McKay, 1967.

C. Books

Andrews, Fannie F. *The Holy Land under Mandate*. Boston: Houghton Mifflin Co., 1931.

Avnery, Uri. *Israel without Zionists: A Plea for Peace in the Middle East*. New York: MacMillan, 1968.

Bell, J. Bowyer. *The Long War: Israel and the Arabs since 1964*. Princeton: Englewood Cliffs, 1969.

Ben-Gurion, David. *Rebirth and Destiny of Israel*. New York: Philosophical Library, 1950.

Berger, Morroe. *The Arab World Today*. New York: Doubleday and Co., 1962.

Bloomfield, L. M. *Egypt, Israel and the Gulf of Aquba in International Law.* Toronto: Carswell Co., 1957.

Bloomfield, Lincoln P. *The United Nations and U.S. Foreign Policy.* New York: Little, Brown, 1961.

Campbell, John C. *Defense of the Middle East.* Revised ed. New York: Council on Foreign Relations, 1960.

Childers, Erskine B. *Common Sense about the Arab World.* New York: Macmillan, 1960.

————. *The Road to Suez.* London: Macgibbon & Kee, 1962.

Churchill, Randolph S. and Winston S. *The Six Day War.* London: Heinemann, 1968.

Davies, David. *The Problem of the Twentieth Century.* London: Ernest Benn Limited, 1930.

Davis, John H. *The Evasive Peace: A Study of the Zionist-Arab Problem.* London: John Murray, 1968.

Draper, Theodore. *Israel and World Politics: Roots of the Third Arab-Israeli War.* New York: Viking, 1968.

Eban, Abba. *Voice of Israel.* New York: Horizon Press, 1957.

Fisher, Sydney Nettleton. *The Middle East.* New York: Alfred A. Knopf, 1960.

Frischwasser, Ra'anan, H. F. *The Frontiers of a Nation.* London: Batchworth Press, 1955.

Frye, William R. *A United Nations Peace Force.* New York: Oceana for the Carnegie Endowment for International Peace, 1957.

Gabby, Rony E. *A Political Study of the Arab Jewish Conflict: The Arab Refugee Problem.* Geneva: Drez, 1959.

Goodrich, Leland M. *Korea: A Study of U.S. Policy in the United Nations.* New York: Council on Foreign Relations, 1956.

Goodrich, Leland M. and Anne P. Simons. *The United Nations and the Maintenance of International Peace and Security.* Washington, D.C.: Brookings Institution, 1955.

Hackworth, Green Haywood. *Digest of International Law.* Vols. I and II. Washington, D.C.: Government Printing Office, 1941.

Hadawi, Sami. *Palestine: Loss of a Heritage.* San Antonio, Texas: The Naylor Company, 1963.

————. Bitter Harvest. *Palestine, 1914-67.* New York: New World Press, 1967.

Hanna, Paul L. *British Policy in Palestine.* Washington: American Council on Public Affairs, 1942.
Hebrew University of Jerusalem. *Israel and the United Nations.* New York: Manhattan Publishing Co., 1956.
Heleben, Sylvester John. *Plans for World Peace through Six Centuries.* Chicago: University of Chicago Press, 1943.
Howard, Harry N. *The King-Crane Commission; An American Inquiry in the Middle East.* Beirut: Khayats, 1963.
Hurewitz, J. C. *The Struggle for Palestine.* New York: W. W. Norton, Inc., 1950.
————. *Diplomacy in the Near and Middle East.* Princeton: D. Van Nostrand Co., Inc., 1956.
Ingrams, Harold, *The Yemen: Imams, Rulers, and Revolutions.* London: Praeger, 1963.
Kelson, Hans. *The Law of the United Nations.* London: Stevens and Sons, 1950.
Kerr, Malcolm H. *The Middle East Conflict.* New York: Foreign Policy Association, 1968.
Khadduri, Majdia D. *The Arab-Israeli Impasse.* Washington, D.C.: Robert B. Luce, 1968.
Khouri, Fred J. *The Arab-Israeli Dilemma.* Syracuse: Syracuse University Press, 1968.
Kirk, George E. *Contemporary Arab Politics.* New York: Praeger, 1961.
————. *The Middle East in the War.* London: Oxford University Press, 1952.
Kraines, Oscar. *Government and Politics in Israel.* Boston: Houghton Mifflin Co., 1961.
Lall, Arthur, *The U.N. and the Middle East Crisis, 1957.* New York: Columbia, 1968.
Lanczowski, George. *The Middle East in World Affairs,* 2nd ed. Ithaca: Cornell University Press, 1956.
Laqueur, Walter Z. *The Soviet Union and the Middle East.* New York: Praeger, 1959.
————. *Communism and Nationalism in the Middle East.* London: Routledge and Kegan Paul Ltd., 1956.
————. *The Road to Jerusalem: The Origins of the Arab-Israeli Conflict, 1967.* New York: MacMillan, 1968.
————. ed. *The Israel-Arab Reader: A Documentary History of the Middle East Conflict.* New York: Citadel, 1968.

254

Larus, Joel. *From Collective Security to Preventive Diplomacy.* New York: John Wiley & Sons, Inc., 1965.

Lash, Joseph P. *Dag Hammarskjöld.* New York: Doubleday and Co., 1961.

Lehrman, Hal. *Israel: The Beginning and Tomorrow.* New York: Sloane, 1952.

Lewis, Bernard. *The Middle East and the West.* Bloomington: Indiana University Press, 1964.

————. *The Arabs in History.* New York: Harper and Row, 1960.

Lilienthal, Alfred M. *What Price Israel?* Chicago: Regnery, 1953.

————. *The Other Side of the Coin.* New York: The Devin-Adair Company, 1965.

Love, Kenneth. *Suez: The Twice-Fought War.* New York: Mc-Graw-Hill, 1969.

Manuel, Frank B. *The Realities of American-Palestine Relations.* Washington: American Council on Public Affairs, 1949.

Marlowe, John. *Arab Nationalism and British Imperialism.* New York: Praeger, 1961.

Mehdi, M. T. *Peace in the Middle East.* New York: New World Press, 1967.

Meo, Leila M. T. *Lebanon: Improbable Nation.* Bloomington: Indiana University Press, 1965.

Murray, G. S. *Political Implications of Peace-Keeping Under the United Nations Charter.* Ottawa: Department of External Affairs, 1963.

Nasser, Gamal Abdel. *The Philosophy of the Revolution.* National Publication House Press, 1955.

Nutting, Anthony. *No End of the Lesson.* New York: Clarkson N. Potter, 1967.

O'Ballance, Edgar. *The Sinai Campaign of 1956.* New York: Praeger, 1959.

Olsen, Arnold. *Inside Jerusalem: City of Destiny.* Glendale, California: Regal Books, 1968.

Padelford, Norman J. and Leland M. Goodrich. *The United Nations in the Balance: Accomplishments and Prospects.* Washington, D.C.: Praeger, 1965.

Pearson, L. B. *The Crisis in the Middle East: October-December 1956.* Government of Canada White Paper.

255

————. *The Crisis in the Middle East: January-March 1957.* Government of Canada White Paper.

Peretz, Don. *The Middle East Today.* New York: Holt, Rinehart and Winston, Inc., 1963.

————. *Israel and the Palestine Arabs.* Washington, D.C.: The Middle East Institute, 1959.

Polk, W. R., D. Stamler and E. Asfour. *Background to Tragedy: The Struggle for Palestine.* Boston: Beacon Press, 1957.

Polk, William R. *The United States and the Arab World.* Cambridge, Massachusetts: Harvard University Press, 1965.

Qubain, Fahim I. *Crisis in Lebanon.* Washington, D.C.: The Middle East Institute, 1961.

Robertson, Terence. *Crisis: The Inside Story of the Suez Conspiracy.* New York: H. Wolff, 1965.

Rodinson, Maxime. *Israel and the Arabs.* New York: Pantheon, 1968.

Rosenne, Shabatai. *Israel's Armistice Agreements with the Arab States: A Juridical Interpretation.* Tel Aviv: Published for the International Law Association, Israel Branch, by Blumstein's Bookstores, 1951.

Safran, Nadav. *From War to War: The Arab-Israeli Confrontation, 1948-1967.* New York: Pegasus, 1969.

Sharabi, Hisham B. *Nationalism and Revolution in the Arab World.* New York: D. Van Nostrand Co., Inc., 1966.

————. *Governments and Politics of the Middle East in the Twentieth Century.* New York: D. Van Nostrand Co., Inc., 1962.

St. John, Robert. *The Boss: The Story of Gamal Abdel Nasser.* New York: McGraw-Hill, 1960.

Stock, Ernest. *Israel on the Road to Sinai, 1949-1956: With a Sequel on the Six-Day War 1967.* Ithaca: Cornell University Press, 1967.

Stone, Julius. *Legal Controls of International Conflict.* London: Stevens and Sons, 1959.

The Suez Canal Report. Suez Canal Authority, United Arab Republic, 1962.

Thomas, Hugh. *The Suez Affair.* New York: Harper & Row, 1967.

Wainhouse, David W. *International Peace Observation: A History and Forecast.* Baltimore: The Johns Hopkins Press, 1966.

Weissberg, Guenter. *The International Status of the United Nations.* New York: Oceana, 1961.

Weizmann, Chaim. *Trial and Error: The Autobiography of Chaim Weizmann.* New York: Harper and Brothers, 1949.

Zurayk, Constantine N. *Palestine: The Meaning of the Disaster.* Beirut: Khayats, 1956.

D. Periodicals

Alami, M. "The Lesson of Palestine," *The Middle East Journal,* 3 (October, 1949), 373-405.

Armstrong, H. F. "U.N. Experience in Gaza," *Foreign Affairs,* XXXV (July, 1957), 600-619.

Aubin, W. de S. "Peace and Refugees in the Middle East," *The Middle East Journal,* 3 (July, 1949), 249-259.

Baldwin, R. "The Palestine Refugees," *Current History,* 33 (November, 1957), 295-298.

Baster, J. "Economic Aspects of the Settlement of the Palestine Refugees," *The Middle East Journal,* 8 (Winter, 1954), 54-68.

————. "Economic Problems in the Gaza Strip," *The Middle East Journal,* 9 (Summer, 1955), 323-327.

Bruhns, F. C. "A Study of Arab Refugees' Attitudes," *The Middle East Journal,* 9 (Spring, 1955), 39-38.

Chapman, Dudley H. "International Law — The United Nations Emergency Force — Legal Status," *Michigan Law Review,* LVII (November, 1958), 56-81.

Cohen, Maxwell. "The United Nations Emergency Force: A Preliminary View," *International Journal,* XII (Spring, 1957), 109-27.

Corbett, Percy E. "Power and Law at Suez," *International Journal,* VII (Winter, 1956-57), 1-12.

Dayan, Moshe. "Israel's Border and Security Problems," *Foreign Affairs,* XXXIII (January, 1955), 250-67.

Draper, H. "Israel's Arab Minority: The Beginning of a Tragedy," *New International,* 22 (Summer, 1956), 86-106.

————. "The Great Land Robbery," *New International,* 23 (Winter, 1957), 7-30.

257

Eban, Abba. "Reality and Vision in the Middle East," *Foreign Affairs*, 43 (July, 1965), 626-638.

Glubb, J. B. "Violence on the Jordan-Israel Border: A Jordanian View," *Foreign Affairs*, 32 (July, 1954), 552-562.

Goodrich, Leland M. and Gabriella E. Rosner. "The United Nations Emergency Force," *International Organization*, XI (Summer, 1957), 413-30.

Gross, Leo. "Passage through the Suez Canal of Israel-Bound Cargo and Israel Ships," *American Journal of International Law*, LI (1957), 530-68.

Hoffman, Stanley. "Sisyphus and the Avalanch: The United Nations, Egypt, and Hungary," *International Organization*, XI (Summer, 1957), 446-69.

Horton, I. E. "The Arab Refugees," *The Spectator*, 185 (July 28, 1950), 166.

Huang, Thomas T. F. "Some International and Legal Aspects of the Suez Canal Problem," *American Journal of International Law*, LI (1957), 277-307.

Hurewitz, Jacob C. "The Israeli-Syrian Crisis in the Light of the Arab-Israel Armistice System," *International Organization*, V (1951), 457-79.

————. "Arab-Israeli Tensions," *Proceedings of the Academy of Political Science*, XXIV (January, 1952), 73-81.

————. "The United Nations Conciliation Commission for Palestine," *International Organization*, VII (1953), 482-97.

Ionides, M. G. "The Refugees and the Jordan," *The Spectator*, 181 (November 19, 1948), 186.

————. Reply to "Refugees Forever?" *The Spectator*, 190 (February 13, 1953), 186.

Jackson, Elmore. "The Developing Role of the Secretary-General," *International Organization*, XI (Summer, 1957), 446-69.

Johnson, D. H. N. "The Effect of the Resolutions of the General Assembly of the United Nations," *British Yearbook of International Law*," XXXII (1955-56), 97-122.

Johnson, Joseph E. "Arab vs. Israeli: A Persistent Challenge to Americans," *The Middle East Journal*, Vol. 18, No. 1 (Winter, 1964).

Khouri, Fred J. "The Policy of Retaliation in Arab-Israeli Relations," *The Middle East Journal*, Vol. 20, No. 4 (Autumn, 1966), 435-455.

258

King, Archibald. "Jurisdiction over Friendly Armed Forces," *American Journal of International Law,* XXXVI (1942), 539-67.

Kunz, Joseph L. "Privileges and Immunities of International Organizations," *American Journal of International Law,* XLI (1947), 328-62.

Mezerik, A. G., ed. "The United Nations Emergency Force (UNEF): Precedents, Creation, Evolution," *International Review Service,* III (May, 1957), 1-55.

Miller, E. M. "Legal Aspects of the United Nations Action in the Congo," *American Journal of International Law,* LV (January, 1961), 1-28.

Munro, Sir Leslie. "The Case for a Standing U.N. Army," *The New York Times* Magazine, (July 27, 1958).

O'Donovan, Patrick. "How the U.N. Troops Were Mobilized," *The Reporter,* XVI (January 10, 1957), 30-32.

Pearson, Lester B. "Force for U.N.," *Foreign Affairs,* XXXV (April, 1957), 395-404.

Peretz, Don. "Arab Blocked Bank Accounts in Israel," *Jewish Social Studies,* 18 (January, 1956), 25-40.

————. "The Arab Refugee Dilemma," *Foreign Affairs,* 41 (April, 1963), 134-148.

————. "The Arab Refugees: A Changing Problem," *Foreign Affairs,* 41 (April, 1963), 558-570.

————. "Problems of Arab Refugee Compensation," *The Middle East Journal,* 8 (Autumn, 1954), 403-416.

————. "The Arab Minority in Israel," *The Middle East Journal,* 8 (Spring, 1954), 139-154.

————. "Arab Refugees: Whose?" *Christian Science Monitor* (October 28, 1957).

————. "Red Star over Islam," *The Reporter,* 14 (1950), 36-38.

Possony, Stefan T. "Peace Enforcement," *Yale Law Journal,* LV (1946), 910-49.

Report of Committee on Study of Legal Problems of the United Nations. "The Establishment of the United Nations Emergency Force," in *Proceedings of the American Society of International Law,* 51st Annual Meeting. Washington, D.C.: American Society of International Law, 1958, 206-29.

Schwadran, B. "Israel-Jordan Border Tension," *Middle Eastern Affairs,* (October, 1950).

259

————. "The Palestine Conciliation Commission," *Middle Eastern Affairs*, 1 (October, 1950), 271-285.

Simpson, Dwight J. "Israel: The State of Siege," *Current History*, 48 (May, 1965), 263-268.

Sohn, L. B. "Authority of the U.N. to Establish and Maintain a Permanent U.N. Force," *American Journal of International Law*, LII (April, 1958), 229-40.

Spry, Graham. "Canada, the United Nations Emergency Force, and the Commonwealth," *International Affairs*, XXXIII (July, 1957), 289-300.

Stoessinger, John G. "Financing the United Nations," *International Conciliation*, No. 535 (November, 1961).

Strange, Susan. "Suez and After," *The Yearbook of World Affairs 1957*, New York: Praeger, 1957.

Wright, Quincy. "Intervention, 1956," *American Journal of International Law*, LVII (1957), 257-76.

Appendices

Appendix A

THE BALFOUR DECLARATION

Foreign Office
November 2nd, 1917

Dear Lord Rothschild,

I have much pleasure in conveying to you, on behalf of His Majesty's Government, the following declaration of sympathy with Jewish Zionist aspirations which has been submitted to, and approved by, the Cabinet.

> His Majesty's Government view with favour the establishment in Palestine of a national home for the Jewish people, and will use their best endeavours to facilitate the achievement of this object, it being clearly understood that nothing shall be done which may prejudice the civil and religious rights of existing non-Jewish communities in Palestine, or the rights and political status enjoyed by Jews in any other country.

I should be grateful if you would bring this declaration to the knowledge of the Zionist Federation.

(signed)
Lord Balfour

Appendix B

PLAN OF PARTITION WITH ECONOMIC UNION

(A/RES/181-II) 29 November 1947

(Selected Excerpts)

The General Assembly,

Having met in special session at the request of the mandatory Power to constitute and instruct a special committee to prepare for the consideration of the question of the future government of Palestine at the second regular session;

Having constituted a Special Committee and instructed it to investigate all questions and issues relevant to the problem of Palestine, and to prepare proposals for the solution of the problem, and

Having received and examined the report of the Special Committee including a number of unanimous recommendations and a plan of partition with economic union approved by the majority of the Special Committee,

Considers that the present situation in Palestine is one which is likely to impair the general welfare and friendly relations among nations;

Takes note of the declaration by the mandatory Power that it plans to complete its evacuation of Palestine by 1 August 1948;

Recommends to the United Kingdom, as the mandatory Power for Palestine, and to all other members of the United Nations the adoption and implementation, with regard to the future government of Palestine, of the Plan of Partition with Economic Union set out below;

Requests that

(a)   The Security Council take the necessary measures as provided for in the plan for its implementation;

(b)   The Security Council consider, if circumstances during the transitional period require such consideration, whether the situation in Palestine constitutes a threat to peace. If it decides that such a threat exists, and in order to maintain international peace and security, the Security Council should supplement the authorization of the General Assembly by taking measures, under Articles 39 and 41 of the Charter, to empower the United Nations Commission, as provided in this resolution, to exercise in Palestine the functions which are assigned to it by this resolution;

(c)   The Security Council determine as a threat to the peace, breach of the peace or act of aggression, in accordance with Article 39 of the Charter, any attempt to alter by force the settlement envisaged by this resolution;

(d)   The Trusteeship Council be informed of the responsibilities envisaged for it in this plan;

Calls upon the inhabitants of Palestine to take such steps as may be necessary on their part to put this plan into effect;

Appeals to all Governments and all peoples to refrain from taking any action which might hamper or delay the carrying out of these recommendations. . . .

Vote: 33 yes, 13 no, 10 abstaining.

In favor: Australia, Belgium, Bolivia, Brazil, Byelorussia, Canada, Costa Rica, Czechoslovakia, Denmark, Dominican Republic, Ecuador, France, Guatemala, Haiti, Iceland, Liberia, Luxembourg, Netherlands, New Zealand, Nicaragua, Norway, Panama, Paraguay, Peru, Philippines, Poland, Sweden, Ukraine, Union of South Africa, U.S.S.R., U.S., Uruguay, Venezuela.

263

Against: Afghanistan, Cuba, Egypt, Greece, India, Iran,
          Iraq, Lebanon, Pakistan, Saudi Arabia, Syria,
          Turkey, Yemen.

Abstaining: Argentina, Chile, China, Colombia, El Sal-
          vador, Ethiopia, Honduras, Mexico, U.K.,
          Yugoslavia.

Appendix C

RESOLUTION ADOPTED BY THE
SECURITY COUNCIL
15 July 1948 (S/902)

The Security Council

Taking into consideration that the Provisional Government of Israel has indicated its acceptance in principle of a prolongation of the truce in Palestine; that the States members of the Arab League have rejected successive appeals of the United Nations Mediator and of the Security Council in its resolution of 7 July 1948, for the prolongation of the truce in Palestine; and that there has consequently developed a renewal of hostilities in Palestine.

Determines that the situation in Palestine constitutes a threat to peace within the meaning of Article 39 of the Charter;

Orders the Governments and authorities concerned, pursuant to Article 40 of the Charter of the United Nations, to desist from further military action and to this end to issue cease-fire orders to their military and paramilitary forces, to take effect not later than three days from the date of the adoption of this resolution;

Declares that failure by any of the Governments or authorities concerned to comply with the preceding paragraph of this resolution would demonstrate the existence of a breach of the peace within the meaning of Article 40 of the Charter requiring immediate consideration by the Security Council with a view to such further action under Chapter VII of the Charter as may be decided upon by the Council;

Calls upon all Governments and authorities concerned to continue to cooperate with the Mediator with a view to the maintenance of peace in Palestine in conformity with the resolution adopted by the Security Council on 29 May 1948;

Orders as a matter of special and urgent necessity an immediate and unconditional cease-fire in the City of Jerusalem to take effect twenty-four hours from the time of the adoption of this resolution and instructs the Truce Commission to take any necessary steps to make this cease-fire effective;

Instructs the Mediator to continue his efforts to bring about the demilitarization of the City of Jerusalem without prejudice to the future political status of Jerusalem and to assure the protection of and access to the Holy Places, religious buildings and sites in Palestine;

Instructs the Mediator to supervise the observance of the truce and to establish procedures for examining alleged breaches of the truce since 11 June 1948; authorizes him to deal with breaches so far as it is within his capacity to do so by appropriate local action; and requests him to keep the Security Council currently informed concerning the operation of the truce and when necessary to take appropriate action;

Decides that, subject to further decision by the Security Council or the General Assembly, the truce shall remain in force in accordance with the present resolution and with that of 29 May 1948, until a peaceful adjustment of the future of Palestine is reached;

Reiterates the appeal to the parties contained in the last paragraph of its resolution of 22 May and urges upon the parties that they continue conversations with the Mediator in a spirit of conciliation and mutual concession in order that all points under dispute may be settled peacefully;

Requests the Secretary-General to provide the Mediator with the necessary staff and facilities to assist in carrying out the function assigned to him under the resolution of the General Assembly of 14 May and under this resolution; and

Requests that the Secretary-General make appropriate arrangements to provide the necessary funds to meet the obligations arising from this resolution.

Appendix D

RESOLUTION ADOPTED BY THE GENERAL ASSEMBLY

11 December 1948. (A/RES/194-III)

The General Assembly,

Having considered further the situation in Palestine,

1. Expresses its deep appreciation of the progress achieved through the good offices of the late United Nations Mediator in promoting a peaceful adjustment of the future situation of Palestine, for which cause he sacrificed his life; and

Extends its thanks to the Acting Mediator and his staff for their continued efforts and devotion to duty in Palestine;

2. Establishes a Conciliation Commission consisting of three States Members of the United Nations which shall have the following functions:

a) To assume, in so far as it considers necessary in existing circumstances, the functions given to the United Nations Mediator on Palestine by resolution 186 (S-2) of the General Assembly of 14 May 1948;

b) To carry out the specific functions and directives given to it by the present resolution and such additional functions and directives as may be given to it by the General Assembly or by the Security Council;

c) To undertake, upon the request of the Security Council, any of the functions now assigned to the United Nations Mediator on Palestine or to the United Nations Truce Commission by resolutions of the Security Council; upon such request to the Conciliation Commission by the Security Council with respect to all the remaining functions of the United Nations Mediator on Palestine under Security Council resolutions, the office of the Mediator shall be terminated.

3. Decides that a Committee of the Assembly, consisting of

China, France, the Union of Soviet Socialist Republics, the United Kingdom and the United States of America, shall present, before the end of the first part of the present session of the General Assembly, for the approval of the Assembly, a proposal concerning the names of the three States which will constitute the Conciliation Commission;

4. Requests the Commission to begin its functions at once, with a view to the establishment of contact between the parties themselves and the Commission at the earliest possible date;

5. Calls upon the Government and authorities concerned to extend the scope of the negotiations provided for in the Security Council's resolution of 16 November 1948 and to seek agreement by negotiations conducted either with the Conciliation Commission or directly, with a view to the final settlement of all questions outstanding between them;

6. Instructs the Conciliation Commission to take steps to assist the Governments and authorities concerned to achieve a final settlement of all questions outstanding between them;

7. Resolves that the Holy Places — including Nazareth — religious buildings and sites in Palestine should be protected and free access to them assured, in accordance with existing rights and historical practice; that arrangements to this end should be under effective United Nations supervision; that the United Nations Conciliation Commission, in presenting to the fourth regular session of the General Assembly its detailed proposals for a permanent international regime for the territory of Jerusalem, should include recommendations concerning the Holy Places in that territory; that with regard to the Holy Places in the rest of Palestine the Commission should call upon the political authorities of the areas concerned to give appropriate formal guarantees as to the protection of the Holy Places and access to them; and that these undertakings should be presented to the General Assembly for approval;

8. Resolves that, in view of its association with three world religions, the Jerusalem area, including the present municipality of Jerusalem plus the surrounding villages and towns, the most eastern of which shall be Abu Dis; the most southern, Bethlehem; the most western, Ein Karim (including also the built

267

up area of Motsa); and the most northern, Shu'fat, should be accorded special and separate treatment from the rest of Palestine and should be placed under effective United Nations control;

Requests the Security Council to take further steps to ensure the demilitarization of Jerusalem at the earliest possible date;

Instructs the Conciliation Commission to present to the fourth regular session of the General Assembly detailed proposals for a permanent international regime for the Jerusalem area which will provide for the maximum local autonomy for distinctive groups consistent with the special international status of the Jerusalem area;

The Conciliation Commission is authorized to appoint a United Nations representative, who shall cooperate with the local authorities with respect to the interim administration of the Jerusalem area;

9. Resolves that, pending agreement on more detailed arrangements among the Governments and authorities concerned, the freest possible access to Jerusalem by road, rail or air should be accorded to all inhabitants of Palestine;

Instructs the Conciliation Commission to report immediately to the Security Council, for appropriate action by that organ, any attempt by any party to impede such access.

10. Instructs the Conciliation Commission to seek arrangements among the Governments and authorities concerned which will facilitate the economic development of the area, including arrangements for access to ports and airfields and the use of transportation and communication facilities;

11. Resolves that the refugees wishing to return to their homes and live in peace with their neighbours should be permitted to do so at the earliest practicable date, and that compensation should be paid for the property of those choosing not to return and for loss of or damage to property which, under principles of international law or in equity, should be made good by the Governments or authorities responsible;

Instructs the Conciliation Commission to facilitate the repatriation, resettlement and economic and social rehabilitation of the refugees and the payment of compensation, and to maintain close relations with the Director of the United Nations

Relief for Palestine Refugees and, through him, with the appropriate organs and agencies of the United Nations;

12. Authorizes the Conciliation Commission to appoint such subsidiary bodies and to employ such technical experts, acting under its authority, as it may find necessary for the effective discharge of its functions and responsibilities under the present resolution;

The Conciliation Commission will have its official headquarters at Jerusalem. The authorities responsible for maintaining order in Jerusalem will be responsible for taking all measures necessary to ensure the security of the Commission. The Secretary-General will provide a limited number of guards for the protection of the staff and premises of the Commission;

13. Instructs the Conciliation Commission to render progress reports periodically to the Secretary-General for transmission to the Security Council and to the Members of the United Nations;

14. Calls upon all Governments and authorities concerned to cooperate with the Conciliation Commission and to take all possible steps to assist in the implementation of the present resolution;

15. Requests the Secretary-General to provide the necessary staff and facilities and to make appropriate arrangements to provide the necessary funds required in carrying out the terms of the present resolution.

Appendix E

RESOLUTION ADOPTED BY THE GENERAL ASSEMBLY

8 December 1949 (A/RES/302 — IV)

The General Assembly,

Recalling its resolutions 212 (III) of 19 November 1948

and 194 (III) of 11 December 1948, affirming in particular the provisions of paragraph 11 of the latter resolution,

Having examined with appreciation the first interim report of the United Nations Economic Survey Mission for the Middle East[1] and the report of the Secretary-General on assistance to Palestine refugees;[2]

1. Expresses its appreciation to the Governments which have generously responded to the appeal embodied in its resolution 212 (III), and to the appeal of the Secretary-General, to contribute in kind or in funds to the alleviation of the conditions of starvation and distress amongst the Palestine refugees;

2. Expresses also its gratitude to the International Committee of the Red Cross, to the League of Red Cross Societies and to the American Friends Service Committee for the contribution they have made to this humanitarian cause by discharging, in the face of great difficulties, the responsibility they voluntarily assumed for the distribution of relief supplies and the general care of the refugees; and welcomes the assurance they have given the Secretary-General that they will continue their cooperation with the United Nations until the end of March 1950 on a mutually acceptable basis;

3. Commends the United Nations International Children's Emergency Fund for the important contribution which it has made towards the United Nations programme of assistance; and commends those specialized agencies which have rendered assistance in their respective fields, in particular the World Health Organization, the United Nations Educational, Scientific and Cultural Organization and the International Refugee Organization;

4. Expresses its thanks to the numerous religious, charitable and humanitarian organizations which have materially assisted in bringing relief to Palestine refugees;

5. Recognizes that, without prejudice to the provisions of paragraph 11 of General Assembly resolution 194 (III) of 11 December 1948, continued assistance for the relief of the

---

1 Document A/1106.
2 Documents A/1060 and A/1060/Add. 1.

Palestine refugees is necessary to prevent conditions of starvation and distress among them and to further conditions of peace and stability, and that constructive measures should be undertaken at an early date with a view to the termination of international assistance for relief;

6. Considers that, subject to provisions of paragraph 9 (d) of the present resolution, the equivalent of approximately $33.7 million will be required for direct relief and works programmes for the period 1 January to 31 December 1950 of which the equivalent of $20.2 million is required for direct relief and $13.5 million for works programmes; that the equivalent of approximately $21.2 million will be required for works programmes from 1 January to 30 June 1951, all inclusive of administrative expenses; and that direct relief should be terminated not later than 31 December 1950 unless otherwise determined by the General Assembly at its fifth regular session;

7. Establishes the United Nations Relief and Works Agency for Palestine Refugees in the Near East:

(a) To carry out in collaboration with local governments the direct relief and works programmes as recommended by the Economic Survey Mission;

(b) To consult with the interested Near Eastern Governments concerning measures to be taken by them preparatory to the time when international assistance for relief and works projects is no longer available;

8. Establishes an Advisory Commission consisting of representatives of France, Turkey, the United Kingdom of Great Britain and Northern Ireland, and the United States of America, with power to add not more than three additional members from contributing Governments, to advise and assist the Director of the United Nations Relief and Works Agency for Palestine Refugees in the Near East in the execution of the programme; the Director and the Advisory Commission shall consult with each Near Eastern Government concerned in the selection, planning and execution of projects;

9. Requests the Secretary-General to appoint the Director of the United Nations Relief and Works Agency for Palestine

Refugees in the Near East in consultation with the Governments represented on the Advisory Commission:

    (a)   The Director shall be the chief executive officer of the United Nations Relief and Works Agency for Palestine Refugees in the Near East responsible to the General Assembly for the operation of the programme;

    (b)   The Director shall select and appoint his staff in accordance with general arrangements made in agreement with the Secretary-General, including such of the staff rules and regulations of the United Nations as the Director and the Secretary-General shall agree are applicable, and to the extent possible utilize the facilities and assistance of the Secretary-General;

    (c)   The Director shall, in consultation with the Secretary-General and the Advisory Committee on Administrative and Budgetary Questions, establish financial regulations for the United Nations Relief and Works Agency for Palestine Refugees in the Near East;

    (d)   Subject to the financial regulations established pursuant to clause (c) of the present paragraph, the Director, in consultation with the Advisory Commission, shall apportion available funds between direct relief and works projects in their discretion, in the event that the estimates in paragraph 6 require revision;

10. Requests the Director to convene the Advisory Commission at the earliest practicable date for the purpose of developing plans for the organization and administration of the programme, and of adopting rules of procedure.

11. Continues the United Nations Relief for Palestine Refugees as established under General Assembly resolution 212 (III) until 1 April 1950, or until such date thereafter as the transfer referred to in paragraph 12 is effected, and requests the Secretary-General in consultation with the operating agencies to continue the endeavour to reduce the numbers of rations by progressive stages in the light of the findings and recommendations of the Economic Survey Mission;

12. Instructs the Secretary-General to transfer to the United Nations Relief and Works Agency for Palestine Refugees in the Near East the assets and liabilities of the United Nations Relief for Palestine Refugees by 1 April, 1950, or at such date as may be agreed by him and the Director of the United Nations Relief and Works Agency for Palestine Refugees in the Near East;

13. Urges all Members of the United Nations and non-members to make voluntary contributions in funds or in kind to ensure that the amount of supplies and funds required is obtained for each period of the programme as set out in paragraph 6; contributions in funds may be made in currencies other than the United States dollar in so far as the programme can be carried out in such currencies;

14. Authorizes the Secretary-General, in consultation with the Advisory Committee on Administrative and Budgetary Questions, to advance funds deemed to be available for this purpose and not exceeding $5 million from the Working Capital Fund to finance operations pursuant to the present resolution, such sum to be repaid not later than 31 December 1950 from the voluntary governmental contributions requested under paragraph 13 above;

15. Authorizes the Secretary-General, in consultation with the Advisory Committee on Administrative and Budgetary Questions, to negotiate with the International Refugee Organization for an interest-free loan in an amount not to exceed the equivalent of $2.8 million to finance the programme subject to mutually satisfactory conditions for repayment;

16. Authorizes the Secretary-General to continue the Special Fund established under General Assembly resolution 212 (III) and to make withdrawals therefrom for the operation of the United Nations Relief for Palestine Refugees and, upon the request of the Director, for the operations of the United Nations Relief and Works Agency for Palestine Refugees in the Near East;

17. Calls upon the Governments concerned to accord to the United Nations Relief and Works Agency for Palestine Refugees in the Near East the privileges, immunities, exemp-

273

tions and facilities which have been granted to the United Nations Relief for Palestine Refugees, together with all other privileges, immunities, exemptions and facilities necessary for the fulfillment of its functions;

18. Urges the United Nations International Children's Emergency Fund, the International Refugee Organization, the World Health Organization, the United Nations Educational, Scientific and Cultural Organization, the Food and Agriculture Organization and other appropriate agencies and private groups and organization, in consultation with the Director of the United Nations Relief and Works Agency for Palestine Refugees in the Near East, to furnish assistance within the framework of the programme;

19. Requests the Director of the United Nations Relief and Works Agency for Palestine Refugees in the Near East:

(a) To appoint a representative to attend the meeting of the Technical Assistance Board as observer so that the technical assistance activities of the United Nations Relief and Works Agency for Palestine Refugees in the Near East may be coordinated with the technical assistance programmes of the United Nations and specialized agencies referred to in Economic and Social Council resolution 222 (IX) A of 15 August 1949;

(b) To place at the disposal of the Technical Assistance Board full information concerning any technical assistance work which may be done by the United Nations Relief and Works Agency for Palestine Refugees in the Near East, in order that it may be included in the reports submitted by the Technical Assistance Board to the Technical Assistance Committee of the Economic and Social Council;

20. Directs the United Nations Relief and Works Agency for Palestine Refugees in the Near East to consult with the United Nations Conciliation Commission for Palestine in the best interests of their respective tasks, with particular reference to paragraph 11 of General Assembly resolution 194 (III) of 11 December 1948;

21. Requests the Director to submit to the General Assembly of the United Nations an annual report on the work of the United Nations Relief and Works Agency for Palestine Refugees in the Near East, including an audit of funds, and invites him to submit to the Secretary-General such other reports as the United Nations Relief and Works Agency for Palestine Refugees in the Near East may wish to bring to the attention of the United Nations, or its appropriate organs.

22. Instructs the United Nations Conciliation Commission for Palestine to transmit the final report of the Economic Survey Mission, with such comments as it may wish to make, to the Secretary-General for transmission to the Members of the United Nations and to the United Nations Relief and Works Agency for Palestine Refugees in the Near East.

Appendix F

SUBJECT OF RESOLUTION: Measures taken by Israel to change the status of the City of Jerusalem

DATE ADOPTED: 4 July 1967

VOTE: 99 in favour, none against, with 20 abstentions (roll call)

DOCUMENT NUMBERS

RESOLUTION SUBMITTED TO ASSEMBLY:
A/L.527/Rev.1

RESOLUTION AS ADOPTED BY ASSEMBLY:
2253 (ES-V)

TEXT OF RESOLUTION

The General Assembly,

Deeply concerned at the situation prevailing in Jerusalem

as a result of the measures taken by Israel to change the status of the City,

1. Considers that these measures are invalid;

2. Calls upon Israel to rescind all measures already taken and to desist forthwith from taking any action which would alter the status of Jerusalem;

3. Requests the Secretary-General to report to the General Assembly and the Security Council on the situation and on the implementation of the present resolution not later than one week from its adoption.

Appendix G

SUBJECT OF RESOLUTION: Measures taken by Israel to change the status of the City of Jerusalem

DATE ADOPTED: 14 July 1967

VOTE: 99 in favour, none against, with 18 abstentions (roll call)

DOCUMENT NUMBERS

RESOLUTION SUBMITTED TO ASSEMBLY:
A/L.528/Rev.2

RESOLUTION AS ADOPTED BY ASSEMBLY:
2254 (ES-V)

TEXT OF RESOLUTION

The General Assembly,

Recalling its resolution 2253 (ES-V) of 4 July 1967,
Having received the report submitted by the Secretary-General,[1]

---

1 A/6753 and S/8052.

Taking note with the deepest regret and concern of the non-compliance by Israel with resolution 2253 (ES-V),

1. Deplores the failure of Israel to implement General Assembly resolution 2253 (ES-V);

2. Reiterates its call to Israel in that resolution to rescind all measures already taken and to desist forthwith from taking any action which would alter the status of Jerusalem;

3. Requests the Secretary-General to report to the Security Council and the General Assembly on the situation and on the implementation of the present resolution.

Appendix H

SECURITY COUNCIL
Document

S/RES/242 (1967)
22 November 1967

RESOLUTION 242 (1967)

Adopted by the Security Council at its 1382nd meeting,
on 22 November 1967

The Security Council

Expressing its continuing concern with the grave situation in the Middle East,

Emphasizing the inadmissibility of the acquisition of territory by war and the need to work for a just and lasting peace in which every State in the area can live in security,

Emphasizing further that all Member States in their acceptance of the Charter of the United Nations have undertaken a commitment to act in accordance with Article 2 of the Charter,

1. Affirms that the fulfillment of Charter principles requires the establishment of a just and lasting peace in the Middle East which should include the application of both the following principles:

(i) Withdrawal of Israeli armed forces from territories occupied in the recent conflict;

(ii) Termination of all claims or states of belligerency and respect for and acknowledgment of the sovereignty, territorial integrity and political independence of every State in the area and their right to live in peace within secure and recognized boundaries free from threats or acts of force;

2. Affirms further the necessity

(a) For guaranteeing freedom of navigation through international waterways in the area;

(b) For achieving a just settlement of the refugee problem;

(c) For guaranteeing the territorial inviolability and political independence of every State in the area, through measures including the establishment of demilitarized zones;

3. Requests the Secretary-General to designate a Special Representative to proceed to the Middle East to establish and maintain contacts with the States concerned in order to promote agreement and assist efforts to achieve a peaceful and accepted settlement in accordance with the provisions and principles in this resolution;

4. Requests the Secretary-General to report to the Security Council on the progress of the efforts of the Special Representative as soon as possible.

Appendix I

TEXT OF THE RESOLUTION ADOPTED ON SUNDAY 24 MARCH 1968 BY THE SECURITY COUNCIL OF THE UNITED NATIONS

The Security Council, late Sunday, unanimously adopted the following resolution (document forthcoming) as read at the request of the President,

The Security Council,

Having heard the statements of the representatives of Jordan and Israel,

Having noted the contents of the letters of the permanent representatives of Jordan and Israel in documents S/8470, S/8475, S/8478, S/8483, S/8484, and S/8486,

Having noted further the supplementary information provided by the Chief of Staff of the United Nations Truce Supervision Organization (UNTSO) as contained in documents S/7930/Add. 64 and Add. 65,

Recalling resolution 236 (1967) by which the Security Council condemned any and all violations of the cease-fire,

Observing that the military action by the armed forces of Israel on the territory of Jordan was of a large scale and carefully planned nature,

Considering that all violent incidents and other violations of the cease-fire should be prevented and not overlooking past incidents of this nature,

Recalling further resolution 237 (1967) which called upon the government of Israel to ensure the safety, welfare and security of the inhabitants of the areas where military operations have taken place,

1. Deplores the loss of life and heavy damage to property;

2. Condemns the military action launched by Israel in flagrant violation of the United Nations Charter and the cease-fire resolutions;

3. Deplores all violent incidents in violation of the cease-fire and declares that such actions of military reprisal and other grave violations of the cease-fire cannot be tolerated and that the Security Council would have to consider further and more effective steps as envisaged in the Charter to ensure against repetition of such acts;

4. Calls upon Israel to desist from acts or activities in contravention of resolution 237 (1967);

5. Requests the Secretary-General to keep the situation under review and to report to the Security Council as appropriate.

279

Appendix J

DR. GUNNAR JARRING'S NOTE TO ISRAEL, JORDAN, EGYPT (U.A.R.) AND LEBANON, AND HIS 14 QUESTIONS REGARDING EACH STATE'S POSITION ON A MIDDLE EAST SETTLEMENT:[1]

[Dr. Gunnar Jarring]

Security Council resolution 242 (1967) sets out provisions and principles in accordance with which a peaceful and accepted settlement of the Middle East Question should be achieved.

Some of these provisions would impose obligations on both sides, some on one side, and some on the other. It has generally been accepted that they should be regarded as a whole.

The following question designed to elicit the attitude of the parties towards the provisions of the Security Council resolution are based on this assumption and are to be understood in the context that each provision is regarded as a part of a "package deal."

1 — Does each of the parties accept Security Council resolution 242 (1967) for implementation of achieving a peaceful and accepted settlement of the Middle East Question in accordance with the provisions and principles contained in the resolution?

2 — Does each of the parties agree to pledge termination of all claims or states of belligerency with other states in the region?

3 — Does each of the parties agree to pledge respect for an acknowledgement of the sovereignty, territorial integrity and political independence of Jordan, Lebanon, the United Arab Republic and Israel?

---

1 *The Boston Globe* (Tuesday, April 22, 1969), p. 2. The reply from Lebanon to Jarring's questions was not available.

4 — Does each of the parties accept the right of Jordan, Lebanon, the United Arab Republic and Israel to live in peace within secure and recognized boundaries free from threats or acts of force?

5 — If so, what is the conception of secure and recognized boundaries held by Israel, Jordan, Lebanon, and the United Arab Republic?

6 — Does Israel agree to withdraw its armed forces from territories occupied by it in the recent conflict?

7 — Does the United Arab Republic agree to guarantee freedom of navigation for Israel through international waterways in the area, in particular: (a) through the Straits of Tiran, and (b) through the Suez Canal?

8 — Does each of the parties agree that, if a plan for the just settlement of the refugee problem is worked out and presented to the parties for their consideration, the acceptance in principle of such a plan by the parties and the declaration of their intention to implement it in good faith constitute sufficient implementation of this provision of the Security Council resolution to justify the implementation of the other provisions?

9 — Does each of the parties agree that the territorial inviolability and political independence of the states in the area should be guaranteed:

(a) by the establishment of demilitarized zones;

(b) through additional measures?

10 — Does Israel agree that such demilitarized zones should include areas on its side of its boundaries?

11 — Does Jordan agree that a demilitarized zone should be established in Jordanian territory from which Israeli armed forces have been withdrawn?

12 — Does the United Arab Republic agree that a demilitarized zone should be established:

(a) at Sharm el-Sheikh;

(b) in other parts of the Sinai peninsula?

281

13 — Does each of the parties agree that demilitarization of such zones should be supervised and maintained by the United Nations?

14 — Would each of the parties accept as a final act of agreement on all provisions a mutually signed multilateral document which would incorporate the agreed conditions for a just and lasting peace?

THE REPLY FROM ISRAEL TO JARRING'S QUESTIONS:

Jerusalem, 2 April 1969

Dear Ambassador Jarring,

Israel's position on all the subjects raised in your eleven questions (Questions 7, 11 and 12 are not addressed to Israel) has been stated in detail in my address to the General Assembly of 8 October 1968, and in the memoranda presented to you on 15 October 1968 and 4 November 1968.

I now enclose specific replies in an affirmative spirit to the questions as formulated. It is my understanding that on the basis of the answers received from the three governments you propose to pursue further mutual clarifications in an effort to promote agreement on all matters at issue in accordance with your mandate (Para 3 of Resolution 242). We are ready to join in this process at any appropriate place.

Israeli's statements of attitude, including her replies to these questions, has taken into account recent developments in Arab policy including the speeches recently delivered by President Nasser and other Arab leaders. We have noted the specific and emphatic reiteration of their refusal to make peace with Israel, to recognize Israel, to negotiate with Israel, to cease terrorist attacks on Israel or to admit the possibility of sovereign coexistence in any field. It would appear at this time that the effective negation by the U.A.R. of the principles of the Charter and of the Security Council's Resolution is obvious and vehement. We hope that this policy, to which effect is given every day, will change, but these authoritative state-

282

ments have caused deep concern and have intensified the tension which we would have wished to see relieved.

It is also our view that highly publicized encounters by four member states (the meetings in New York among the representatives of the U.S., U.S.S.R., U.K. and France) have weakened the attention which should have been concentrated on the efforts of the parties themselves to move towards agreement. The [Big Four meetings] are causing a duplication and dispersal of effort. They have also encouraged a wrong impression in some quarters that a solution can be sought outside the region and without its governments. Israel recognizes your mission as the authoritative international framework within which peace between the States in the Middle East should be promoted.

I recall the idea which we discussed some weeks ago that the Foreign Ministers of the three governments should meet with you soon at a suitable place to pursue the promotion of agreements. As you will remember, I reacted positively to this idea. I wish to reaffirm that Israel will continue to cooperate with you in the fulfillment of your mission.

Yours sincerely,
Abba Eban

Confidential

Answer to Question One:

Israel accepts the Security Council Resolution (242) for the promotion of agreement on the establishment of a just and lasting peace, to be reached by negotiation and agreements between the governments concerned. Implementation of agreements should begin when agreement has been concluded on all their provisions.

Answer to Question Two:

It is the Arab States, not Israel, which claimed and originated states of belligerency. They declared themselves for two decades to be in a state of unilateral war with Israel. It is therefore primarily incumbent upon them to terminate the state of war with Israel.

On the establishment of peace with her Arab neighbours,

Israel agrees to the termination, on a reciprocal basis, of all claims or states of belligerency with each state with which peace is established. A declaration specifying each state by name would be made by Israel in each case.

The corresponding statement by any Arab state must specifically renounce belligerency "with Israel" and not "with any state in the area." Legal obligations must be specific in regard to those by whom they are bound.

Renunciation of belligerency includes the cessation of all maritime interference; the cessation of boycott measures involving third parties; the annulment of reservations made by Arab states on the applicability to Israel of their obligations under international conventions to which they have adhered; non-adherence to political and military alliances and pacts directed against Israel or including states unwilling to renounce claims or states of belligerency with Israel and maintain peaceful relations with it; the non-stationing of armed forces of such other states on the territory of the contracting states and the prohibition and prevention in the territory of Arab states of all preparations, actions or expeditions by irregular or paramilitary groups or by individuals directed against the lives, security or property of Israel in any part of the world.

The last stipulation is without prejudice to the fact that the responsibility of Arab governments for preventing such activities is legally binding under the cease-fire established by the parties in June 1967.

Answer to Question Three:

Israel agrees to respect and acknowledge the sovereignty, territorial integrity and political independence of neighboring Arab states; this principle would be embodied in peace treaties establishing agreed boundaries.

Answer to Question Four:

Israel accepts the right of Jordan, Lebanon, the United Arab Republic and other neighboring states to live in peace within secure and recognized boundaries, free from threats or acts of force. Explicit and unequivocal reciprocity is Israel's only condition for this acceptance. "Acts of force" include all preparations, actions or expeditions by irregular or para-

284

military groups or by individuals directed against the life, security or property of Israel in any part of the world.

Answer to Question Five:

Secure and recognized boundaries have never yet existed between Israel and the Arab states; accordingly, they would now be established as part of the peace-making process. The cease-fire should be replaced by peace treaties establishing permanent, secure and recognized boundaries as agreed upon through negotiation between the governments concerned.

Answer to Question Six:

When permanent, secure and recognized boundaries are agreed upon and established between Israel and each of the neighboring Arab states, the deposition of forces will be carried out in full accordance with the boundaries determined in the peace treaties.

Answer to Question Seven:

The refugee problem was caused by the wars launched against Israel by Arab states, and has been perpetuated through the refusal of Arab states to establish peaceful relations with Israel. In view of the human problems involved in this issue Israel has expressed its willingness to give priority to the attainment of an agreement for the solution of this problem through regional and international co-operation. We believe that agreement could be sought even in advance of peace negotiations. We suggest that a conference of Middle Eastern states should be convened, together with the governments contributing to refugee relief and the specialized agencies of the United Nations, in order to chart a five-year plan for the solution of the refugee problem in the framework of a lasting peace and the integration of refugees into productive life. This conference can be called in advance of peace negotiations.

Joint refugee integration and rehabilitation commissions should be established by the governments concerned in order to work out agreed projects for refugee integration on a regional basis with international assistance.

In view of the special humanitarian nature of this issue we do not make agreement on plans for a solution of the refugee problem contingent on agreement on any other aspect of the Middle Eastern problem. For the same reason it should not be invoked by Arab states to obstruct agreement on other problems.

Answer to Question Eight:

The effective guarantee for the territorial inviolability and political independence of states lies in the strict observance by the governments of their treaty obligations. In the context of peace providing for full respect for the sovereignty of states and the establishment of agreed boundaries, other security measures may be discussed by the contracting governments.

Answer to Questions Nine and Ten:

Without prejudice to what is stated in answer to Question Eight, it is pointed out that experience has shown that the measures mentioned in Questions Nine and Ten have not prevented the preparation and carrying out of aggression against Israel.

Answer to Question Eleven:

Peace must be juridically expressed, contractually defined and reciprocally binding in accordance with established norms of international law and practice. Accordingly, Israel's position is that the peace should be embodied in bilateral peace treaties between Israel and each Arab state incorporating all the agreed conditions for a just and lasting peace. The treaties, once signed and ratified, should be registered with the Secretariat of the United Nations in accordance with Article 102 of the United Nations Charter.

2 April 1969

The Reply from Jordan to Jarring's Questions:

March 23 1969

Your Excellency,

Following are the answers of my government to the questions which you presented to us in Amman, on Saturday, March 8th, 1969. The answers as numbered, hereunder, correspond to your questions.

These answers explain my government's position, which position has repeatedly been stated to Your Excellency throughout our past meetings.

Yours sincerely,
Abdul Monem Rifa'i
Minister of Foreign Affairs

Answer (1)

Jordan, as it has declared before, accepts the Security Council Resolution 242 (1967) and is ready to implement it in order to achieve a peaceful and accepted settlement in accordance with the provisions and principles contained in the Resolution.

Answer (2)

Jordan agrees to pledge termination of all claims or states of belligerency. Such a pledge becomes effective upon withdrawal of Israeli forces from all Arab territories which Israel occupied as a result of its aggression of June 5th, 1967.

A pledge by Israel to terminate the state of belligerency would be meaningful only when Israel withdraws its forces from all Arab territories, it occupied since June 5th, 1967.

Answer (3)

On June 5th, 1967 Israel launched its aggression against three Arab states violating their sovereignty and territorial integrity. Agreement to pledge respect for an acknowledgement of the sovereignty, territorial integrity and political independence of every state in the area requires the termination by Israel of its occupation and the withdrawal of its forces from all the Arab territories it occupied as a result of its aggression of June 5th.

Answer (4)

Jordan accepts the right of every state in the area to live in peace within secure and recognized boundaries free from threats or acts of force, provided that Israel withdraws its

287

forces from all Arab territories it occupied since June 5th, 1967, and implements the Security Council Resolution of November 22nd, 1967.

Answer (5)

When the question of Palestine was brought before the United Nations in 1947, the General Assembly adopted its resolution 181 (II) of November 29th, 1947 for the partition of Palestine and defined Israel's boundaries.

Answer (6)   (general question 8)

It has always been our position that the just settlement of the refugees problem is embodied in paragraph II of the General Assembly resolution 194 of December 1948 which has been repeatedly reaffirmed by each and every General Assembly session ever since its adoption.

If a plan on the basis of that paragraph is presented for consideration to the parties concerned, its acceptance by the parties and the declaration of their intention to implement it in good faith, with adequate guarantees for its full implementation, would justify the implementation of the other provisions of the resolution.

Answer (7)   (general questions 9 and 11)

We do not believe that the establishment of demilitarized zones is a necessity. However, Jordan shall not oppose the establishment of such zones if they are astride the boundaries.

Answer (9)   (general question 13)

In case demilitarized zones are established Jordan accepts that such zones be supervised and maintained by the United Nations.

Answer (10)   (general question 14)

In view of our past experience with Israel and her denunciation of four agreements signed by her with Arab States, we consider that the instrument to be signed by Jordan en-

288

gaging her to carry out her obligations, would be addressed to the Security Council. Israel would likewise sign and address to the Security Council an instrument engaging her to carry out her obligations emanating from the Security Council Resolution of November 22nd, 1967. The endorsement by the Security Council of these documents would constitute the final multilateral act of agreement.

The Reply from Egypt (U.A.R.) to Jarring's Questions:

The memorandum handed to you on March 5th, 1969, during your recent visit to Cairo clearly expresses the realities of the present situation. It expounds Israel's persistence in rejecting the Security Council Resolution and its refusal to carry out its obligations emanating from it as well as Israel's plans for annexation of Arab lands through war; a policy which not only is prohibited by the Charter of the United Nations but also violates the Security Council Resolution which specifically emphasizes the inadmissibility of the acquisition of territory by war. It has become obvious that Israel, in its endeavour to realize its expansionist aims, is no longer satisfied with the actual rejection of the Security Council Resolution but actively works against it.

The same memorandum also states Israel's expansion plan as revealed by the quoted statements of Israeli leaders. This plan aims at:

(1)   Annexation of Jerusalem;

(2)   Keeping the Syrian Heights under its occupation;

(3)   Occupation of the West Bank in Jordan and its complete domination, practically terminating Jordan's sovereignty in that part;

(4)   Economic and administrative integration of the Gaza Strip into Israel and the systematic eviction of its inhabitants;

(5)   Occupation of Sharm el-Sheikh and the Gulf of Aqaba

289

area as well as the continued military presence in eastern part of Sinai;

(6) The establishment of Israeli settlements in the occupied territories.

This Israeli position constitutes a flagrant violation and clear rejection of the Security Council Resolution of November 22nd, 1967, and of the peaceful settlement for which it provides.

In the light of these undeniable facts, I find it incumbent upon me to state categorically, at the outset of the replies to the specific questions you addressed to the U.A.R. on March 5th, 1969, that all the answers of the United Arab Republic, which reaffirm its acceptance of the Security Council Resolution and its readiness to carry out the obligations emanating from it require, likewise, that Israel accept the Resolution and carry out all its obligations emanating from it and in particular withdrawal from all Arab territories it occupied as a result of its aggression of June 5th, 1967.

Question (1):

The United Arab Republic, as it has declared before, accepts the Security Council Resolution 242 (1967) and is ready to implement it in order to achieve a peaceful and accepted settlement in accordance with the provisions and principles contained therein.

Question (2):

The United Arab Republic agrees to pledge termination of all claims or state of belligerency. Such a pledge becomes effective upon withdrawal of Israel's forces from all Arab territories occupied as a result of Israel's aggression of June 5th, 1967.
A declaration by Israel terminating the state of belligerency would be meaningful only when Israel withdraws her forces from all Arab territories it occupied since June 5th, 1967.

Question (3):

On June 5th, 1967, Israel launched its aggression against

290

three Arab states violating their sovereignty and territorial integrity. Acceptance by the U.A.R. to pledge respect for an acknowledgement of the sovereignty, territorial integrity and political independence of every state in the area requires the termination by Israel of its occupation and the withdrawal of its forces from all the Arab territories it occupied as a result of its aggression of June 5th, and the full implementation of the Security Council Resolution of 22nd November, 1967.

Question (4) :

The U.A.R. accepts the right of every state in the area to live in peace within secure and recognized boundaries, free from threats or acts of force, provided that Israel withdraws its forces from all Arab territories occupied as a result of its aggression of June 5th, 1967, and implements the Security Council Resolution of November 22nd, 1967.

Question (5)

When the question of Palestine was brought before the United Nations in 1947, the General Assembly adopted its resolution 181 of November 29th, 1947, for the partition of Palestine and defined Israel's armistice boundaries.

Question (6)   (general question 7) :

We have declared our readiness to implement all the provisions of the Security Council Resolution covering, inter alia, the freedom of navigation in international waterways in the area; provided that Israel, likewise, implement all provisions of the Security Council Resolution.

Question (7)   (general question 8) :

It has always been our position that the just settlement of the refugee problem is embodied in paragraph II of the General Assembly resolution 194 of December 1948, which has been unfailingly reaffirmed by each and every General Assembly session ever since its adoption.
   If a plan on the basis of that paragraph is presented for consideration to the parties concerned, its acceptance by the

parties and the declaration of their intention to implement it in good faith, with adequate guarantees for its full implementation, would justify the implementation of the other provisions of the Security Council Resolution.

Questions (8), (9) (general questions 9 and 12):

We do not believe that the establishment of demilitarized zones is a necessity. However, the United Arab Republic will not oppose the establishment of such zones if they are astride the boundaries.

Question (10) (general question 13):

In case demilitarized zones are established the United Arab Republic accepts that such zones be supervised and maintained by the United Nations.

Question (11) (general question 14):

In view of our past experience with Israel and her denunciation of four agreements signed by her with Arab States, we consider that the instrument to be signed by the U.A.R. engaging her to carry out her obligations, should be addressed to the Security Council. Israel should, likewise, sign and address to the Security Council an instrument engaging her to carry out her obligations emanating from the Security Council Resolution of November 22nd, 1967. The endorsement by the Security Council of these documents would constitute the final multilateral document.

Mahmoud Riad
Cairo, March 27, 1969

Appendix K

UNITED NATIONS ORGANS IN THE MIDDLE EAST

UNSCOP   U.N. Special Committee on Palestine. Committee created by Special General Assembly on 15

May 1947 to prepare Palestine item for regular 1947 Assembly session. Committee members: Australia, Canada, Czechoslovakia, Guatemala, India, Iran, Netherlands, Peru, Sweden, Uruguay, Yugoslavia. Work ended on 31 August 1947 with report to General Assembly.

Palestine Commission

Commission created on 29 November 1947 by General Assembly to implement "Plan of Partition with Economic Union of Palestine." Commission members: Bolivia, Czechoslovakia, Denmark, Panama, Philippines. Commission dissolved on 20 May 1948.

Truce Commission

Organization created by Security Council on 23 April 1948 to supervise truce in Palestine. Advisory countries: U.S., France, Belgium. Truce Commission superseded by UNTSO.

Mediator for Palestine

Count Folke Bernadotte appointed by General Assembly on 20 May 1948 to mediate Palestine dispute and replace Palestine Commission. Count Bernadotte was assassinated on 17 September 1948 and was succeeded by Dr. Ralph Bunche. Office of Mediator ended with signing of armistice agreements.

UNTSO

U.N. Truce Supervision Organization. Organ created in June-July 1948 by U.N. Mediator to observe truce in Palestine and investigate violations. Formation of this group was in accord with Security Council resolution of 29 May 1948. Members: U.S., France, Belgium (members of former Truce Commission), Australia, Canada, Denmark, Netherlands, New Zealand, Sweden. UNTSO still legally exists.

UNRPR

U.N. Relief for Palestine Refugees. Agency created by General Assembly on 19 November 1948 to plan and implement relief program for

293

Palestine refugees. UNRPR dissolved on 8 December 1949.

CCP   U.N. Conciliation Committee for Palestine. Commission created by General Assembly on 11 December 1948 to assist governments of Arab countries and Israel in reaching final settlement of all outstanding questions between them. Membership (as chosen by U.S., U.S.S.R., U.K., China, France) : U.S., Turkey, France. CCP still legally exists.

Mixed Armistice Commissions   Four separate commissions established in armistice agreements between Israel and Egypt (24 February 1949), Israel and Lebanon (23 March 1949), Israel and Jordan (3 April 1949), Israel and Syria (20 July 1949). Each commission composed of three representatives from military organizations of both of the parties, headed by UNTSO Chief of Staff or his representative. Mixed Armistice Commissions may also employ U.N. observers who are responsible to command of UNTSO Chief of Staff. All commissions still legally exist.

Technical Committee on Refugees   Committee established by CCP, as directed by General Assembly, on 29 June 1949 to study number, place of origin and distribution of refugees with view to economic solution of the problem. Work ended in report to CCP.

Economic Survey Mission   Mission established by CCP on 23 August 1949 to study conditions for economic integration of refugees into Arab countries. Mission headed by Gordon R. Clapp (U.S.). Work ended 28 December 1948 in final report to CCP.

UNRWA   U.N. Relief and Works Agency for Palestine Refugees in the Near East. Agency established by General Assembly, 8 December 1949, on basis of recommendations of Economic Survey Mission, to replace UNRPR and carry out relief and works projects in collaboration with Arab governments. Agency continues to function but has dropped works projects and operates solely as relief organization.

UNEF   United Nations Emergency Force. International force established by Special Emergency General Assembly on 5 November 1956 to "secure and supervise cessation of hostilities" between Israel and Egypt. Seven-nation Advisory Committee composed of Brazil, Canada, Ceylon, Colombia, India, Norway, Pakistan supervises nontechnical planning and operation of UNEF. The Force withdrew at the request of the United Arab Republic on May 18, 1967.

UNOGIL   United Nations Observation Group in Lebanon. An observation mission established by the Security Council on June 11, 1958, to proceed to Lebanon so as to insure that there would be no illegal infiltration of personnel or supply of arms from the United Arab Republic across the Lebanese borders. UNOGIL withdrew on December 10, 1958.

UNYOM   United Nations Observation Mission in Yemen. An observation mission established by the Security Council on June 11, 1963, to proceed to Yemen to observe, certify, and report the situation that involves both Saudi Arabia and the Yemeni royalists on one side, and the United Arab Republic and the Yemeni republicans on the other. UNYOM withdrew on September 4, 1964.

SGSR   Secretary-General Special Representative. In accordance with the Security Council Resolution of November 22, 1967, Dr. Gunnar Jarring was

295

designated as the Secretary-General Special Representative to proceed to the Middle East to establish and maintain contacts in order to secure the implementation of the provisions and principles envisaged in the Resolution. This peace-making mission has not yet been terminated.